EXPERIENCING BLACK SABBATH

The Listener's Companion
Kenneth LaFave, Series Editor

Titles in **The Listener's Companion** provide readers with a deeper understanding of key musical genres and the work of major artists and composers. Aimed at nonspecialists, each volume explains in clear and accessible language how to *listen* to works from particular artists, composers, and genres. Looking at both the context in which the music first appeared and has since been heard, authors explore with readers the environments in which key musical works were written and performed.

EXPERIENCING BLACK SABBATH

A Listener's Companion

Nolan Stolz

ROWMAN & LITTLEFIELD
Lanham • Boulder • New York • London

Published by Rowman & Littlefield
A wholly owned subsidiary of The Rowman & Littlefield Publishing Group,
Inc.
4501 Forbes Boulevard, Suite 200, Lanham, Maryland 20706
www.rowman.com

Unit A, Whitacre Mews, 26-34 Stannary Street, London SE11 4AB

British Library Cataloguing in Publication Information Available

Library of Congress Cataloging-in-Publication Data

Names: Stolz, Nolan, 1981- author.
Title: Experiencing Black Sabbath : a listener's companion / Nolan Stolz.
Description: Lanham : Rowman & Littlefield, [2018] | Series: The listener's companion | Includes
    bibliographical references and index.
Identifiers: LCCN 2017020547 (print) | LCCN 2017020807 (ebook) | ISBN 9781442256927 (elec-
    tronic) | ISBN 9781442256910 (cloth : alk. paper)
Subjects: LCSH: Black Sabbath (Musical group) | Heavy metal (Music)—History and criticism
Classification: LCC ML421.B57 (ebook) | LCC ML421.B57 S76 2018 (print) | DDC
    782.42166092/2—dc23 LC record available at https://lccn.loc.gov/2017020547

♾ ™ The paper used in this publication meets the minimum requirements of
American National Standard for Information Sciences Permanence of Paper
for Printed Library Materials, ANSI/NISO Z39.48-1992.

Printed in the United States of America

CONTENTS

SERIES EDITOR'S FOREWORD

The goal of the Listener's Companion series is to give readers a deeper understanding of pivotal musical genres and the creative work of its iconic composers and performers. This is accomplished in an inclusive manner that does not necessitate extensive music training or elitist shoulder rubbing. Authors of the series place the reader in specific listening experiences in which the music is examined in its historical context with regard to both compositional and societal parameters. By positioning the reader in the real or supposed environment of the music's creation, the author provides for a deeper enjoyment and appreciation of the art form. Series authors, often drawing on their own expertise as both performers and scholars, deliver to readers a broad understanding of major musical genres and the achievements of artists within those genres as lived listening experiences.

Nolan Stolz's book on Black Sabbath is a study in musical identity within musical differences. He avoids sensationalism and the "usual suspects" of rock criticism—politics and personal foibles—to bring greater attention to the distinctly musical aspects of his subject. This is not easy. Music resists being reduced to mere prose. Stolz's answer is to use words to focus the ears intently on each song, each track, bringing to bear such English-language description as might illuminate for the listener what is making the song sound as it does.

If it's tricky to deal with music in words, it can be even trickier to negotiate the maze of changes in a band that endured as long as Black Sabbath. Some band names are umbrellas for a wide range of different

sounds and personnel over decades, and as Stolz makes clear in this
ultimate guide to one of heavy metal's earliest progenitors, that is un-
doubtedly true here. Stolz tracks the lineup changes from the band's
founding in 1968 as "Earth" to its final hurrah in the album and tour
fittingly called "The End" in 2016/2017—nearly fifty years of transfor-
mations and restorations. In detailed, track-by-track examinations of
every recording ever made by the legendary group, the author describes the musical differences made when a singer or a drummer is
replaced. The personnel changeups in Black Sabbath were so frequent
that one of this book's chapters is aptly called "Stonehenge and the
Revolving Door of Musicians." Stolz notes, "I have calculated thirty-
four different lineups. That only includes lineups that rehearsed and
performed live or rehearsed and recorded, and does not include one-
offs, substitute musicians, or brief rehearsals. If one does include the
very brief other lineups, then that would be thirty-nine."

In addition to the musical style changes brought on by personnel
changes, there were also exterior influences that affected the band's
sound over the years. Because Black Sabbath's history spanned a period
of incredible musical changes, stylistic and production trends in the
general culture seeped in. For instance, Stolz mentions the band's flir-
tation with progressive (prog) rock in the seventies and later the introduction of gated reverb for the drums, typical of the eighties.

And yet, the author observes, certain fundamental musical features
remain throughout the decades, characteristics that define a core approach bridging the maze of personnel swaps and the changing styles of
music production from the sixties to the present. Most importantly,
Stolz grasps the foundational influence of the blues and traces its persistence throughout the years. He also traces the repeated appearance in
Sabbath's music of the tritone, a relationship of two notes also known as
"the devil in music." Fittingly, this "devilish" harmonic element distin-
guished the band's sound from day one. (Stolz at one point flat out calls
it "an evil sound.") In the context of the band's blues framework, the
persistence of the tritone suggests that one particularly revealing way of
hearing Black Sabbath is as an insistent exploration of blues harmonies
in their "dark" potential.

Blues harmonies consist of certain patterns that play on the relationship of music's primary chords: the I, the IV, and the V. But in Sabbath's music, as Stolz points out, the tritone is not merely used as a

blues scale inflection but instead brought front and center as a defining feature. It's as if someone reedited Hitchcock's films so as to loop the violent scenes, revealing the dark content that in the original shows up only as a small part of the overall structure. It's *Psycho* with the shower scene every five minutes.

The blues as a form has always projected an ambivalent worldview. On the one hand, the bending of standard scale notes and the addition of nonscale notes expanded the expressive potential of the blues performer. On the other, these alterations clouded the tonal stability associated with classical music and nonblues popular song. The tension inherent in even the simplest twelve-bar blues engages this ambivalence. The form has endured for well over a century and shows no sign of flagging, though its structure is fundamentally the same from blues to blues, in the same way that sonata form bloomed for two centuries, maintaining an integrity-within-diversity that ended only with the takedown of traditional tonality in classical music. The blues may stick around longer, as the fundaments of its tonal language have never been challenged. And the longer it sticks around, the more musicians will explore and exploit its rich ambivalence. In some manner, Black Sabbath could be said to have successfully exploited the darker shades of that ambivalence, with the tritone—an interval that knows no definite tonal home—an emblem of that exploitation.

Stolz gives us the facts we need to locate the Sabbath's work in the timeline of the band's own history and within the larger history of rock music itself. He contextualizes the music in respect to where the members were when they wrote and recorded the songs, as well as what was happening with them at the time. He pulls in quotes to illuminate certain aspects of the music, and makes connections from song to song, or album to album, sometimes across decades, showing commonalities throughout the band's oeuvre. As always in the hurly-burly of the record business, there were often errors in album credits; Stolz corrects these and clarifies just who did what.

Stolz's descriptions are extremely detailed. He gives each observation—and there are sometimes dozens per song—a corresponding time stamp on the recording, and often the observations are only two to five seconds apart. This is necessary with a band in which swift instrument-to-instrument shifts and an almost constant vocal displacement of register or at least of vocal production style occur (from screams to growls to vocal fries and sustained notes). But it can also make for slow reading on its own. How does one get past this? I would suggest starting with the album that means most to you and locating its corresponding treatment in the book. Track by track, play the songs first, without reading about them. Then read Stolz's comments, and finally listen once more. Listen, read, and listen. Again, do this track by track, song by song, in order to focus on a single musical expression and the author's description of it. Move on to the next album, and repeat. Or you could make this a chronological journey, following Stolz's play by play from front to finish.

Written commentary can, of course, go only so far. Ultimately, it's the experience of a song, an album, or a group that counts. But just as it is helpful to know facts about any object of emotional attachment, from a cat to a cathedral, it is enlightening to know the truth about why Ozzy left and came back; what drummer Bill Ward meant by "playing to the words"; how the songwriting process might start with a guitar riff, move on to chord progressions, and finally produce several versions of a vocal line; or how influences from Ravel's *Bolero* to Frank Zappa managed to find their way into Sabbath's music.

How will history treat Black Sabbath? Perhaps, after all, it really is the music that matters. Beyond the image, the social commentary, and the personalities, it is that use of a tritone or that extension of the blues, or that sudden, shocking high note, that merits our attention. This is what Stolz's book seeks, with precise scholarship and passion for the subject, to persuade us to believe.

Kenneth LaFave

ACKNOWLEDGMENTS

- Samantha for all the patience
- Bennett, Gregg, Ken, Monica, Natalie, and the anonymous peer reviewer for helping make this book happen
- To all the members of Black Sabbath for your hard work
- Malcolm Cope, Laurence Cottle, Tony Martin, Louis Osbourne, Bobby Rondinelli, Jim Simpson, and Jezz Woodroffe for additional insight and information
- Osage Arts Community for the time and space to work on the book, and to the Goldwell Open Air Museum, the Sitka Center for Art and Ecology, and the Virginia Center for the Creative Arts for the time and space to research
- The research for, and the writing of, this book was supported in part by the Office of Sponsored Awards and Research Support at the University of South Carolina Upstate through the Scholarly Course Reallocation Program and the Scholarly Startup Package Program. Special thanks to Adrian, Elaine, and Melissa for everything you do.
- Mary at USC Upstate's interlibrary loan, the librarians at Beatty Library and Osage County Library, Brian ("Tri"), James B., and Robby for all your help
- Cody and James (aka GeezerABDE) for the jams, and to Mom, Chrisse, and Linda for letting us jam
- Brad, Christine, Ciro, Dave, Eric, Griffin, Justin, Megan, Nick, Philippe, Sarah, Thomas, and too many other popular music scholars to mention

- Garry, Joe, and Martin for their research and to countless Sabbath fans for sharing old articles and recordings
- Neville (of Eclipse) from the Newtown Community Centre
- Mike Judge for having Beavis and Butt-Head chant "Electric Funeral" and "Iron Man," introducing another generation to Sabbath's music

INTRODUCTION

Black Sabbath is one of the earliest and most influential heavy metal bands. Some say they invented heavy metal with their first album. In the late 1960s and early 1970s, they were a band like no other: they were harder, louder, darker, and heavier than their contemporaries. As time went on, heavy metal sprouted countless subgenres, all of which can be traced back to Black Sabbath. Any successful metal band of the last thirty-plus years would cite them as an influence. This new style of music was not created overnight in a vacuum; rather, there were stylistic elements that developed over time, and these can be found in Sabbath's music.

Before they were Black Sabbath, they were known as Earth. Based out of Birmingham, England, Earth was a blues band fronted by vocalist Ozzy Osbourne with Tony Iommi on guitar, Geezer Butler on bass, and Bill Ward on drums. It is important to know their blues background in order to understand the musical direction and style of the band. The blues played an enormous role in the melodies, chords, riffs, rhythms, forms, and grooves they play. Before they were known as Earth, they briefly called themselves the "Polka Tulk Blues Band" and had a saxophonist and a slide guitar player. And before that, Geezer and Ozzy were in a band called the Rare Breed, and Bill and Tony were in a band called Mythology. Have a listen to the live recording of Mythology's July 13, 1968, performance in Silloth (northwest England) to hear the unabated blues style, especially in Tony's solos. Ozzy and Tony were literally card-carrying blues fans: they had a membership to "Henry's Blueshouse," Jim Simpson's Tuesday-night blues series at the Crown in Birmingham. It was through this series that Jim became Earth's manager. Their blues roots should not be overlooked, as it was an important element that shaped the band. Geezer explains, "Heavy metal would not exist without the blues. Black Sabbath would not exist without the blues."[1] Bill says, "I can't say enough about coming back to shuffles and the blues, especially English blues music that was so dominant during the midsixties."[2] Geezer said they also did soul music such as Sam & Dave, Otis Redding, and Wilson Pickett when they were still Earth. Tony said, "When we started, both Geezer and I were playing guitar, and we learned everything we knew from the blues. Anyone who was serious about an instrument was either learning blues or jazz."[3]

Yes, jazz was another important influence on Bill, Geezer, and Tony. Bill was exposed to big band jazz records at an early age and has cited Gene Krupa and Joe Morello as important influences. You can hear the jazz drumming influence on many songs but most overtly on "Wicked World," "Rat Salad," and "Song for Jim." Tony said that in Mythology he would play some jazz and Chet Atkins. He said, "Bill Ward and I both liked jazz and jazz drumming, and we would try to put that in the songs. Then when we formed Earth with Geezer and Ozzy, we were mostly playing blues with jazzy bits."[4] Ozzy said in 1972 that they started playing jazz around 1968, the time around which Earth was formed.[5] Geezer said, "I started off as a blues and jazz player."[6] Tom Allom, the engineer for their earliest albums, said, "What [Bill] and Geezer were doing together was incredible, actually. They were almost a jazz band, really."[7] Tony says, "My influences are mainly jazz."[8] Jazz guitarists such as Wes Montgomery and Joe Pass were influences on Tony, but Django Reinhardt was not only an influence but inspirational. The tips of two fingers of Tony's fretting hand were cut off whilst working in a sheet metal factory as a teenager. Django had an injury limiting the use of some of the fingers on his fretting hand. Once Tony learned that he and Django had a similar "handicap," yet Django still managed to be a virtuosic guitarist, it inspired him to continue as a guitarist. In 1970, he told *New Musical Express* that he is very interested in jazz, including jazz-rock bands Chicago and Blood, Sweat & Tears. Jim said, "We listened to jazz- and blues-related records. They discovered their riff music [their "repetitive riff idea"] from artists like Jimmy Rushing. . . . In fact, their stage show at that time included covers of some Jimmy Rushing songs. They liked the riffs small jazz bands played and it started a trend within Sabbath."[9] Tony told *Melody Maker* in 1971 that they would play jazz in rehearsals to "loosen up."[10] A recording of a 1985 rehearsal shows that they did the same many years later as well. Ozzy said in 2006 that they "never used to write a structured song. There'd be a long intro that would go into a jazz piece, then go all folky."[11]

Another influence on Tony was Alvin Lee of Ten Years After; listen for the fusion of jazz, blues, and rock found in Tony's and Alvin's playing. Tony also cited the instrumental band the Shadows as an influence, which makes sense because Sabbath was such a guitar-driven band with long instrumental sections in their songs. Geezer cited Frank Zappa and the Mothers of Invention as his favorite band after the Beatles. Ozzy said the members of Sabbath "looked up to Zappa, especially Geezer."[12] Tony writes, "As a musician I think Frank was very clever, especially at arranging, and his band was tight."[13] Geezer calls Jack Bruce of Cream his "number one inspiration" as a bassist.[14] They cite the Beatles as influences, and Ozzy in 1972 said he liked "anything that was heavy," mentioning the Kinks, the Who, and Led Zeppelin.[15]

Another aspect to consider is the environment in which they lived. Birmingham in the 1960s was an industrial town, and that surely had an impact on them as people and as musicians. Bill said, "I would go past the factories and put rhythms in my head to different machine sounds."[16] The area of Birmingham where they lived was, and still is, considered to be among the roughest parts of the city. Tony lived in the Newtown part of Aston, less than two miles north of the city center. Geezer lived just a five-minute walk north of him, and Ozzy lived less than a mile north of Geezer. It's amazing all three of them lived in such proximity to one another. Bill lived in a nicer neighborhood a few miles north of the rest of the band but still close. Having grown up in the same area and all being roughly the same age, they had similar experiences that shaped the band.

For a brief time in December 1968, Tony played with Jethro Tull. He decided to return to Earth. From that experience, he was inspired to learn flute. Although it was never a focus for him, he played it on several songs. He also gained knowledge of how to make rehearsals more productive. After his time with Tull, Tony got Earth to be very serious about rehearsals, being on a schedule, and so forth. They rehearsed in the Newtown Community Centre, which is only about eight hundred feet from where Tony lived. They were regimented about rehearsals thanks to Tony's experience with Tull: "We're going to do it seriously and really work at it, starting with rehearsals at nine o'clock in the morning," he recounts. [17]

To get a sense of what the band sounded like around this time, the best available example is from a concert in Dumfries (southwestern Scotland) on November 16, 1969. The live set included at least three twelve-bar blues covers: Willie Dixon's "Let Me Love You Baby," Elmore James and Marshall Sehorn's "Early One Morning," and an up-tempo version of Eddie Boyd's "Blue Coat Man." Aside from an original called "Song for Jim," the rest of the recording consists of songs from their first album. Having listened to these blues covers, when you listen to Black Sabbath's original compositions, notice how the blues have influenced Ozzy's vocal melodies, Tony's guitar solos, Geezer's bass lines, and Bill's drumming. Listen for how the standard twelve-bar blues form was expanded, developed, and abandoned in their original songs. Lastly, and perhaps what is most important, listen for what set them apart from other blues bands. Tony said, "We couldn't keep playing 12-bar [blues]." [18] They became a hard-hitting, high-energy band with some very nonblues riffs and lyrics. Also in the set was "Black Sabbath," so lyrics such as "Satan's coming around the bend" certainly stood out against the blues numbers.

In addition to that live concert, having a listen to the demos they recorded in the months leading up to the album sessions will paint a clearer picture of the development of the band. On August 22, 1969, Earth recorded a two-song demo at the famed Trident Studios in London (it is no longer there, but a new studio named Trident Sound Studios is on an upper floor in the same building). It must have been quite the experience for the young band to record in the same studio the Beatles had recorded "Hey Jude" only one year prior. At Jim's suggestion, they recorded "The Rebel," a song written by Norman Haines, with the composer at the piano. It hasn't been released officially, but it is available. Although there are pop elements (the chords, background vocals, etc.), listen for Tony's power chords, which together with aggressive solos give the song its hard edge.

They also recorded "Song for Jim" on that session. It is closer to jazz than it is to rock with its "swung" rhythms in the melody, walking bass line, and jazz swing pattern in the drums. A clip of that song appears on *The Black Sabbath Story Vol. 1* video, but it is labeled as a demo from 1968. It is possible that the recording in the film was from the August 22, 1969, session, but the performance isn't as polished as "The Rebel," so it could have come from a 1968 rehearsal or session. A live version of "Song for Jim" from the aforementioned Dumfries concert shines some light on the song. Here, the melody is played on the flute instead of on guitar. The song is used in this performance to feature Bill; from 0:49 to 10:17 it's only Bill, as Geezer and Tony only return for the final thirty seconds. Drum solos over nine minutes were not unusual for them, as they would stretch out solos to fill a set in their early days.

By the end of August, they had changed the name of the band to "Black Sabbath." They returned to Trident about a month later to record a session that likely included "Wicked World." On October 7, Sabbath recorded "When I Came Down," another Norman Haines composition, in Ladbrooke Sound Studios (later called "Zella") in Birmingham, in a small studio behind a music store. (The music store has since become an Eritrean/Ethiopian restaurant, and the studio behind it became a room for private parties.) Tony's intro riff on the guitar is taken from Norman's keyboard parts, as Norman does not appear on the demo. Bill does some interesting tom work in the bridge section, breaking away from a typical rock drumbeat, an approach he would return to many times. Only less than a minute of this recording has been released, but to get a sense of what the rest of the song is like, check out "When I Come Down" (different spelling) on the Norman Haines Band's 1971 release *Den of Iniquity*. They also recorded "The Wizard" in this session, but it was rerecorded at Regent Studios in London for their first album. According to the owner of the disc, "The Wizard" has "slightly different lyrics" than on the album.

On November 10, Sabbath returned to Trident to record a version of Crow's "Evil Woman." It was Jim's idea to record that song, and the band "reluctantly agreed."[19] It was released as a single on Fontana Records and later on the European releases of their first album. The B side was "Wicked World," which likely came from the September session. After recording four songs for BBC One on November 11, Sabbath went to Regent Sound Studio A (off Tottenham Court Road, not the one on Denmark Street) to record the rest of their first album. Some sources say it was in October, but according to Martin Popoff's *Black Sabbath FAQ* book, the tape with "Behind the Wall of Sleep," "Black Sabbath," "The Wizard" and "N.I.B." was dated November 17, and the tape with "Sleeping Village" and "The Warning" was dated November 18. Those dates are also listed on some of the more recent releases, meaning it was recorded the day after the concert in Dumfries, Scotland.

Throughout this book, I invite you to take a closer listen to the songs. Although it is tempting to sing along to the vocal parts, or to your favorite riff or drum fill, take a step back and listen to all that is happening in the music. In fact, try to ignore your favorite parts and listen for other things happening at the same time that you may have missed in previous listenings. You may wish to listen to the song several times, focusing on a different band member each time. For instance, you could listen to "N.I.B." and pay attention to Geezer exclusively; you may hear things that you hadn't noticed before because you were paying attention to a particular vocal line, guitar riff, or drum part at that same moment in the song.

Beyond the blues, jazz, and rock influences mentioned earlier, there are other stylistic elements about Sabbath to listen for. For instance, Tony plays through heavy distortion and occasionally "palm mutes" the strings, giving the guitar sound a crunch. Partially due to his injury, he played two-note chords eventually referred to as "power" chords. Rock musicians have credited him as the "master of the riff" who developed and popularized the use of the power chord. Rather than reserving the vibrato technique for single notes, Tony would use vibrato on chords as well in order to make the guitar, as he described it, sound "more full" and "as heavy as I could."[20] For the same reasons, Geezer often uses vibrato when he plays.

Geezer uses distortion as well, which was not common for bass at the time. They would turn up the amps in the studio, at times letting the bass distort, something most studios in the late sixties/early seventies would not do. "Luckily we got the right producer that said 'yeah, this is the sound that I want,'" Geezer said. The producer didn't care that the bass was distorted, "which was unheard of in those days."[21] Geezer prefers natural distortion (by turning the volume so loud that the sound distorts) to distortion pedals. He said they would put the speaker cabi-

nets in another room when recording. His bass lines often follow the
guitar riffs to add weight and heaviness to them. "I always wanted to
back the riff up to make it deeper and heavier, so I'd play the same that
Tony is playing," he explains.[22] For additional thickness on certain
notes, Geezer will play a different note than Tony or he will bend the
string (putting him slightly out of tune with Tony's chord), thus creating
a dissonant—hence thick—sound. Instead of keeping to primarily one
note, as do most bass players, Tony explains that "[Geezer would] be
playing all over the place, bending the strings. . . . I'd bend the string,
and Geezer'd bend the string to make it bigger, to make it a wider
sound."[23]

   The sound of Ozzy's voice has a character that is quite recognizable.
Not regarding effects on his voice, there are moments where he
changes his sound enough where it doesn't sound like him (e.g., "Planet
Caravan" and "Solitude") due to the change of technique, volume, and
style. There are certain blues-derived mannerisms he gravitates toward
and small inflections he uses that are distinct to his style. He sings in a
"rock tenor" range, usually in his medium and high registers. Only
occasionally would he sing in his lower register. It should be noted that
although Ozzy has contributed somewhat to the lyric writing, it was
Geezer who was the band's primary lyricist. Tony describes the usual
process: "Ozzy would improvise lyrics, but then later, Geezer would
write the actual lyrics, sometimes incorporating what Ozzy had come up
with."[24] Aside from the melodies that followed Tony's riffs, Ozzy wrote
many of the vocal melodies from improvising with the band and trying
things out. Geezer comments, "I don't think [Ozzy] gets enough credit
for the talent he had for coming up with these incredible vocal lines."[25]

   Bill's drumming is very aggressive, loud and heavy. He said there
was "rage" in their music.[26] Also notice how he doesn't usually play
typical rock drumbeats, placing the snare drum and bass drum on different parts of the beat and incorporating toms into his drum parts. He
is like Ginger Baker of Cream in that respect, who also had jazz elements in his playing. Bill pairs crash cymbals with drums as do big band
jazz drummers to accent certain notes played by other musicians. He
describes this approach as playing "orchestrationally." Thus, instead of
playing a drumbeat, he "plays to the riff" in a reactionary way. Bill
explains, "From a musical point of view, I react to Geezer and I react to
Tony. If Tony's playing unbelievably loud, then I try to be as intimate as

possible with those loud parts as a percussionist."[27] In the song "Black Sabbath," Bill describes his approach as "playing drums to the words."[28]

When listening along to Sabbath's catalog while reading this book, I recommend listening with a good set of headphones and stereo system to good-quality vinyl from an earlier pressing whenever possible. Some of the newer remasters on CD and vinyl have problems, and streaming audio (e.g., YouTube) is very poor. Some of the intricacies of the music are lost with a poor stereo system or low-quality digital files. Second, the timings used in the text correspond to the audio when pulled into audio editing software. Be aware that certain playback programs such as iTunes and QuickTime Player will sometimes differ by one or two seconds. Lastly, I represent the pace of the basic beat, or pulse, of the songs ("tempo") in "beats per minute," commonly abbreviated as "bpm," in order to express the relationships among their slow, moderate, and fast riffs. There are free metronomes online that you can use as a reference to the bpms listed in the text.

TIMELINE

1968   Aston, Birmingham, England: Bill Ward, Geezer Butler, Ozzy Osbourne, and Tony Iommi form a blues band named Earth. Tony leaves the band only briefly to play in Jethro Tull.

1969   Earth changes their name to Black Sabbath, records demos in Birmingham and London, records album in London.

1970   Their first album, *Black Sabbath*, released. Second album, *Paranoid*, recorded in London, released in the UK in September. First concerts in the United States.

1971   *Paranoid* released in the United States in January. Sabbath writes, records, and releases third album, *Master of Reality*. Six weeks (May/June) in Wales writing new material.

1972   January: Some recording in London for a fourth album. May: Relocated to LA to write and record. June: Completed album in London; *Vol. 4* released.

1973   Went to LA to write more songs; then returned to UK to continue working. Recorded fifth album, *Sabbath, Bloody Sabbath* (*SBS*), in London with guest keyboardist Rick Wakeman (Yes). *SBS* released.

1974   Tour to promote *SBS*. April performance at famed Cal Jam.

1975   Recorded sixth album, *Sabotage*, in London and released. Jezz Woodroffe hired to play keyboards on the tour.

1976   Sabbath, with Jezz, goes to Miami to record seventh album, *Technical Ecstasy*, released in autumn. Tour to promote *Technical Ecstasy* includes Jezz.

1977   *Technical Ecstasy* tour continues to April. In autumn, Ozzy leaves band and is replaced by Dave Walker (Fleetwood Mac).

1978   Ozzy returns in time to write and record *Never Say Die!* in Toronto. Don Airey (Colosseum II) hired to play keyboards on the album but not for the tour. *Never Say Die!* released, and a tour follows.

1979   Sabbath goes to LA to write songs for a new album. Ozzy fired, replaced by Ronnie James Dio (Rainbow). Geezer leaves, and Geoff Nicholls (Quartz) and Craig Gruber (Rainbow) brought in. Band relocates to Miami in the first week of September to continue writing. Two weeks into the recording sessions, Geezer returns and replaces Craig's bass parts. Geoff remains and plays keyboards on the album.

1980   Sabbath relocates to Paris in early January to write and record "Neon Knights." *Heaven and Hell* is released, and they tour to promote it, including Geoff on keyboards and background vocals. Bill leaves midtour and is replaced by Vinny Appice (Derringer) in August. Mid-December, band goes to England to write and record "E5150" and "The Mob Rules" for the film *Heavy Metal*.

1981   *Heaven and Hell* tour continues to February. Band goes to LA to write and record *Mob Rules*. "The Mob Rules" is rerecorded for the album, but most of "E5150" is retained aside for some guitar overdubs. *Mob Rules* released and a tour follows. The twenty-minute short film *Spinal Tap: The Final Tour* goes into production, including the infamous Stonehenge scene, predating Sabbath's "Stonehenge."

1982   Ronnie and Vinny quit. Geezer and Tony meet Ian Gillan (Deep Purple) in Woodstock, Oxfordshire.

1983   Ian officially joins the band in February. Bill invited to return, but stays in LA to detox and is temporarily replaced by Malcolm Cope (Quartz). Geoff, Geezer, Malcolm, and

Tony work up new songs in Birmingham. Ian soon joins rehearsals but does not sing due to nodules on his vocal folds. The band, including Bill, goes to Shipton-on-Cherwell, Oxfordshire, to write and record album. Bill relapses, quits the band, and returns to LA. *Born Again* is released, and tour with Bev Bevan (Electric Light Orchestra) on drums follows.

1984   Ian quits, replaced by David Donato, and Bill returns. Bill and Geezer quit, and the band becomes temporarily inactive.

1985   Retaining Geoff from Sabbath, Tony begins work on a solo album in LA and hires Gordon Copley (bass) and Eric Singer (drums) of Lita Ford's band and singer Jeff Fenholt (original Broadway production of *Jesus Christ Superstar*) to make demo recordings. In June, Tony invites Glenn Hughes (Deep Purple) to sing on the album, and they record in LA in July. Bassist Dave Spitz replaces most of Gordon's recorded tracks. Original lineup reunites for one concert: *Live Aid*, in mid-July. Album completed in Atlanta in late August.

1986   Tony's solo album is released as "Black Sabbath Featuring Tony Iommi," titled *Seventh Star*. Rehearsals in LA in winter. In mid-March, Glenn gets into a fight that affects his voice. One week into the tour, he is fired and replaced by Ray Gillen in late March. After the tour, Sabbath goes to England and then Wales to write new material. The band records in Montserrat in September, but Dave leaves the band by the end of the month. Bob Daisley (Ozzy, Rainbow) replaces Dave's bass parts in early October. Later that month, the band relocates to London to continue work on the album.

1987   Eric and Ray quit, and Tony Martin replaces Ray's vocal parts. Album completed in London, with percussion on a new composition, "Scarlet Pimpernel," played by Bev. Geezer and Bev rehearse with Geoff and both Tonys in mid-July, but Geezer quits and is replaced by Dave in time for their July 21 concert in Greece. Bev quits and is replaced by Terry Chimes (the Clash) for concerts in South Africa, after which Dave quits and is replaced by Jo Burt (Virginia Wolf). *The Eternal Idol* is released in autumn, and Sabbath plays a brief tour in Europe.

1988 Drummer Cozy Powell (Rainbow) joins, and the band writes and records new album in England. Laurence Cottle (Alan Parsons and many others) records bass parts, and Brian May (Queen) records a guitar solo on "When Death Calls."

1989 *Headless Cross* is released, and bassist Neil Murray (Whitesnake) is hired for the tour.

1990 January: The band, including Neil, writes new material in Birmingham. February: The band goes to Wales to continue writing and begin recording, relocating later that month to Berkshire to complete new album by June. *Tyr* is released in August, and a tour follows into November. Meanwhile, Geezer "sits in" with Ronnie's solo band Dio in August and "sits in" with Sabbath in September, prompting talks of a reunion.

1991 Cozy, Geezer, Geoff, Ronnie, and Tony write material for a new album in Henley-in-Arden. Tony Martin is also involved during this time with Ronnie temporarily away. Vinny returns, replacing Cozy. The band, with Ronnie, goes to Surrey to record "Time Machine" for *Wayne's World* and then to Wales to record demos and the album, including rerecording "Time Machine."

1992 *Dehumanizer* is released. Ronnie quits midtour, replaced by Rob Halford (Judas Priest) for the final two nights of the tour. Tour ends in November with a reunion of the original Bill/Geezer/Ozzy/Tony lineup at the end of the final night. Vinny quits, and negotiations to continue an Ozzy-led Sabbath begin.

1993 Tony Martin returns, and Sabbath goes to Henley-in-Arden to resume work on new material. Drummer Bobby Rondinelli (Rainbow) joins in mid-March. Guitarist Eddie Van Halen comes to April 26 rehearsal and helps write "Evil Eye." The band goes to Wales in mid-May to record album, which is finished in the summer. Ozzy backs out of the reunion plans in August. Ray dies of AIDS in December.

1994 *Cross Purposes* is released, and a tour follows. Bill replaces Bobby for the South American dates at the end of the tour.

With Cozy and Neil rejoining, Sabbath goes to Wales in October to write new material, with producer Ernie C (Body Count) sometimes present. Rhythm tracks recorded in Liverpool in early December.

1995   *Forbidden* album completed in LA and Surrey, and then released in June. Sabbath tours in summer. In August, Bobby replaces Cozy midtour.

1996   Sabbath inactive, but Tony Iommi begins recording a solo album with Don, Geoff, and Glenn, and drummer Dave Holland (Judas Priest).

1997   Ozzy and Geezer rejoin Sabbath with Mike Bordin (Faith No More, Ozzy) on drums and Geoff on keyboards (and likely background vocals and guitar) for the Ozzfest '97 tour. Shannon Larkin (Ugly Kid Joe) plays drums on final concert of the tour. Bill joins band for two concerts in Birmingham.

1998   Cozy dies in a car accident in April. In April and May, the original lineup records two new songs (one of which with a drum machine) released on *Reunion* with recordings from the 1997 concerts with Bill. He suffers a heart attack, and Vinny is hired for a brief European tour. Bill rejoins in late October for a performance on *The David Letterman Show* and a tour that begins New Year's Eve.

1999   Tour continues into December.

2000   Band largely inactive, aside from one brief performance near LA. Tony releases solo album *Iommi* with guest appearances by Bill, Laurence, and Ozzy.

2001   Sabbath writes new material with the intention of making a new album. On Ozzfest 2001 tour; set list included the new song "Scary Dreams."

2002   Band largely inactive, aside from a performance of "Paranoid" in London with Ozzy and Tony, with Phil Collins (Genesis) and Pino Palladino (the Who and many others) on drums and bass, respectively.

2003   Band inactive, but various Sabbath alumni work on other projects.

2004   Band is on Ozzfest 2004 tour but with Adam Wakeman replacing Geoff as side-stage keyboards and eventually rhythm guitar as well. Rob Halford returns to sing for an ill Ozzy on August 26.

2005   The Adam/Bill/Geezer/Ozzy/Tony lineup tours in Europe and then does Ozzfest 2005 for the rest of the summer. Ronnie announces in October that he will work with Tony on new material.

2006   Bill and Geezer join Ronnie and Tony (essentially reuniting the *Heaven and Hell* lineup without Geoff) and write three new songs. Bill quits in November and is replaced by Vinny. Mike Exeter (Iommi) plays keyboards on the new tracks, but his primary role is engineer.

2007   The new studio tracks are included on the compilation album *The Dio Years*. Band tours under the moniker "Heaven & Hell" with Scott Warren (Dio) on keyboards. In October, the band decides to make another album.

2008   Band writes new material in the summer and then goes on a brief tour in August with the 2007 lineup. Band goes to LA to continue writing songs and then to Wales to record in the fall. Mike provides the keyboards for the album but is primarily an engineer and coproducer.

2009   *The Devil You Know* is released, and a tour follows.

2010   Ronnie dies from stomach cancer in May. Heaven & Hell performs a tribute concert on July 24 with Glenn and another guest vocalist, Jørn Lande.

2011   Mike and Tony show demos of new material to Ozzy and go to LA in February to work up demos with Tommy Clufetos (Ozzy) on drums and Mike temporarily on bass. Mike and Tony return to England to continue writing. Bill and Geezer enter the project, working at Ozzy's home studio in LA. Mike and Tony then return to LA to work on material with Bill, Geezer, and Ozzy. On November 11, at 11:11 a.m., Sabbath announces a reunion of the original lineup. Tony diagnosed with cancer in December.

2012   January: Geezer, Mike, Ozzy, and Tony go to England to continue working, but Bill remains in LA and then quits. The band continues to write in the UK until April, after which they play a few concerts with Tommy on drums. Drummer Brad Wilk (Rage Against the Machine) joins the project, and the band resumes writing in mid-August and begins recording in LA. After a short break, they resume recording sessions in October, and the album is close to done by mid-December.

2013   Mike and Tony record additional parts in England. LA-based Stanley Behrens likely adds harmonica to "Damaged Soul." Album mixed from mid-January to mid-March. The album *13* released in June, their first number one album in the United States and their first number one album in the UK since *Paranoid*. Tour starts in April with Adam on keyboards and Tommy on drums.

2014   Tour continues until mid-July.

2015   Band largely inactive; members take time off. Band rehearses in December in preparation for *The End* tour.

2016   *The End* EP, consisting of four leftover tracks from the *13* sessions and four live recordings from the 2013–2014 tour, is released. Band tours for most of the year.

2017   Geoff dies from lung cancer in January. Sabbath concludes *The End* tour in their hometown of Birmingham in February.

I

THE BIRTH OF METAL

The origins of heavy metal can be traced back further than February 13, 1970, the date when Black Sabbath's first album was released. Those musical moments were the sparks that ignited what was to be known as heavy metal. The heaviness and darkness (musical and lyrical) heard on *Black Sabbath* set them apart from other bands at that time. It really was the first true heavy metal album.

BLACK SABBATH

The album begins ominously with sounds of rain, thunder, and a distant tolling bell. With a band named after a horror film, this atmosphere fits. The lyrics and main riff of the opening track, "Black Sabbath," define what was distinctive about the band. This was no ordinary blues band; this was the emergence of heavy metal. The song is like a horror movie, with its intention of sounding frightening. The lyrics were written after Geezer Butler had a supernatural experience. He explained that the night after receiving an old book of black magic, he woke up suddenly and saw an apparition—a black shape—at the foot of his bed.

The music sounds as frightening as that experience. The main riff emphasizes two different notes, and the interval between them is what is called a "tritone," or the "*diabolus in musica*" (the "devil in music"). Its nickname was unbeknownst to Tony Iommi, but he liked the evil sound. In rehearsal one day, Geezer played the first three notes to the theme from the "Mars" movement of Gustav Holst's orchestral suite *The Planets*. Tony played it at rehearsal the next day, changing the second note to be the same pitch as the first, only higher, and that became the main riff of "Black Sabbath." They repeat that riff for nearly four minutes with very little variation. The interest lies in the different ways that it's played over the course of those four minutes: sometimes loudly with much distortion; other times softly behind Ozzy Osbourne's vocal lines. When played loudly, Tony plays a "trill" (a rapid alternation of two notes) every other time through the riff to give emphasis and variation. In this trill, he alternates between the evil-sounding "tritone" note and the missing note from the Holst theme (that "missing note" is actually present in the power chord at the beginning of the riff, where it is not used melodically, but instead to thicken up the sound). Geezer also makes the riff dramatic, especially with his bass slides (0:44, etc.). Bill Ward's drumming makes the verses dramatic in a different way by creating an earthy backdrop for Ozzy's vocal parts. To achieve that, he focuses on the toms by avoiding the use of the snare drum and cymbals (aside from gently keeping time with his left foot on the hi-hat). Notice that he avoids playing a rock drumbeat but instead approaches the drum set like a percussionist. The tolling bell (which is also the missing note from Holst's theme) eventually ceases at 1:22 just before Ozzy's entrance, but it returns for the loud section at 2:20. Ozzy's vocal delivery is as intense and scary as the supporting music, the tone of his voice rich.

Another element of the music that makes it so "doomy" is the dreadfully slow tempo. Although one could feel the tempo at about 64–68 beats per minute (bpm), in the loud sections, Bill plays a "backbeat" that implies a slow rock beat at about 32–34 bpm. That backbeat is played on the snare drum with the second note of the riff (the higher one, 0:40, 0:47, etc.). The tempo picks up fourfold at 4:36 with a new riff and feel, yet the horror-like emotional affect remains. Introducing a new riff at a faster tempo is a device that Sabbath will return to many times in their career. The new tempo fits the drama of the lyrics, for instance, "people running 'cause they're scared." In some early recordings, but not on the *Black Sabbath* studio release, there is a third slow verse that occurs after they briefly go to the faster riff. It is definitely worth a listen, if only for the especially creepy lyrics. It must have been a very strange experience for those visiting or working at the Newtown

Community Centre hearing these young men rehearsing and writing this song, as there wasn't anything like it at the time. The guitar solo is classic Tony Iommi. In it you will hear "Tony-isms" such as bends, trills (5:48), repetitions of a brief idea (5:38–5:41), and of course the blues roots. With Tony's guitar solo in the left channel and his wah-wah-drenched rhythm guitar in the right channel, Bill and Geezer provide support aggressively. After a second of silence, the band returns for a surprise "tag" to end the song. It is notable that they did not play this tag in live performance from around this time, so perhaps it was a musical suggestion from the producer or engineer.

The very beginning of "The Wizard" shows the band's blues roots with the use of the harmonica played by Ozzy. The harmonica, guitar, and bass together blend well to give a heavy blues-derived sound. Notice their riffs are a bit different, adding interest to the music. In the first two notes of the main riff, the harmonica goes down, but Geezer and Tony go up (0:21). The same thing happens in the outro riffs of "Black Sabbath"; there, Tony goes up, but Geezer goes down. In both cases, they play at the same time to create a heavy sound, but the contrary motion gives the music another dimension. Bill's drumming is also interesting in this song. Again, he doesn't play a typical rock beat. He "plays to the riff" by accenting with Geezer and Tony, and fills in the space between those hits (1:07–1:12, etc.). He even plays to Ozzy's melody: notice the three snare drum hits that are in the same rhythm on words such as "misty morn—," "without warn—," "long grey cloak," and others (1:17, 1:22, etc.). The ending uses the blues and jazz band convention of the "tag," where a band repeats the very last bit of a song three times (4:10–4:17). With this track being done in only one take, it makes sense that they employ a convention from their experience as a working band to execute a solid ending.

The working title for "The Wizard" was "Sign of the Sorcerer," as can be seen on a lyric sheet written on a log sheet from Regent. Contrary to some reports, it was not originally called "Devil's Island," which was a working title for "Sleeping Village." On the studio outtakes, someone announces "Devil's Island" because that was the next scheduled to be recorded, not because it was a working title for "The Wizard." Some have assumed that was the case because Ozzy is heard on the recording saying, "It isn't 'Devil's Island.' It's 'The Wizard.'"

The next track, "Wasp/Behind the Wall of Sleep/Bassically/N.I.B.," is listed as two tracks on the European releases as "Behind the Wall of Sleep" and "N.I.B." Although "Wasp" and "Behind the Wall of Sleep" are registered as separate titles with ASCAP (American Society of Composers, Authors and Publishers), they are essentially two parts of the same song. The extra song titles on the U.S. versions of their early albums was for royalty purposes, a "publishing trick" as Bill described it.[1] Tony says the extra titles were added "not particularly by us" but by the record company (likely the publishing company).[2] He said in one case they didn't know about the additional titles until they saw the record. If anything, "Wasp" would be the first thirty or so seconds of the song, as it has a different key, tempo, feel, meter, and rhythm. That section comes back briefly at 2:34 but not in its entirety. The meter is three, which is highly unusual for Sabbath, and the rhythms are swung as in jazz. Thus, it's like a hard-rock version of the jazz waltz. Bill said, "What I like about the first album is the swing time, and the very subtle jazz qualities."[3] At 0:11, however, the two hits break up the waltz-like three-meter feel, as they are answered by guitar licks over four beats. So, they approach it as if it were six beats (two plus four), an interesting variation of the "three" feel. After briefly returning to the jazz waltz, the tempo drops suddenly, and the feel changes for Bill's funk groove. The key also drops, heard when Tony returns at 0:37 for the verse riff.[4] The blues influence is heard here, but as Tony said they wanted to get away from playing twelve-bar blues, so they rethought how to approach it. The verses still imply three-chord blues but over ten bars instead of twelve (a "bar" refers in this case to a group of four beats, about 2.7 seconds long in this part of the song). Notice how it implies the blues with changes at 0:44, 0:48, 0:55, 0:58, and 1:00. Also, they shorten the riff slightly by skipping a beat at 1:00. At 1:29, they change the key by going to the original but keeping the same feel. By raising the key here, Geezer and Tony give a sudden boost to the music and increase the momentum.

Key changes are an important aspect of Sabbath's songs; they are used for emotional effect and for variety's sake. Instead of using a wide variety of chords, Tony keeps the chords relatively simple but may use several keys in a single song to keep the music sounding fresh. When they return to the jazz waltz at 2:30, it doesn't sound too jarring because they are already in the original key. However, the element of change is still there because the tempo, meter, and feel change suddenly. It's quite impressive how well the band changes tempo together without issue, clearly an indication of a band that has been performing together for a while. At 3:36, the drums fade out on Bill's funk groove. Recordings of live performances at this time reveal that the song at this point goes into a multisection, up-tempo jazz-rock instrumental part to end the song.

"Bassically," the bass solo intro to "N.I.B.," is not registered as a separate title with ASCAP, so it's clear the intro had its own title so that the U.S. release would appear to have ten different songs. "N.I.B." was named after Bill's beard, which looked like a pen nib, not an abbreviation for "nativity in black," as it has sometimes been reported. In "Bassically," Geezer plays through a wah-wah pedal, an effect much more common for guitar than for bass guitar. He adds distortion to introduce the main riff of "N.I.B.," another effect not normally used on bass. Ozzy compared "N.I.B." to Cream's "Sunshine of Your Love," and if you sing the first four notes of each song's main riff, you will hear the similarity. "N.I.B." has two examples of Geezer and Tony playing similar but different lines: in the postverses, Geezer descends as Tony stays the same by repeating the riff three times (1:19–1:26, 2:53–3:00, and 5:03–5:09), and they switch roles in the choruses by Tony's chords descending and Geezer staying the same for three times (1:56–2:03, etc.). Another nice touch to the choruses is the tambourine in the right channel and its reverb in the left. The second postverse melody becomes a guitar solo, which is actually a duet with each guitar in separate channels (left and right). The two guitars play nearly identically to each other except in a couple of parts (3:12–3:15 and 3:35–3:37). Tony approaches many of his solos as duets on the studio recordings by keeping them quite similar, only diverting at key moments. A second guitar duet at the end of the song develops the same way as before: it begins with the postverse melody that becomes a double-tracked solo with only brief moments where they play differently. The lyrics are a twist on the love song genre, as the song is sung from Lucifer's perspective, and it is he who falls in love. The lyrics on the Dumfries concert are almost entirely different; only the chorus resembles the studio version ("your love for me" sung as "my love for you"). If the concert was indeed on November 16 and the song was indeed recorded at Regent the next day on November 17, the lyrics were likely written shortly before or during the studio sessions, as it doesn't sound as if Ozzy forgot the lyrics and improvised new ones.

Side two of the U.S. release begins with "Wicked World," the first song they wrote as a band ("Black Sabbath" being the second). Although Tony is best known for playing a Gibson SG, his primary guitar used to be a Fender Stratocaster, which was used for "Wicked World." In his 2011 book, Tony said the pickups stopped working in the recording session, so he switched to his "backup" SG for the rest of the session. This song was not recorded during the Regent sessions, so this must have happened at the earlier session. However, this contradicts a 1974 interview with *Guitar Player* where he recalled that this happened in a gig in Germany. The jazz influence is most overt on the intro and outro of the song, especially with Bill's jazz hi-hat work (0:00, 3:55) and when he switches to the ride cymbal and "comps" on the snare drum (0:21, 4:11). Ozzy confirms: "If you listened closely, you could also hear a lot of jazz influences in our sound—like Bill's swing-style intro to . . . 'Wicked World.' It's just that we played at eight hundred times the volume of a jazz band."5 The first drum fill (0:35) also appears at 0:17 in the Dumfries performance of "Song for Jim," demonstrating Bill's jazz approach to drum solos. At 0:54, the tempo and feel change drastically and a new riff appears. It is nearly identical to the main riff in the Doors's "Wild Child" (1968). Tony's riff omits the last note of the "Wild Child" riff, but Geezer plays it. It was probably unintentional because, when asked about it, Tony says he wasn't inspired by the Doors, nor did he like that band.

Side two of the European releases have "Evil Woman" in its place. It being a cover, one can get an idea of Sabbath's style and sound by comparing it to the original version by Crow. For instance, the bass part is mostly the same, but Geezer uses his distinctive bends on certain notes (0:30–0:37, etc.) and a much different tone. The Crow version has a liberal use of a horn section, including a trumpet feature, something highly unusual for Sabbath. The horn section on the Sabbath version is way back in the mix, and it can only be heard in the intro and sometimes with the two-note guitar riff in the verses and choruses (the baritone sax being the most prominent). Another mix of the song reveals that the horns were used in other places and that flute (likely played by Tony) was used as well.

The final track, "A Bit of Finger/Sleeping Village/Warning," is listed as two tracks on the European releases as "Sleeping Village" and "Warning." "A Bit of Finger" is registered as a separate title with AS-CAP, but because the opening of the song contains the words "sleeping village," it is clear that this not a separate song but a way to have the track count twice with ASCAP for royalty purposes. A reference to his injury, Tony called "A Bit of Finger" one of their "silly titles."

Tony starts the song with a solemn guitar part, letting his strings ring for greatest resonance. With Tony mostly in the left channel, the producer, Rodger Bain, is heard in the right channel playing the "Jew's harp" (mouth harp). Geezer enters gently at 0:05, and Bill lightly taps the cymbal only three times (0:11, 0:44, and 0:49). The sparse instrumentation leaves plenty of sonic room for Ozzy to enter in his softer, medium-low register. Like several of his melodies from other songs, he goes higher on the third phrase (0:32) and comes back down for the fourth.

The music changes feel, tempo, key, and mood suddenly at 0:54. If the argument were to be made that it is a separate song, then this would be "A Bit of Finger" and the track should have been labeled "Sleeping Village/A Bit of Finger/Warning." The music has little to do with the first minute and with "Warning" heard a few minutes later. Tony's guitar riff gives the impression that the music is faster, but when Bill plays a backbeat (1:00, 1:04, etc.), he implies a half-time feel (about 71 bpm) that is actually slower than the "Sleeping Village" part. The music is more active, so it sounds faster. At 1:21, Bill changes the groove, and the faster feel (142 bpm) could be felt here, especially considering the cowbell and shaker parts. This section has a Beatles-like sound and style to it (an amalgamation of the "Paperback Writer" and "Run for Your Life" riffs), "A Bit of Beatles" if you will. Bill, Geezer, and Ozzy all cited the Beatles as an influence, as any rock band of this generation would likely do. But a very Sabbath/non-Beatles power chord riff comes in at 1:38. The mood is darker, thanks to change of key, the heavy power chord, and the confirmation of the slower, half-time feel. The primary guitar in the left channel plays the riff, but to thicken up the sound, a second guitar adds power chords on the second half of the riff (1:49, 1:56, and 2:03).

The guitar in the right channel is awkwardly muted at 2:05, and Bill begins a Latin jazz–like groove on the ride cymbal bell not unlike the famous ride cymbal part in the Louis Prima/Keely Smith version of "That Old Black Magic." Moreover, his snare drum and bass drum work is not unlike what a jazz drummer would do. Geezer enters at 2:10 with what sounds like a pick, giving it a different sound because he usually plays with his fingers. But with the fast rhythms he plays behind Tony's guitar duet (2:14–3:06), it gives the bass the definition it needs. Each of the simultaneous solos could stand on its own; try listening to them separately by muting one channel at a time. But the two solos work well together due to Tony's phrasing and conservative note choice, thus they don't "step on each other's toes" when heard at the same time. Tony would revisit the idea of two simultaneous guitar solos on other songs.

The power chord section from 1:38 returns at 3:08, but instead of Bill's cymbal work, both of Tony's guitars (still panned hard left and right) holds out their last note, shaking it and getting it to feedback in the same manner as Jimi Hendrix at the beginning of "Foxey Lady." Instead of a Hendrix cover, we get Sabbath's version of "Warning" by Aynsley Dunbar's Retaliation. The original was a 1967 single not included on ADR's LP releases at the time. The writing credit on the single was given only to Aynsley, the drummer, but credit was also given to all four members of the band on the U.S. release of *Black Sabbath*. ADR had broken up by the time *Black Sabbath* was released, and two of the members, Aynsley and Alex, went on to work with Frank Zappa.

Like "Evil Woman," "Warning" gives the listener insight into Sabbath's sound and style by comparing the two versions. An important distinction to make is Sabbath wanted to cover "Warning" and was part of their live set, whereas they were reluctant to record "Evil Woman." Ozzy keeps the same bluesy vocal line, and it fits nicely in his medium register. In both versions, the guitar plays background lines that support the vocals, but Tony's is more aggressive. The ADR version uses organ heavily to accompany the guitar and vocals, but keyboards are rarely a major part of Sabbath's sound, so Geezer's loud, lightly distorted bass takes its role. Aynsley's approach is similar to Bill's in that he plays like a percussionist instead of playing a typical rock beat. However, Bill's version is much busier with more frequent rhythmic activity and the use of the entire drum set.

With the background guitar melodies solely in the left channel, the guitar suddenly moves to the center when the solo starts at 5:17. It's not really in the center but in the right channel with the slapback echo (delay) in the left channel. It gives the impression that he's standing to the right and echoing off the left wall in a small room. The way Rodger and Tom Allom captured the sound of the band being in one room is remarkable. (Barry Sheffield engineered the Trident sessions and also captured their sound well.) The solo continues at 5:52, but it moves to the left channel keeping the sonic image moving and fresh to the ears.

At the end of the final verse (7:01), Ozzy keeps the original vocal melody on the repetition of "just a little bit too strong" by leaping down into his low register. You can hear him struggle to hit the low note on the word "too," as he is a true rock tenor. You can hear two Ozzys on the word "just," so this line was probably an overdubbed additional take. If the song were an original, I doubt he would have written that low note in his melody. He only goes that low on "Hand of Doom," "Never Say Die," and in some songs much later in his career.

Instead of going back to the main riff as in the ADR version, Bill, Geezer, and Tony go into a free, unmetered jam from 7:04 to 8:20. Bill and Geezer provide a low rumble for Tony to solo over. By 7:23, it changes key, going higher, to heighten the vibe. Bill becomes more intense, and he and Geezer accent Tony's chords. They all progressively get more intense, but by 7:57 they all begin to dissipate the energy.

At 8:20, Tony introduces a new melody in a moderately paced shuffle feel so it sounds like a new song, and he begins another solo at 8:36. With the same rhythm and contour, his melody at 8:57 resembles 2:42 of "Fairies Wear Boots" but without the bend. The extended instrumental jams they would do live were breeding grounds for riffs and melodies for future songs, so this resemblance is not surprising. Interestingly, listed beneath the title "Warning" on a session log sheet is "Fairies." It appears they may have referred to that shuffle section as "Fairies," so perhaps "Fairies Wear Boots," which also has a shuffle feel, was an outgrowth of this particular jam.

By 9:50, Tony returns to the free, unmetered style while Bill and Geezer continue the groove, but they fade out at 10:06 leaving only Tony. The separation on the guitar here is so wide (both temporally and spatially) that it sounds as if it's two guitars and is double-tracked, but it's just one with slapback echo. Tony starts yet another section to his solo at 10:46 with a new melody/riff, this one especially blues derived. At 11:37 it transitions to a brief fingerstyle-picked passage resembling "Orchid" or the live intro to "Black Sabbath." Tony kicks on the distortion at 11:57 for an aggressive section ending with an eerie passage that foreshadows the end of "Children of the Grave" (aka "The Haunting"). At 12:51, Tony hits three chords that cue Bill and Geezer to come back in. Before it settles in the new tempo (around 126 bpm), they seamlessly change tempo at 12:59, dropping the speed by one-third to 84 bpm. It's common for bands to drop into half time but by a third is unusual and not as easy. To coincide with the drop in tempo, the key drops down back to the original, and it settles back into the groove for "Warning." This six-minute-plus middle section is a good representation of their live set jams. Geezer recalled it being much longer before it was edited down for the album.

At 13:27, Ozzy returns to repeat the final verse and, as before, struggles with the low note on the word "too" (14:00), his voice cracking a bit. It's wonderful to hear Ozzy stretch his vocal range and to hear him sounding so natural doing it. At over ten minutes, their cover of "Warning" is the longest Sabbath studio track, but that is due to the extended guitar solo and the insertion of other material in the middle. Notice they end the song the same way they do "N.I.B.": with a guitar solo finishing with the so-called Picardy third, a tom roll, and a final chord hit.

PARANOID

Only several weeks after *Black Sabbath* was released in the UK, Tony said "the songs on [*Black Sabbath*] are representative of us nine months ago. We recorded them six months ago,"[6] implying that they changed as a band from June 1969 to March 1970. None of the songs from their second album, *Paranoid*, appear on the November 1969 Dumfries concert, so they would have developed the material during the several months leading up to the June 1970 recording sessions. Any musical ideas that ended up on *Paranoid* were probably not ready for stage performance in November 1969. Jim Simpson said that *Paranoid* was developed on the road by rehearsing before gigs and at sound check. Ozzy said they also wrote new songs "in the van going to the gig" and "road tested" and "stage tested" them by including them in their live set as a song or as part of an instrumental jam.[7] Not all of their time was spent on the road, as they had gigs in Birmingham at Mothers and at the Crown ("Henry's Blueshouse"). Some of the material for *Paranoid* (e.g., "Iron Man") was worked out in their rehearsals in the Newtown Community Centre. Bill called the process "still jamming but it became team writing."[8] The band also spent time at Rockfield Studios (in rural southeast Wales about seventy-five miles southwest of Birmingham), rehearsing and writing in preparation for the recording sessions for what would become *Paranoid*. Tom Allom, the engineer, does not recall Sabbath having all of the melodies and lyrics done before the June 16/ 17 sessions at Regent. In fact, during those sessions, they were asked to write an additional song, as the album would have been too short. They quickly wrote the music for "Paranoid," and Ozzy recorded a guide vocal with temporary lyrics. Only the basic tracks were done at Regent; the vocals and overdubbed guitars were done at Island Studios, another famous London studio located a few miles west of Regent.

Tony says that "War Pigs (Interpolating Luke's Wall)" came from one of the "jams in the clubs."[9] Geezer said that the two-note verse riff (0:52) came from the middle instrumental jam in their live performances of "Warning." Originally titled "Walpurgis," it was about a black mass (e.g., "see them anoint my head with dead rat's blood"). The opening line "witches gather at black masses," however, was changed only slightly to "generals gathered in their masses, just like witches at black masses." Have a listen to the March 4, 1970, Cologne concert, the April 26 recording for John Peel's BBC show, or the April 29 Lausanne concert to hear the earlier lyrics. Geezer said they sent the original lyrics to the record company and that their response was "no, you're not going to call it that—too Satanic." "So I changed it to 'War Pigs,'" he clarified.[10] Interestingly, Ozzy used earlier lyrics in live performances after the album was recorded (e.g., the June 21 Germany, June 26 Germany, and August 31 Switzerland concerts) and even after the album was released (e.g., the October 3 so-called Paris 1970 concert). The album lyrics were used by the U.S. tour (see November concerts).

The song begins with guitars (one in each channel) dramatically holding out chords, with the left guitar tastefully generating feedback. It is one of the few examples of Sabbath playing in a moderate three-meter feel (about 111 bpm). Although the rhythms are swung, it does not have the jazz waltz feel of "Behind the Wall of Sleep" because Bill plays a backbeat on the snare drum (0:02, 0:05, etc.) implying a very slow rock feel (37 bpm). Because of Bill's backbeat, it's not a true three-meter feel but closer to what some blues musicians might call a "slow, 12/8 blues." For as "metal" as we may hear this introduction to be, there remains a connection to their blues roots.

If you listen closely, you will hear two simultaneous bass tracks from Geezer on this song: one placed only in the left channel, the other placed center right. The two parts are nearly identical for a majority of the song, so it could easily go unnoticed. However, some of the bass fills in the instrumental sections are noticeably different, revealing that there are two Geezers. The most noticeable moments in the intro are at 0:02 and 0:11, when the bass in the left channel comes in a fraction of a second early. If you listen to only the right channel, you can hear just the one bass locking in with Bill. For this, I suspect that it was the left-channel-only bass that was the overdubbed one. The practice of using two bass tracks is not usual for Geezer (if not the only time, certainly the most noticeable one).

At 0:31, Rodger added air-raid sirens to enhance the war-themed lyrics. At 0:39, the chords change twice as fast (every three seconds instead of six), increasing the momentum. The famous two-chord riff enters at 0:52, suddenly changing the tempo, meter, feel, and vibe. Although the riff is repeated every five seconds, we can think of it as being Sabbath's shortest riff ever (at only one second long) because of the four seconds of silence between each iteration. Bill keeps time throughout the silence with the hi-hat, giving a short open hi-hat cue a second before the big hits. Ozzy's vocal line begins in his low register, ascends to his medium register, and then descends back to where he started. Notice the difference between the notes he sings on the way up and the ones on the way down. The blues inflections can be heard on the way down: compare "gathered" (1:04) with the "blue" note on "masses" (1:11), or compare "minds that" (1:15) with "construction" (1:22). Tony's right channel guitar adds a couple of fills (1:29 and 1:34), and Bill plays a brief fill at 1:38 to enhance the vocal line. On the fourth time, they both remain silent to allow the space for Ozzy's iconic "Oh, Lord, yeah!" at 1:45.

Geezer and Tony expand the two-chord riff at 1:46 with some added chords, and Bill comes to the foreground by playing drum fills in the brief silences. At 2:07, Geezer and Tony introduce a new riff, and Bill settles into a moderate rock feel enhanced by tambourine to smooth out and connect the rhythms. When Ozzy returns at 2:18, Tony's riff changes, but Bill and Geezer more or less keep the same with very slight variations. They briefly recall the 2:07 riff at 2:38 but head to another verse at 2:49. At 3:09, Ozzy anticipates the return of the two-note riff by singing it over "yeah." Geezer and Tony answer Ozzy with the expanded version of the riff at 3:10, and again Bill has the space to play several drum fills.

At 3:31, the guitar solo begins like many of his solos do—simply and focused on melody. By 3:41, the guitars play slightly differently, so it becomes a duet. The basses here are quite busy and are played very melodically, so it's as if Geezer is "soloing" as well. One could think of this "guitar solo" section of a quartet of two guitars and two basses. By 3:44, a third guitar heard only in the right channel diverts from the others, and by 3:47, it descends to its middle register while the other guitars are playing much higher. It's like a quintet of three Tonys and two Geezers all soloing at once! After a brief lull of busyness (3:52–3:55), Tony launches into a series of bends and trills that are distinctive to his style, and Geezer continues to play soloistically (especially 4:08–4:11). To close his solo, Tony recalls the opening solo melody but varies it. The two held-out chords from the introduction return, which is clever because they are presented in a different context because the tempo and meter are different (compare 0:39–0:52 to 4:19–4:29).

After a few minutes of being absent, the two-chord riff returns as a backdrop for Ozzy's final verse. Like before (0:57), Geezer makes the second iteration of the riff extra dramatic by sliding down from it (4:35). He also slides down from the riff at 5:18 just before Ozzy sings, "Satan, laughing, spreads his wings." On live performances, he slides down at a much slower pace to make that moment especially dramatic.

After recalling the postverse riff that features Bill, they head into a two-minute coda that is referred to as "Luke's Wall" by some. "Luke's Wall" is one of the extra titles for the U.S. versions. Although it is registered as a separate title with ASCAP, it's not really a separate song but rather the instrumental coda of "War Pigs." It has several riffs and sections, so it's not throwaway material by any means. Tony's melody at 6:35 is so integral to the song that audiences sing along to the guitar part. The chords are based off the alternating two chords from the introduction and the end of the middle section, so it sounds like a logical outgrowth of the song. They bring back the first riff of the coda

(5:44) to close the song. Rodger and/or Tom decided to speed up the tape from 7:47 to the very end, so the song ends in a different tempo and key. Tony said, "We were shocked when we heard the sped up bit at the end."[11] A track without the tape being sped up reveals that, from 7:45 to the end, Bill speeds up from 87 to 92 bpm. Perhaps the intention was to add interest, to give a sudden boost of excitement, to obscure that the next track is in the same key, or to obscure and exaggerate the band rushing the tempo.

The next track, "Paranoid," became Sabbath's most well-known song. The music was written at Regent in a very short time period (some accounts say about twenty-five minutes). They knew it would have to be a short song, and although it has been said they didn't intend to write a single, the word "single" was written in green marker on the tape from Regent—that is, before it was completed at Island. Geezer calls the song an "afterthought" because it was written so late into the recording process.[12] He didn't want to record the song for the album, thinking it was too similar to Led Zeppelin's "Communication Breakdown." Although the chords are different, the rhythm of the ends of both songs' main riffs is the same. "Everybody else just couldn't see it," Geezer said.[13] The tempo is quite quick for an Ozzy-era Sabbath song (164 bpm). The song consists of a series of very short sections, only twelve seconds each. The only exception is the guitar solo, which is twice as long. The solo is split into two channels: the one on the left is Tony's usual sound, but the one on the right is the signal being sent through a ring modulator. Regarding the lyrics, Geezer says they relate to the depression he suffered from as a teenager. "I couldn't relate to anybody when I was getting into my depressions," he said.[14] It should be noted that the band intended the album to be titled *War Pigs*, but due to the political climate (i.e., Vietnam War), it would have to be changed. Joe Smith, the executive vice president of Warner Bros., said they would not allow the album to be called *War Pigs*, and based on the strength of "Paranoid," they decided to title it *Paranoid*.

The next track, "Planet Caravan," shows another side to the band. Tony said it "was very different to anything we'd done before."[15] Geezer called it a "smokey jazz number."[16] The volume is much lower, the performance is gentler, and the mood is relaxed. Tony plays without distortion, and Bill plays bongos instead of a drum set. Geezer explains the inclusion of a soft song on the album: "We've always liked variation.

I think that's another Beatles influence, if you like. Every album they did, none of the songs were the same—different feels to each song. We always tried to get that. We didn't make a heavy metal album from [start to finish]."[17] The song has a structure even simpler than "Paranoid": brief introduction, verse, ten-second interlude, another verse, and guitar solo. The material for each of those sections is the same and very simple, merely two alternating chords. Multiple times throughout the song there is a synthesizer sound in the right channel that echoes in the left (0:58, 1:04, etc.). Tom explains that the "funny little synthy-thing" is "not a keyboard at all. It's a knob" that controls the synthesized sound.[18] I wonder if it was an EMS VCS3, because it was a keyboard-less synthesizer from 1969 England. It had a ring modulator, so perhaps they used it for Tony's solo on "Paranoid." The last two minutes of the song features Tony, for what he calls a "jazzy solo."[19] His solo is clearly influenced by jazz as heard in the tone, phrasing, and the collection of notes (i.e., the scale) used. He will employ this scale in some of his other solos to evoke the sound of jazz. Citing Django Reinhardt and Joe Pass as two of Tony's influences, Geezer said the solo on "Planet Caravan" gave Tony "the chance to show his jazz roots as that didn't really fit with the heavier stuff."[20] With Tony in the right channel, Tom's piano is heard in the left channel from 3:11 to the end. Ozzy's voice sounds almost unrecognizable because he sings softer with a slightly different technique and his voice was recorded through a rotating Leslie speaker cabinet. Only temporary lyrics appear on the Regent sessions, so, like "Paranoid," it was completed at Island. The earlier lyrics, which were also love themed, do not have the space-themed imagery of the final version (aside from the mention of "moon" and "sun"). Geezer offers insight: "['Planet Caravan'] was really laid back. I didn't want to come up with the usual love crap, so it was about floating through the universe with your loved one . . . taking a spaceship out into the stars, having the ultimate romantic weekend."[21]

The beginning of "Iron Man" has to be one of the most iconic intros in rock music. In the first eight seconds, Bill's bass drum moves from the right channel to the center as if it's Iron Man himself approaching. Tony's guitar bend also moves from right to center (0:08, 0:15, and 0:22). At 0:11, Ozzy's voice sounds as if it's sent through a ring modulator, probably the same one used on the "Paranoid" guitar solo but with different settings. The "Iron Man" riff (0:28) came first, and the song's title and lyrics were inspired by the riff. Geezer said that Ozzy said the riff "sounds like a big iron bloke walking about."[22] When an interviewer asked Tony if it was true that the "Iron Man" riff was inspired by tea, he replied, "Coffee actually! We rehearsed in [the Newtown Community Centre], and it was all they had. I had a cup and out came that riff."[23] The vocal melody follows the riff, an approach for which he has been unfairly criticized. Ozzy said, "If I couldn't come up with a melody over the top of what Tony was doing—what his riff was, I'd sing the riff."[24] Having the vocal follow the riff should not be viewed as lazy or unimaginative; it is very effective because it keeps the music focused and powerful. Tony concurs: "It seemed to be the right approach for it, I think."[25] The vocals are double-tracked (notice the slight differences between the left and the right channels) and also fill the sound. Notice during the main riff that Bill plays more than just a rock beat; he plays fills nearly all the time yet never disrupts the flow. Geezer is heard entirely in the left channel, thus Tony sounds as if he's off to the right even though he can be heard on both channels. With Bill and Ozzy in the center, the stereo image is the same as they usually appear on stage.

Ozzy said that Geezer wrote the lyrics about "a guy who travels through time and he sees what is going to happen in the future . . . a Sci-Fi thing."[26] On the hand-written lyric sheet, it says, "Written as a science fiction song by Geezer Butler." Geezer expands on that, explaining that it was "all about the future of the world. I was really into [writing about] pollution back then. . . . You could just see that a lot of things were going wrong in the world and nobody was saying anything about it. . . . There was nobody talking about the stuff that I wanted to talk about—political stuff—so that's what inspired me."[27]

The song is divided into several sections, each with different riffs and/or chords. There are verses, a postverse riff, a chorus (or another postverse section), a solo section, and an instrumental coda. They play in generally two different tempos, so the song has a slow-fast-slow-fast structure. The song uses three different keys, with some changes being very subtle and others jarring for dramatic effect. Constructing songs with multiple keys and tempos is something the band would continue to explore, especially in their longer songs, to keep the music sounding fresh throughout the course of the song.

After repeating the riff seven times for a couple of verses, a post-verse riff (1:14) heard three times provides contrast. Geezer and Tony break for Bill's simple three-drum fill to take it back to the main riff for a third verse. Instead of recalling the postverse riff at 1:58, a chorus-like section uses a new riff. This section is like a chorus in that Ozzy sings over it and for its placement after the second verse. It doesn't seem like a chorus because it only comes back once more over the next four minutes and with mostly different words. From 2:22 to 2:34, the main riff is heard twice more before the fourth verse begins. These twelve seconds are an excellent example of a band playing, feeling, and listening to one another. Notice how at 2:27 Bill hesitates in the middle of the fill (the second tom hit coming in a bit late). It doesn't seem to faze Geezer and Tony at all, because they delay the final note of their riff to line up right with him. Although this is a matter of a fraction of a second (probably fifty milliseconds), it's enough to notice, and the fact that Geezer and Tony adjusted in real time (assuming these aren't overdubs) is quite astonishing.

After a fourth verse, the second "chorus" ends with the line "now he has his revenge," setting up a sudden tempo change to more than twice as fast (79 to 169 bpm). The key goes higher, as in the solo in "Warning," adding another dimension to the sudden change. Changing the key or tempo for a different section, especially for a solo, is something Sabbath will do many times in their career. To open and close this brief solo (3:11, 3:40), Bill, Geezer, and Tony together play a syncopated riff based on the blues scale. Although the focus is on the guitar in this solo section, Geezer plays some interesting moving lines as well (3:23–3:26, for instance); mute the right channel to listen to just him and Bill.

At 3:45, the second half of the "chorus" riff is played four times. Because of the sudden change of tempo and key, this moment is as dramatic as 3:11. Having come from a fast section, when they return to the slower feel (81 bpm), it makes the riff seem even heavier. With the main riff absent for over a minute, the listener craves its return. When it comes back at 3:57, it sounds broader and heavier because the tempo decreases slightly (to 78 bpm), effectively making it more intense.

At the end of the fifth and final verse, one of the Ozzys stretches out the word "again" as the other Ozzy sings it short. As Ozzy holds out his note (4:22–4:25), the tape is sped up, raising his pitch. At 4:22, the postriff from three minutes prior returns. Ozzy's rising note matches Geezer's and Tony's in the second half of that riff (4:25) and fades out.

That last line, "Iron Man lives again," sets up a return to the faster feel (158 bpm) for the instrumental coda. It's not as fast as before, but it seems faster because of the more active rhythms used. The coda is in a third key, which is established by Geezer at 4:41. This change is much more subtle because the main riff ends on this note. Tony cleverly brings back the intro guitar bend at 4:49. When it first appeared, it was played over a slow tempo and without any context of a key. It returns in a much different context, breathing new life into the musical gesture. As in "War Pigs," the guitar solo opens and closes with a simple, singable melody. By 5:15, the guitars split into a duet. Unlike Tony's other guitar duets, the guitar in the left channel cuts out several times, so its role is more to accentuate what is happening in the right channel than to function on its own. At 5:42 and 5:49, Bill and Geezer pick up on a rhythmic idea from Tony's melody. The three of them together play a three-note "stinger" to end it.

Side two of *Paranoid* opens with "Electric Funeral," a slow (61 bpm), doomy song describing a world destroyed by nuclear war. Tony plays through a wah-wah pedal for the main riffs, giving it a postapocalyptic sound. Aside from a few notes to offer variation, Geezer follows Tony for the riff used in the intro and between verses. As in "Iron Man," the vocal melody (for the verse) follows the riff, keeping the music focused, with Tony again calling it "the right approach."[28] At 1:49, the tempo picks up more than twice as fast (from 62 to 130 bpm) and even faster by 1:56 (140 bpm) to build intensity. In this transitional section, notice the third chord of Tony's three-chord hits progressively get shorter (1:58, 2:03, and 2:06), giving it an anxious quality. A new riff in an even faster tempo (224–236 bpm) starts another section with its own verse riff; here Ozzy follows Tony's melody, as does Geezer for the most part. Bill doesn't play a backbeat proto-punk drumbeat but instead follows the riff with a swing-like feel. From 2:50 to 2:58, Ozzy sings the song's title three times in his low register. The timbre of his voice sounds altered, so it was likely recorded at a higher tape speed (thus a higher note in his middle register) so he can project those low notes. At 3:09, they drop the tempo by nearly four times (!) to return to the original feel for the song's main riffs, making them seem even heavier than before—the same technique used in "Iron Man."

Geezer explained that "Hand of Doom" was about Vietnam War troops using heroin, specifically U.S. troops that were temporarily stationed in Germany or England before returning home. It has an eerie, serious tone to the music, illustrated by Ozzy singing at the bottom of his range for the first half of the verses. This allows him to sing the same melody an octave higher in his medium-high register when the band comes in loudly for the second half of the verses (0:45, 1:29, 5:44, and 6:28). In the soft parts, Bill plays a funk-like groove at a low volume, placing his left drumstick across the head of the snare drum and playing on the metal rim. The middle part of the song (2:05–4:59) is in a different key, tempo, and feel (faster and swung), giving the music a much different character.

"Rat Salad" may offer insight into the drum solos Bill would take in live concerts. Tony said they wanted to have a drum feature on *Paranoid*, so they came up with a riff to open and close the song. From 0:17–0:27 and 2:07–2:17, Tony and Bill "trade twos" (two-bar phrases) in an up-tempo swing feel, evoking jazz. Tony's solo, although with distortion, uses jazz phrasing and scales. The drum solo in the middle lasts less than a minute, but in live performances, Bill's solos usually were longer. In live performances of "Hand of Doom" around 1970, they would go directly into "Rat Salad" but without the drum solo in the middle. The extended drum solo (over nine minutes) in "Song for Jim" from the Dumfries is a better example of Bill as a soloist.

The intro to "Fairies Wear Boots" goes through five different keys for four different riffs and a guitar solo. Tony says bands doing long intros "doesn't happen so much these days, but that is what we tended to do on the songs."[29] This part is called "Jack the Stripper" on the U.S. releases and is registered as a separate song with ASCAP, but it's another case of the "publishing trick." The song goes into a new tempo and feel at 1:15, but it returns to the very first key. It is a moderate shuffle, showing their blues and jazz roots. Bill describes the feel as "like swing with power." He continues: "I can't say enough about coming back to shuffles and the blues, especially English blues music that was so dominant during the midsixties."[30] Some of the accents have a jazz feel about them (e.g., Tony's higher chord at 1:17). On the *Classic Albums: Paranoid* DVD, Bill says, "What reminds me of the jazz in ['Fairies Wear Boots'] is the . . ." and then he demonstrates big-band-style "kicks" on bass the drum with cymbal hits. It's not only Bill who recalls the blues; listen to Geezer and Tony in the guitar solo (2:54–3:15).

Geezer, attributing the lyrics to Ozzy, says that the song starts about an encounter of being attacked by a gang of skinheads, calling them "fairies" and referencing the boots they'd wear. At the end of song, the subject changes to being about drugs, about LSD "I think," says Ozzy.[31] Geezer recalls: "This other time we did this gig in the seaside town of Weston-super-Mare [southwestern England], and we had a fight with all these skinheads. I think that's where the lyrics for 'Fairies Wear Boots' came from."[32] That would have been the June 13 performance. Tony recalls still having a black eye from the events when entering the studio, which would have been just three days later. The song is on their April 26 and 29 performances, both predating this event, thus it couldn't have been about this particular altercation as it has been reported and assumed. It's possible the lyrics were written to reference skinheads in general, or perhaps the "fairies" were originally not skinheads after all but instead the hallucinations referenced in the final verse, explaining the sudden shift in subject matter. In either case, the lyrics became to be about skinheads and the fight. In an August 1970 interview, manager Jim Simpson said the song was a "subtle go at skinheads,"[33] confirming the song's meaning before the album's release.

"PARIS 1970" AND OTHER CONCERTS

The best audio and video document of the band around this time is the "Paris 1970" concert, which was filmed in Brussels on October 3, not Paris in December. It is nearly an hour long and certainly worth watching. There is additional footage from German TV (Frankfurt and Bremen) and Dutch TV (Bilzen and another, albeit the band miming). There are audio recordings from Berlin, Cologne, Lausanne, London (John Peel/BBC), Montreux, San Francisco, and Sheffield. Listening to these recordings reveals how the band developed in the ten months from promoting their first album to preparing for their third.

2

SWEET LEAF AND SNOWBLIND

"**S**weet Leaf" (1971) and "Snowblind" (1972) are two classic Sabbath songs about drugs from their third and fourth albums: cannabis in the former, cocaine in the latter. Although there are certain stylistic elements common to both albums, there are some key differences discussed in this chapter. These two songs may be used as a point of comparison, but many other songs could as well. Considering what Ozzy Osbourne said about *Vol. 4*, "we're getting more into melody,"[1] compare the songs from that album to vocal melodies from songs such as "After Forever" and "Into the Void" from *Master of Reality*. They became more interested in experimentation. With their relocation from England to Los Angeles, think about how far they traveled geographically and musically in only one year. Their music changed. Even their preferred drug changed.

Stylistically, *Master of Reality* pairs with *Paranoid* for similarity in riffage, use of melody, song structure, and production. It was written around the time they were touring to promote the recently or yet-to-be-released *Paranoid*, thus those songs were in their live repertoire. Tony Iommi says that "musically, *Master of Reality* was a continuation of *Paranoid*."[2] It was done at Island Studios, the same place where they completed *Paranoid*, in the first couple of weeks in February before they left for their second U.S. tour. They completed the album in early April upon their return from the tour. The rehearsal-room writing sessions Tony has mentioned likely took place in late December 1970 and/ or late January 1971 between tours. "Into the Void" and "After Forever" were performed on January 14, 1971, with different lyrics, so at least two songs were in the works by that point. Ozzy said he didn't like the *Master of Reality* album, calling the songwriting and recording process "too rushed." "It was done so quickly, in three weeks," he said, "we didn't have the chance to do what we wanted."[3]

Just as "Planet Caravan" is a soft song to contrast the heaviness of "Iron Man," there are songs on *Master of Reality* to create "light and shade" as Tony describes it: "Embryo" before "Children of the Grave," "Orchid" before "Lord of This World," and "Solitude" before "Into the Void." Tony explains, "If you listen to an album or even a song from start to finish and it's all pounding away, you don't notice the heaviness of it because there is no light in between it. And that's why, sometimes in the middle of songs as well, I put a light part in, to make the riff sound heavy when it comes back in."[4]

MASTER OF REALITY

"Sweet Leaf" begins with a cough, the end of which is looped, moves from the left to the right channel, and becomes progressively distorted over the course of five seconds. The cough comes from Tony, having just taken a toke on a joint given to him by Ozzy. Although it was recorded during a session for a different song, its inclusion for the beginning of "Sweet Leaf" make sense, as the lyrics are essentially a love letter to cannabis. The cough sets up not only the lyrical theme of the song but the tempo as well. It is looped at a rate of about 417 milliseconds (or shall we round up to 420 to keep with the theme of the song?), which is 144 beats per minute (bpm). The band enters with a moderately slow groove at 72 bpm, half of that. For comparison, Bill Ward's hi-hat plays at the same pace as the cough loop.

The main riff is played by two guitars (one in each channel) and bass. It sounds like one guitar because they play the same thing, but there are small differences (e.g., fret noise, squealing, etc.) heard in one channel and not the other. Geezer Butler slides down from the second note, giving it a fatter sound. At the end of the riff, Geezer goes higher and plays a different note than Tony, creating a nice harmony (0:07). On the second time, he stays on the same note as Tony. Although the riff is three seconds in duration, Geezer's pattern is six seconds because he alternates going up or staying the same. He also lines up with Bill's bass drum pattern.

The riff is played six times (three for Geezer's pattern) before each verse begins. Ozzy sings "alright now" at the end of the second; he sings "won't you listen?" at the end of the fourth; and the pickups to the first verse ("when I first") occur at the end of the sixth. The lyrics are set in second person, and the subject to whom Ozzy sings is cannabis itself. Aside from the cough, this is not given away until the second verse with "I love you, sweet leaf." However, it sounds as if it could be an endearing term for someone. In fact, an earlier version of lyrics were not drug related at all and included lines such as "I want you, baby, to be my wife, to love and cherish for the rest of my life." The love-song tone remained, but the subject became an inanimate object. The earlier version had the same melody for the most part and was fully developed: same riffs, interlude, guitar solo, and so forth.

On the subject of melody, Ozzy sings a strange note on the last syllable of "introduced" (0:37). It is not in the key, and he doesn't sing the note again, nor does Tony or Geezer play that note. On the second verse he changes it by singing a bit higher, this time in the key ("free" at 1:49). On the third verse he changes it again, this time singing a bit lower, and also in the key ("me" at 3:55). In live performances, he sings "introduced" with the note used in the second verse, leading me to believe it was a mistake that they decided to keep or did not notice. Having heard it "fixed" in the second and third verses and in live performances, the note in the first verse is attention grabbing. On the other hand, one could hear it like a blues inflection (although it is certainly not a part of the blues scale, it has a similar effect).

After the verse, a six-second riff is played four times. Tony's post-verse riff ends with a held power chord that allows Bill and Geezer to fill during the last two seconds of each iteration. Geezer's fill on the second one (1:01–1:03) has a bluesy character and has the most motion—it starts high and goes down the scale. Bill and Geezer more or less play together on the fourth one (1:14–1:16) to bring it back to the main riff.

A third guitar enters at 1:16 to play the main riff in a higher register as a single-line melody (instead of the lower power chords in guitars one and two). Like the intro, the second verse begins after the main riff is played six times with Ozzy singing at the end of the second, fourth, and sixth. The melody is changed only slightly, with the "fixed" note for "free now" (1:49) and the words "sweet leaf" (1:55) matching the notes for "free now" instead of the note for the word "wanting" (0:44) from the first verse. These slight changes give the music a living and improvisatory quality instead of it feeling fixed and tied down. The third guitar remains in the texture for the postverse (2:02), still doubling the riff as a single-line melody in a higher register. The switch (lever) for the snare drum comes loose at 2:24 and remains that way for the rest of the song; it is difficult to hear in the mix but quite evident in the isolated tracks. It loosens the snares enough that it changes the timbre of the drum. Compare the snare drum sound in the first verse to the third verse to hear it.

At 2:27, the music suddenly changes. The tempo is bumped up to 82 bpm from 76 (which is up from 72 where it started). Here, Tony plays four big power chords, each answered by five quick floor tom hits from Bill. The tempo changes yet again to a much faster 173 bpm (more than double time). To coincide with the tempo change, the key is also changed. The key change is ambiguous with the first chord change (2:33), but it is established with the chord at 2:36. The new key is confirmed with Tony's fast melodic figure, which he plays sixteen times (2:48–2:59). In this transitional section, a tam-tam (often incorrectly called a gong) is struck three times, the third time the loudest (2:33, 2:39, and 2:44). This is the same tam-tam used for the beginning of "After Forever," which is clear if you hear the isolated tracks from "Sweet Leaf" and play the beginning of "After Forever" in reverse. It is gong-like because it has a pitch (E-flat), but it has so many other overtones it would be classified as a tam-tam. With all the guitars playing in this section, the pitch is inaudible so it certainly sounds like a tam-tam. Bill and Geezer really drive the band here, especially with Bill's fast tom work, bass drum on all beats ("four on the floor" it's sometimes called), and occasional crash cymbals. Bill refrains from the cymbals from 2:47 to 2:54, allowing Tony the sonic space to begin his repeated figure. From 2:54 to 2:59, Bill and Geezer play "stop time" hits behind Tony. When the figure ends at 2:59, Geezer and Tony hold out the note, allowing Bill to fill all the way to 3:02, the start of the "guitar solo."

I am hesitant to call the next section the "guitar solo" because Bill and Geezer are so busy and prominent that one could hear it as instrumental trio. Bill plays mostly on the snare drum with the occasional tom hit. Geezer moves around quite a bit, refraining from staying on the same bass note throughout. Tony's part is double-tracked, each part playing almost exactly the same thing, giving the effect of one guitar with a delay or chorus effect. Tony's part could be heard as a short, simple solo consisting of a five-second phrase played twice, the second with slight variation. Each begins with bended notes in the higher register and descends to the lower register. In the middle of each phrase, he recalls the bends but starts them a beat early (3:04 and 3:10), preventing it from sounding too symmetrical. It could also be heard as four short phrases (each lasting less than three seconds and starting with bends), with the first and third being similar and the second and fourth being similar.

The first and last notes of the postsolo riff (3:13) outline that infamous tritone, cleverly connecting the key of the instrumental section with the original key. Geezer and Tony play the riff three times, and the "instrumental trio" becomes a Bill drum solo, as he becomes the focus. The time and beat break down, and they return to the original tempo and riff. Guitar three returns to double the main riff in the higher register, as it did starting at 1:16. The melody for the third verse is mostly the same, with the small change for "gave to me" (3:54) avoiding the strange note from "introduced" and the higher note on "free now" from the first and second verses, respectively.

The postverse at 4:08 is cut in half, returning to the main riff after only thirteen seconds. When Geezer plays long notes, he often plays them with vibrato to give a fatter sound. He does this on the postverses, but it is especially evident at 4:08. Hear how the note goes slightly sharp (raised) as he bends it with vibrato. Bill's bass drum is busier and quite punchy here for this final postverse section.

The outro repeats the main riff into a fade-out, and it sounds like a jam with Ozzy's improvisatory style and the odd phrasing. Bill begins by playing on the crash cymbals, but after three times through Tony's riff (one earlier than expected), he switches to the hi-hat. As expected, Ozzy sings at the end of the second riff, but instead of waiting until the fourth as before (0:17, 1:28, and 3:34), he comes in one early for "oh yeah." Ozzy's original guide vocal is different than the recorded take, so it is clear he overdubbed the vocals later. Thus, Ozzy follows Bill's phrasing by shortening the phrase. That doesn't affect Tony's pattern, but because Geezer's is twice as long, Bill and Ozzy's phrase overlaps with his pattern. Even though Bill goes to the hi-hat making it sound like the start of a new phrase, he plays a fill at the end of the fourth riff to match Geezer's pattern (4:32). By singing the words "sweet leaf" (4:40), it sounds as if the next phrase starts there, which is after three bars (4:31–4:39). The riff played before each verse is played six times by Tony (three by Geezer because his pattern is twice as long), but this time Bill and Ozzy divide it three plus three, overlapping Geezer's pattern. To complicate matters, the tam-tam is struck every bar (three seconds) starting at 4:37 (before "sweet leaf"), making it sound as if the phrase might start earlier. Then Ozzy sings more short vocal motifs for an uneven five bars (fifteen seconds) before singing "sweet leaf" again (4:55). Geezer doesn't adjust his two-bar phrase to fit the odd-length phrases from Bill and Ozzy. Tony's riff is only one bar long, so it doesn't get affected and acts as the glue for the rest of the band. Sabbath usually stays even with their number of riffs per phrase and remain consistent from member to member. But here, they overlap with different ambiguous phrase lengths, giving it a jam-like quality instead of a worked-out, calculated sense.

What's also interesting about the vocal phrasing is that if one is to play a standard twelve-bar blues progression over what Ozzy is singing (ignoring the rest of the band), his vocal phrasing actually fits. Here, their blues roots show: not just the notes but the phrases too. Even though the phrases are asymmetrical at the end of "Sweet Leaf," they are, in a way, birthed from a more symmetrical blues form. For some reason, they deleted "yeah" from Ozzy's final "oh yeah" (compare the isolated tracks to the final studio version at 4:56). Perhaps the "oh yeah" sounded too final and they wanted to continue the momentum throughout the fade-out.

The next track, "After Forever," is likely the first Christian metal song. Although some critics unfortunately cherry-picked the line "the pope on the end of a rope" and took it out of context, lines such as "God is the only way to love" and "open your eyes, just realize that he's the one" are but two examples of the Christian message. After eight seconds of a tam-tam played in reverse, synthesizer sounds drone in a two-second tape loop. Tony enters with a melody supported by a repeated open string, a texture not unlike "Embryo."

The up-tempo feel, major-key melody, synthesizer, tambourine, and shaker give it a pop-like sound. This section is called "The Elegy" on some releases, but it is not registered as a separate song with the American Society of Composers, Authors and Publishers (ASCAP). At 0:34, it drops to half time, the key is minor, the guitars play power chords, and although the shaker remains, the music takes on a darker, riff-rock character instead. The "elegy" section returns, and they head into a second verse. After playing the "elegy" section again, a bridge section changes the key, taking it back to the original key for the third iteration of the "elegy" section. Ozzy's vocal melody for the verses is simple; he only sings three different notes, primarily just two. His melody in the bridge is just as simple: only two notes, three if you include the key change. After the third verse, a bluesy riff functions as an introduction to the solo. The song changes key for the solo, giving it a boost of energy. The first half of the solo (3:36–3:46) is melody driven; it sounds like melodies Ozzy might sing. Tony plays four short phrases that answer one another: the second answers the first, the third is similar to the first, and the fourth takes the solo in another direction. The second half is more guitar-like with its blues and early rock 'n' roll guitar licks such as the series of bends. After the solo, the "elegy" section returns, and Ozzy sings a fourth and final verse. The song closes with the "elegy" section, its fifth appearance, and fades out with the synth loop.

"Embryo" is a twenty-eight-second track for solo guitar that serves as an introduction to "Children of the Grave" on the album and in many live performances. The ear gravitates to the lower part because it has the melody and because the higher part begins as a repeated open string. But pay attention to the upper part too, because it has more going on than just a repeated note: at 0:02 it moves with the lower part in harmony, and it has moving lines at 0:18 and 0:21. The melodic climax of the lower part occurs at 0:12 when it jumps as high as the repeated open string. Only two of the guitar's six strings are required to play "Embryo," as if it were imagined on some sort of medieval two-stringed folk instrument. That, the use of the open strings, and the simplicity of the melody give it a folklike quality.

"Children of the Grave" starts ominously with the first half of the main riff looped quietly on palm-muted guitar (left channel only), bass, and toms with Bill's left foot lightly keeping time on the hi-hat. A timpani roll lasts thirteen seconds and crescendos into the main riff. Here, the full band kicks in with a second guitar added, both partially palm-muted so that the crunch of the distortion is still strong, yet there is more resonance to the string than in the intro. This riff is one of Sabbath's heaviest thanks in part to the palm-muting and detuning of the strings (one and a half steps). Ozzy calls it the "most kick-ass song we'd ever recorded."[5] Geezer opts out of using the lowest range of his instrument and instead plays in Tony's register; in fact, he never plays below a low "E" so the whole song could be played on a regularly tuned bass guitar. To create extra heaviness, however, Geezer at times plays two notes at a time (0:36, 0:52, 1:33, 2:52, and 3:08). Bill aggressively bashes away on the crash cymbals instead of using hi-hats or a ride cymbal. At the end of the riff are two big hits played by Bill, Geezer, and Tony, the most characteristic part of that famous riff.

At nine seconds in duration, riff 2 (0:20) is three times as long as the first. Bill and Geezer remain busy, but Tony provides contrast in this section by holding out the chords. The held-out chords allow the sonic space for Bill's timbale part. The two timbales are close mic'ed with the higher drum placed in the right channel and the lower one in the center. The effect is that they create a large space by moving around the stereo image quite a bit, yet Bill is going back and forth between only two drums that are actually next to each other. The first riff is played twice more, riff 2 is played once again, and the first riff is played two more times before the verse begins.

The verse riff is a slight variation of the first, so I will call it riff 1B. The difference is a hit at the end of riff 1B that occurs in the space between where the two big hits in riff 1A are. That hit is played by the two guitars, bass, drums, and a third guitar in a very high register drenched in reverb. It never gets in the way of Ozzy's vocal melodies, but it is omitted on the eighth time when Ozzy yells "yeah." The timbales cease in the middle of Ozzy's first vocal phrase also not to get in the way of the vocal parts. The lyrics have an antiwar sentiment, and to put it in historical context, the Vietnam War was still raging on at this time. It is a continuation of "War Pigs" in that sense. An earlier recording of the song reveals that the lyrics were totally different, but the vocal melodies were fairly similar.

The postverse (1:18–1:34) consists of riff 2 once and riff 1A twice. Instead of going through that sequence twice such as from 0:20 to 0:52, it goes directly into the second verse. The timbales return for this section but cease in the middle of Ozzy's first vocal phrase of the second verse. The postverse after the second verse is even shorter, this time only using riff 2. It skips riff 1A and goes to riff 3, a triplet rhythm riff based on the blues scale. Riff 3 is so "ahead of the beat" that it shortens the pause between each riff just enough that it pushes the tempo from 150 bpm to 160, giving it an anxious quality. They drop into a half-time feel (75 bpm, half of 150, not 160) at 2:21 for riff 4, which has a relaxed feel instead of the rushed, anxious quality of riff 3. Tony and Geezer play a riff that sounds sinister because it features the "flat 5," the note a tritone away from the first chord (heard twice: 2:24 and 2:36). Bill plays a tribal-like pattern on the toms and bass drum at first, but at 2:34 he and Geezer move into a bolero-like rhythm. Also in the texture is an uncredited keyboard instrument that has a reedy sound very similar to an accordion. It can be heard on Ozzy's isolated vocal track, and the key clicks are audible, thus it is most likely a Mellotron with the accordion tape set or a harmonium. There are two; both keyboards play low notes that match and harmonize the guitar/bass riff, but the one in the right channel also plays a melody that brings out the evil-sounding "flat 5" four times (2:24, 2:30, 2:36, and 2:43). The lower notes of the keyboard are buried in the final mix, but the higher melody comes through, clearly giving the music an eerie quality.

Riff 1A returns at 2:46 as if restarting where it left off at 2:09. Then riff 2 and riff 1A are played twice more, completing the instrumental interlude that is essentially an expansion of the postverse. In verse 3, Ozzy addresses the listeners, the "children of today," directly. He warns that they will become "children of the grave" if they don't "show the world that love is still alive." The wish for peace gives Geezer's antiwar message a hopeful, positive tone. The final postverse is short like the second one, as it only uses riff 2. It skips riff 1A and heads directly into the guitar duet.

The guitar duet sounds like a guitar solo because both parts are playing the same thing for the first six seconds. When they split apart at 3:50, they play similar notes, rhythms, and gestures so they blend nicely. They come back together briefly at 3:56, but from 3:58 to 4:01 the guitar in the right channel plays the same thing as the guitar in the left channel, but shifted one beat (a fraction of a second) later. This canonic technique gives it a chasing feel. After the duet, riff 2 is played once more followed by some outro hits to close the song.

The song could end at 4:30, but the studio version continues with a coda section that is sometimes called "The Haunting." Although some releases label it as such, the words "children of the grave" are whispered, so it is very much a part of "Children of the Grave." Tony keeps the bottom string open and uses the "whammy" bar to change the pitch. That allows for various harmonics and feedback to come out because there isn't a finger touching the string to stop it from ringing. Two guitars navigate this eerie, haunting soundscape.

"Orchid" is a short acoustic guitar piece accentuated by delayed bass swells. The first seven seconds is a true introduction, as the material never returns. Not only does the intro have its own distinctive rhythm, but also it implies a different—but closely related—key than the rest of the work. Thus, the material is different enough to have its own character but similar enough to not sound out of place. The middle section (0:36–0:57) makes use of the original implied key by making it the basis for the harmony (0:36–0:39 and 0:43–0:46). From 0:50 to 0:57, Tony uses what are called "diminished" chords, which are surprisingly rare for him considering his fondness for the tritone. The harmonies in this piece (especially those diminished chords) are more closely related to classical music than the power chord riffing for which Tony is most known. The fingerstyle guitar technique he uses in "Orchid" evokes classical guitar playing. To end the piece, the harmonies suddenly change at a faster pace and the music gets softer (1:24); the effect created is the music unraveling itself before the listener.

"Step Up" is the first riff of "Lord of This World," labeled as a separate track on some releases but not registered as a separate title with ASCAP. The moderately slow (about 86 bpm) "step-up" riff is heavy, but the guitar plays it softly at first. The guitar is turned down, but you can hear the timbre of the string as it's being picked with light distortion. Bill starts to keep time with his left foot on the hi-hat, but after a squeak (likely the hi-hat stand) he stops. They had played the riff twice before coming in heavy, but the first one was edited out for the album. At 0:28, the tempo drops about 22 percent to about 67 bpm, and the feel abruptly changes from "straight" rhythms to "swung" rhythms. This verse riff supports lyrics that are, according to Geezer, how "the world was going at the time. It wasn't God's world; it was Satan's world."[6] Geezer calls it "our one and only Satan song."[7] After the second verse, the instrumental section gradually brings it up to the original tempo. At 2:04, the music suddenly changes feel ("swung" rhythms back to "straight" again), key (one step higher), and tempo (up 10 percent, to 74 bpm) to provide contrast and to propel the energy. Two cowbells (one in the right channel, the other in the center) drive the new, faster tempo. Aside from the extra hit in the right cowbell at 2:16, they play exactly the same thing. At 2:17, it returns to the original key but the tempo is faster yet (80 bpm). By the end of the guitar duet, the tempo is up to around 84–85 bpm for the return of the "Step Up" riff and the bridge section. By making the shift of speed gradual, it builds intensity over time instead of at one instant. The bridge section (2:59–3:09) is the climax of the song, and here Ozzy sings the highest: "lord of this world." Behind "evil possessor" (3:03), Tony has an evil-sounding downwards pitch bend with the whammy bar. Bill stumbles a bit here, his six bass drum and snare drum hits not played evenly enough for the band to come in together at 3:04; it's as if his triplet rhythm caught everyone by surprise. After the "Step Up" riff is played a final time (3:10), the tempo drops to about 67 bpm and the feel changes abruptly as it did at 0:28. After a third verse, the instrumental transition from 2:04 returns at 4:11, again with the same change in feel, key, and tempo. At 4:24, the tempo and key changes as it did at 2:17. As the guitar duet continues, the tempo increases to 84 bpm by 4:40, thus gradually pushing the tempo from the verse tempo to the original "Step Up" tempo. At 4:59, Tony picks up on Geezer's bass line used for the guitar duet and turns it into an outro riff. It is also worth checking out the earlier mix of the song that contained a piano doubling the "Step Up" and verse riffs and some Robert Johnson–esque slide guitar, recall-ing Tony's early blues roots.

"Solitude" is a soft song that provides contrast, for it is placed be-tween "Lord of This World" and "Into the Void" on the album. Geezer lightly drives the song while Tony provides light strumming on the guitar. Bill adds some very light finger cymbal work that is colored by a delay effect. Tony also plays flute on this track, an instrument he started to play after his time working in Jethro Tull. Although he had only been playing flute for a couple of years at most by this point, he sounds quite competent here, better than "amateurish" as he described it.[8] When the flute takes the melody at 4:00, its first phrase is like the first phrase in his guitar solo, a bit of cross-instrument self-quotation. The third and fourth phrases of the flute melody (4:24 and 4:34) are like Ozzy's vocal melodies. Starting at 1:40, there is an uncredited piano part. It sounds as if it's in reverse, but when played backward it's still not clear. Thus, it's probably not reversed but has reverse reverb, the same effect they used on the vocals for "Megalomania" on *Sabotage* four years later. Tony said he had not played piano before 1972, so it was likely engineer Tom Allom who played it. Tom, not credited at all on the album, has since taken credit for engineering duties on *Master of Reality*. Tom played piano on "Planet Caravan," and the parts are quite similar. Ozzy's voice is almost unrecognizable, as the timbre of his voice on this song is so different than how he usually sounds. His melodic apex comes at 3:04 and 3:28 ("the world is a lonely place" and "crying and thinking") when he alters the melody to go higher, yet he refrains from singing loudly.

The intro riff to "Into the Void" is labeled on some releases as part of "Death Mask." It is very doomy, partly because of its slow tempo (51 bpm). The riff dates back at least to November 20, 1970, as Tony played it in his extended solo in "Wicked World" in concert. He also excerpted the riff for his extended solo in "Wicked World" on the 1973 recording *Live at Last* (released 1980). "Death Mask" is listed as 3:08 in duration, which is approximately where the fast section starts, but that section lasts only twenty-three seconds. It makes more sense to think of "Death Mask" as being the first seventy-four seconds because that material never comes back and it has a clear ABA structure (riff 1, riff 2, riff 1). It is not registered as a separate title with ASCAP, so it makes the most sense to consider "Death Mask" not its own song but the long intro to "Into the Void," it being labeled that way to make it appear there are more tracks on the album.

At the start of "Death Mask/Into the Void," the guitar in the left channel starts with a long slide setting up the tempo joined soon thereafter by a second guitar (right channel) for riff 1. The first and lowest note of the riff is so low that it requires detuning the strings three half steps, giving it the same low-range heaviness as "Lord of This World" and "Children of the Grave." The other notes of the riff fall in the normal range of the guitar, so it's not as obvious. Geezer enters on his lowest note (requiring the same detuning), and it is very low and fierce sounding when they hit together at 0:10. He opts to go higher at 0:14, playing mostly in Tony's register and reserving his very low note for opportune moments (e.g., 0:56–0:59). Throughout the song Geezer mostly avoids the lowest register but "drops" using his open low string occasionally—only twelve more times for the entire song, so they are especially effective when they do occur. He sometimes plays two notes at a time to thicken it up (e.g., 0:39, etc.) and plays in harmony to Tony to give the riffs another dimension (e.g., 0:50, etc.).

The tempo changes suddenly for riff 3 (increasing to around 73–76 bpm), the main riff for "Into the Void." It is slightly different behind the vocal lines, so one could refer to the verse riff as riff 3B. Ozzy sings a simple, direct melody consisting of only three different notes but mostly staying on just one. The postverses (2:05, 2:53, and 4:24) use riff 3A and riff 4, a new riff derived from riff 1 (also similar to the transitional riff at 1:56 in "Electric Funeral"). Notice the overdubbed "trashy" hi-hats in the right channel whilst Bill's regular hi-hats play at half its pace. Tony introduces riff 5 at 3:05, and it is at three and a half times the previous tempo—252 bpm—making it one of Sabbath's very fastest ("The Law Maker" nineteen years later is even faster). Bill's overdubbed fast toms/bass drum pattern fill out the sound with a rumbling effect. Riff 4 is inserted at 3:27 and 3:31 to bring the fast section to a close. After a third verse and postverse, there is a guitar duet starting at 4:46, but like many of Tony's solos, it sounds like a solo at first because both parts play the same thing until 4:57. The outro riff, riff 6, is introduced at 5:04, and it is loosely based on the postverse riff; it has the same overdubbed hi-hat part too, further connecting riffs 4 and 6. The band enters a stop-time feel at 5:16; the left and right channel guitars trade licks from 5:29 to 5:39, at which point Bill comes back in with the groove, Geezer plays the outro riff, and the guitar duet resumes. After six seconds, the guitars split again into two solo parts, but by 5:57 all guitars come together for the outro riff to end the song. Although the song ends abruptly on the last note of the riff, copious amounts of reverb are added to the last note to extend its length.

BLACK SABBATH VOL. 4

As the name implies, *Black Sabbath Vol. 4* was the band's fourth album. Recorded and released in 1972, it was the first of several albums with experimental, progressive-rock-like elements. Describing the new direction for the band, Ozzy said *Vol. 4* was the "beginning of a new trip for us. . . . On *Vol. 4* we opened up [audiences'] eyes to what we can do, to what we can eventually do. It's like opening another door."[9] Tony said *Vol. 4* was a "complete change; we felt we had jumped an album, really. It didn't follow suit."[10] He later said, "The first three albums could've all been from the same batch really, but *Vol. 4* was when we started introducing different things."[11] Ozzy told *Billboard* in 1972, "This album isn't going to be quite as raw and heavy as the first three. We're getting more into melody."[12] He said that instead of singing the guitar riff, the aim was to be more melodic.

Geezer called it "more lyrical, more melodic" than the last album.[13] Ozzy said, "We're getting some weird effects in the studio and doing insane things."[14] He told *Melody Maker* in 1972, "We experimented a lot on this album."[15] Geezer's thoughts were the same: "We were experimenting a lot with different sounds. We had a grand piano in the [rehearsal] house; that's where 'Changes' came about. We had a Mellotron, all different kinds of instruments at our disposal."[16] One of the primary areas of experimentation on *Vol. 4* was timbre (i.e., sounds, instruments, etc.), especially the use of piano, Mellotron, a string orchestra, and sound effects. They also wrote in longer, multisectional forms; for instance, the opening track, "Wheels of Confusion/The Straightener" is eight minutes in duration with several sections. Tony said before *Master of Reality* was completed that he would "like to listen to and play a lot more classical and jazz styles,"[17] which may explain the use of strings and long forms on *Vol. 4*. Regarding the use of Mellotron and strings, Ozzy said, "It's a good change for us to use other instruments or to dub on something else that we don't use on stage. It's good for our ears as well as other people. We like our own music better if we can experiment on albums."[18] Listen, for example, to the string orchestra on "Laguna Sunrise," the piano and Mellotron on "Changes," and to "FX," a piece that consists of no melody, harmony, or meter, just sound effects created from objects hitting the guitar. Compare that timbral variety to the guitar-driven music found on the first three albums.

What led Sabbath to become more experimental? Perhaps we can look at what they were doing immediately preceding the June 1972 recording sessions for *Vol. 4*. In March 1972, they played nine or ten concerts with Yes, mostly in cities on the West Coast of the United States. It was during this leg of the tour that members of Sabbath befriended Yes's keyboard player Rick Wakeman. Sabbath performed additional dates with Yes, two in 1970 and two in 1971. According to a book written by two longtime members of the Sabbath road crew David Tangye and Graham Wright, "There were nights when Yes stole the show."[19] They shared the bill with many other progressive rock bands before 1972, for instance, three performances with Gentle Giant (one in 1970, two in 1971) and twelve performances with Curved Air (of which ten were in January 1971). They performed with several progressive rock bands in 1970, such as Renaissance, King Crimson, ELP, the Nice, Caravan, and Pink Floyd. They even performed with Van Der Graaf Generator when Sabbath still went by "Earth"; this was in March 1969 before Van Der Graaf Generator had released their first album. According to Tangye and Wright, the January 1971 tour with Curved Air "went generally well for Sabbath, although there were nights when they had to concede that Curved Air stole their limelight."[20]

It is likely that performing alongside progressive rock bands, such as Curved Air and Yes, inspired Sabbath to expand creatively. Certainly they had heard recordings of progressive rock music in the early 1970s, but more importantly, they had come in close contact with a variety of progressive rock bands. It is conceivable, then, that this influenced their own performing, compositional, and songwriting style. Tony said, "I used to watch [guitarist Steve Howe] when Yes used to tour with us in America—great players, great musicians." Tony described Steve as "very technical," calling him a "great player, superb musician."[21] Geezer said in 2004, "I remember trying to sound like [Yes's bassist] Chris Squire . . . but it didn't fit my playing style."[22] Tangye and Wright say that Sabbath was "more interested in creating art, something they could be proud of."[23] Ozzy said years later, "We still really cared about the music. We wanted to impress ourselves before we impressed anyone else."[24] They also had more time to write and record *Vol. 4* than with *Master of Reality*, which Ozzy called "too rushed."[25] Bill said, "We had this change of attitude where we had decided to slow down a bit and feel less hurried about getting an album out."[26]

Although it's generally thought that *Vol. 4* was made in Los Angeles, it was recorded in three studios: two in London and one in LA. According to Tangye and Wright, Sabbath spent three days in January 1972 at Marquee Studios recording "Snowblind," "FX," and "a couple of backing tracks."[27] A January 22 article in *Sounds* states that they had completed "Snowblind" and recorded "several backing tracks."[28] "Snowblind" and "Tomorrow's Dream" were performed on tour in March

1972, and the latter was performed in January in Birmingham. Thus, it is likely that backing tracks for "Tomorrow's Dream" were recorded at this session as well. Some of the songs may date back to May and June 1971, as they returned to Rockfield Studios for six weeks working up new material. Ozzy told *Creem* in 1971, "We've got a little cottage in the country. We'll stay there a few weeks, get loaded all the time and write some new songs."[29] *Sounds* reported that the album would be mixed in the United States and released as early as March 1972. Instead, they went to LA in May to continue writing songs and rehearsing. They recorded the rest of the album at the Record Plant, located about twenty minutes from their rented mansion in Bel Air. In June, they returned to London for additional sessions (including Bill's drums on "Under the Sun") at Island Studios.

It was party time for Sabbath at the Bel Air house; although other substances were (ab)used, they treated themselves to copious amounts of cocaine, cannabis, and beer. When asked if drugs enhanced their music, Bill replied simply, "Well, we wrote 'Sweet Leaf' [and] 'Snowblind.'"[30] Perhaps, then, the drugs were more inspiration than distraction. It's amazing they were able to make an album under those conditions from the stories that have been told. Bill Bruford (the drummer for Yes at that time) told me that when they toured together, he sees Ozzy with a fork in one nostril, a knife in the other, and a look on his face as if he was lost to the world. Then Bill turns to the other members of Yes and says, "This guy's not going to make it to 1973!" Decades later, in 2014, Bill is telling me this story and Ozzy's still out there performing!

Vol. 4 begins with an eight-minute track titled "Wheels of Confusion/The Straightener." "The Straightener" starts at 5:20 and is registered with ASCAP as a separate title (not an alternate title) for royalty and publishing purposes. It also appears as a separate song in the 1974 songbook from their publisher TRO Essex. Some releases list it as one song titled "Wheels of Confusion," and all releases have the timings combined. The introduction is somber with its slow tempo (47 bpm), minor key, and Tony playing in a sad, crying tone. The guitar in the right channel with its delay in the left augments the spaciousness of the music. The tempo picks up (59 bpm) at 0:21 with a new riff in a new key (although at first it sounds as if it is a chord from the previous key, it actually establishes a new key). Bill's groove here is not a typical rock drumbeat: he has double snare drum hits on the backbeat and ends most measures with a short, "mini" fill on the toms. After Ozzy's verses (1:09 and 2:00), Tony's riff features three-note groupings that syncopate against the beat, and Bill takes advantage of this rhythm by playing fills throughout it. After the second postverse section, they introduce another riff in yet another key and tempo/feel (fast, about 200–212 bpm; swing/boogie feel). At 2:36, Tony's higher guitars and Bill's cymbals and toms play a syncopated feel against the beat like during the postverses. They also play against the four-beat meter: at 2:41 and 2:46, there are nine-beat breaks for harmonized guitar (left and right channels), and when Geezer and Bill come back in at 2:48, they play only fifteen beats before the next section. At 2:52, Geezer stays on one note as Tony plays some psychedelic-sounding slides. But metal takes over psychedelia with a new, heavy riff at 3:33. Ozzy returns with another set of vocals (3:41, "lost in the wheels of confusion"), supported by harmonized guitars in the left and right channels. By now, the tempo has crept up from 200 to 222, so the energy is high. At 3:57, they return to the postverse but slightly faster than before, keeping the energy up. Returning to the second key, the main riff returns at 4:16, it too slightly faster than before.

The song (or part one of the song, if you will) ends after another verse and postverse. It never returns to the introductory material, so the intro, having its own tempo and key, really stands out like Chekhov's gun. Anton Chekhov's playwriting principle (i.e., whatever is presented must eventually have a function in the story line) may be applied to music: the audience has been introduced to something, but what is to come of it? As the last chord of "Wheels of Confusion" sustains, a new guitar part sneaks in, and it is "The Straightener." Two big chords announce the arrival of the new song (or part two). It is back in the original key for the remainder of the eight-minute piece, connecting this music to the introduction over five minutes prior. The tempo of the intro can be felt in a slow "four" (at 47 bpm) or in fast "three" (141 bpm), and because "The Straightener" is at 142 bpm, it feels connected to the intro with a similar pulse and the same key. Thus, the Chekhov principle delivers: the gun is finally fired. The rest of the track is instrumental, featuring Tony in a guitar duet. At 5:47, the two guitars play the same lines but harmonized. They come together at 6:14, but at 6:41, they split apart and play independently of one another.

"Tomorrow's Dream" is a relatively short song with a fairly simple structure. It was written before they went on tour in early 1972, but new lyrics were written for the studio version (they only kept the first four words and the title, but the melody is almost exactly the same). The chords, form/structure, drumbeat, and even the guitar solo are also the same, suggesting that it may be the other "backing tracks" recorded at Marquee months before the LA sessions. Listen for the tasteful simplicity in this track. For example, the guitar solo is a simple melody played in a medium-low register—no need to show off his technical ability here. Also, Bill's incorporation of the cowbell into the groove in the main riff is done subtly (not "clank-clank-clank-clank" as in so many seventies rock songs). The song starts with its main riff as an intro, followed by a verse. The postverse riff (0:36) feels relaxed and suggests a key one step lower, so when it goes back to the main riff (0:45), the energy returns as the key steps back up. The bridge (1:28) is also in the lower key of the postverse, so there is that same propelled energy when it steps up to the original key for the guitar solo (1:55). The synth tone that slowly rises from 1:55 to 2:06 (fade-out) also increases the energy for the solo. The bridge (1:28–1:45) feels even more relaxed than the postverse, as if it's in half time. It's not really in half time, but Bill gives that impression by delaying the snare drum backbeat and making it feel more "open." Geezer also makes it feel open by staying on the same note. If the song is propelled by the disagreement of two keys, then the lower key wins out because after the third verse, the postverse ends the song.

A side note about the development of "Tomorrow's Dream" is that the tempo on the studio recording is at 110 bpm, but it was noticeably faster when they toured in March. That isn't normally something notable, but it was remarkably consistent on three different concerts: all at 117 bpm. However, it was noticeably slower (103–104) when they played it in Birmingham in January, around the time of the Marquee sessions. The studio track plays at a slightly higher pitch than what they usually tune to. I wonder if they recorded the backing tracks in January at a slower tempo and decided after touring that a faster tempo works better, so they sped up the tracks by 5 percent, effectively raising the pitch and tempo ever so slightly. Speeding up rhythm tracks is not unusual, an old studio trick to make a band sound tighter. Then Ozzy recorded new vocals over those tracks in LA. If you listen to these five versions, you will hear the difference in feel.

Although there are softer tracks such as "Planet Caravan" and "Solitude," "Changes" was a departure for the band. For one, it lacks guitar, and Tony plays piano instead. It has a very serious tone—musically and lyrically—so the choice to not include a guitar solo or drums makes sense. In addition to bass, Geezer played Mellotron (strings tape set), giving the song an almost orchestral sound. Ozzy delivers the lyrics with such sincerity you would believe he is singing about himself. However, Geezer wrote the lyrics about Bill splitting up with his wife, having left her for someone he met while in California. Geoff "Luke" Lucas, then a member of the crew, described Bill and his first wife as "childhood sweethearts."[31] Knowing the backstory makes the lines "I've lost the best friend that I ever had" and "it's too late now, I've let her go" all the more sad. The piano part is simple, keeping to the white keys, as this was Tony's first foray into playing piano. The song structure is simple, with only three sections: verse, chorus, and postchorus. The three postchorus sections (1:03–1:33, 2:27–3:15, and 4:09–end) allow the Mellotron to take the fore. Instead of a guitar solo, the Mellotron continues over three-fourths of a verse (2:49–3:15) before the third verse begins. Although the song is in a hopeful C major, it ends on an A minor chord in a very sad feeling. To me, when I hear the last chord, I want—almost expect—the C major chord to return to give hope. It never comes, and in my mind, I hear that C major representing Bill's first wife and the A minor that ends the song to represent the sadness of letting her go.

Tony years later said, "If 'Changes' was unusual, 'FX' certainly was way out there."[32] It is the typifying example of their experimental aesthetic that started at this time. Think of "FX" as a piece for guitar and delay in which the guitar is used as a percussion instrument. Although there are pitches produced from the strings, there is no melody in the traditional sense. But there is rhythm, and it is intentional and not random as implied from Tony and Geezer's descriptions. The delay, set at about 195 milliseconds, creates the rhythm and tempo. Notice from 0:15 to 0:28 that it is consistently struck after eight or sixteen iterations of the delay. The regularity gives it a feeling of a regular beat at 77 bpm. The hits in those thirteen seconds were not coincidental because from 0:40 to 1:02 it is struck every sixteenth iteration (once every 3.12 seconds). After 1:10, it becomes denser as the guitar is struck more often.

To add interest, the sound moves around the stereo image a bit (left to right to left, etc.). To get the sounds, Tony tapped the guitar with the cross he wears. Geezer said Tony was nude for the recording, but Tony said "we were mostly naked . . . everybody then danced past the guitar, hitting it."[33] You don't hear the dancing footsteps, only some faint talking at the beginning.

From Bill's opening hi-hat part to the repeated riff in the fade-out, "Supernaut" has an incessant energy, the song's most defining feature. Keeping with that energy, Ozzy remains in his upper register throughout. Bill bashes away on the cymbals and at times (e.g., 0:27–0:29) plays double bass drum figures, a new setup for him at the time. Tony's guitar tone, enhanced by wah-wah in the left channel, is stellar on this track. The main riff does not use power chords but instead uses a single-line melody. This allows him to harmonize the riff on a third guitar in the right channel (0:13, 1:01, 2:29, and 3:56). Tony does this again on the single-line riff on "A National Acrobat" on their next album. Years later, guitarists would use harmonizer pedals to achieve similar results. Tony's guitar solo (1:41–2:22) is a fine example of his style. Tony-isms such as unison bends (e.g., 1:57–2:01) and trill figures (e.g., 2:01–2:09) are heard throughout. The last lick (2:16–2:22) uses a scale ubiquitous in rock music but is delivered in his unique way. Tony likes to use short ideas and repeat them; for example, the lick at 2:12–2:16 uses a repeated three-note idea. That same lick appears in the second solo in "Snowblind" (4:55–5:01). At 2:37, the guitars cease, but the energy remains. It is Bill alone, and he uses the double bass drums more liberally. At 2:45, percussion is added: in the left channel, guiro, agogo bells, and a woodblock playing a clave pattern; and in the right, additional drums (probably snare drum and timbales). Led Zeppelin's drummer John "Bonzo" Bonham said he "really liked" this song. Years later, he recorded his own overdubbed percussion ensemble: "Bonzo's Montreaux" on *Coda* (1982). Bonham wasn't the only rock legend that appreciated "Supernaut": Frank Zappa told *Let It Rock* in 1975 that he had it at number one in his top ten, ranking among the Beatles, the Rolling Stones, Krzysztof Penderecki, and Edgar Varèse. Later, Zappa replaced "Supernaut" with "Iron Man" as his favorite.

Side two of *Vol. 4* opens with "Snowblind," one of Sabbath's most oft-performed songs. It was written before their time in LA, as they performed it on tour in March. Like "Tomorrow's Dream," most of the lyrics were rewritten for the album, but the song was fully formed in terms of chords, melody, form, and even the guitar solo. The lyrical concept was there, as they kept the title and the theme of cocaine. The first verse was the same, but they wrote three new verses for the album. In concerts before and after the album's release, Ozzy says, sings, or yells "cocaine" after each verse. Ozzy told *Creem* in March 1972 (published July), "You can interpret ['Snowblind'], I suppose, as being about taking cocaine."[34] How would a listener *not* interpret it that way? On the album, however, "cocaine" is only heard once, when Geezer whispers the word after the first verse. They intended *Snowblind* to be the album's title, but the record company objected to having a drug reference in the title, so it was released as *Black Sabbath Vol. 4*. They did manage, however, to keep the song's title and to include a little note to their drug suppliers: "We wish to thank the great COKE-Cola Company of Los Angeles" (their all caps).

The song begins with five big power chords in the guitar accented by bass guitar, bass drum, and cymbals. The intro riff continues with Bill's and Geezer's groove backing up two chords, of which Tony lets each note ring to bring out the harmony. In many cases, Tony will play a chord in that way in order to bring out its characteristics, especially when the chord has three or more different notes in it. Compare this part of the riff to the "when sadness fills my days" section of "Tomorrow's Dream" (1:29–1:46); there, he also plays one note at a time and lets them sustain. The tempo is slow (58 bpm)—especially for a song about cocaine—and the overall sound is heavy.

The intro riff is played twice, and it settles into the verse riff (0:17). Bill's drum part isn't a typical rock drumbeat but is more stylized to his personal approach. As in "Wheels of Confusion," he plays two successive snare drum hits on the backbeat (0:18, 0:20, 0:22, etc.) and "mini-fills" (0:25, 0:33, 0:37, etc.). He also plays one-handed "mini" snare drum rolls, like soft grace-note ruffs, just before a bass drum hit (e.g., there are two at 0:19). It is more apparent in the second verse (0:50–1:14). Geezer also adds his personal touch to the riff. Although he follows Tony for the most part, on occasion he plays slightly differently (e.g., at the end of the riff: 0:21) or adds little ornaments (e.g., the fast two-note ornament just before Tony changes the chord: 0:19). If Bill played a standard rock beat and Geezer followed Tony exactly, it would not be so interesting or effective.

At the end of the first verse, Ozzy sings the song's first snow-as-cocaine metaphor: "icicles within my brain." In case you didn't catch the reference, Geezer whispers "cocaine" in the right channel. The postverse riff (0:42) is related to the intro riff. They both have several hits with guitars, drums, and cymbals in the first half, and then Tony ringing out the two chords in the second half. This section is a perfect example of how Bill "plays to the riff" instead of playing a drumbeat. He plays the first half (0:42–0:44) with crash cymbals and bass drum matching Tony's line and the second half pairing ride cymbal with bass drum for the first chord (0:44) and snare drum with crash cymbal for the second chord (0:45). Bill would describe this approach to drumming as playing "orchestrationally"; he is a self-described "orchestrationist" (not an orchestrator along the lines of Wil Malone or Mike Lewis from the next four albums but his own term: "orchestrationist").

The second verse (0:58) has more winter-themed lyrics (e.g., "winds of ice" as snorting coke) and goes directly to the postverse without Geezer's reminder that the song is about cocaine. The postverse (1:15) goes back to the intro riff (1:23) before going to the bridge (1:40). Tony applies the held-out chord/one-note-at-a-time texture of the second halves of the intro and postverse riffs to the bridge. A part of the chord stays the same throughout the bridge, but the other part (including the bass note) moves down for each chord change. In that respect, it is similar to what he and Geezer do four years later in the end section of "Dirty Women" (3:57–end). Once Ozzy enters (1:49), Geezer becomes busier by adding several notes between each chord change. In the bridge, Ozzy sings additional references to snow (cocaine) but also perhaps a reference to LSD: "the sun no longer sets me free." LSD was sometimes called "sunshine" or "orange sunshine," so the line could imply a preference for cocaine over LSD. In the third verse, Ozzy sings "winter sunshine," continuing the sun imagery.

The bridge continues as a guitar solo takes over the melody. Tony saves his fast licks for the second solo (4:30–end) and keeps this one simple, melodic, and well constructed. It consists of four phrases, each about eight seconds long. The first phrase (2:22) is almost the same as the last (2:47), and the two middle phrases (2:30 and 2:38) are the same, giving it an organization that is clear. The first phrase features four bends (2:22), a descending blues scale (2:24), and a leap down at 2:26. When the four bends return at 2:47, it again goes down the blues scale

(2:49) but leaps up instead (2:51). After the leap down at 2:26, the second phrase remains in the lower register and develops a little five-note idea (2:30) by shortening it to four notes (2:32) and then to just two (2:34). The entire phrase is repeated (2:38–2:47), and Bill marks the halfway point of the solo with double bass drums at 2:37. The solo ends with Tony going down the blues scale and Bill accenting all eleven of Tony's notes (2:51–2:54). The solo is wonderfully designed and executed and without the "fireworks" of technical display.

The band comes down in volume for the verse riff, and Bill plays a little syncopated rhythm on the bass drum to bring it into Ozzy's third verse. After another postverse, Tony plays a new riff to start the middle section. It is more than twice as fast (130 bpm) and in a swing/shuffle feel. Bill does some interesting things in this section. First, he plays a cross rhythm on the ride cymbal, playing three beats for every two (i.e., 195 bpm against the 130). Second, he syncopates the backbeat on the snare drum by playing it early, locking with the cross rhythm of the cymbal. Third, he incorporates the toms into the pattern (3:38, 3:42, 3:45, etc.). Lastly, he plays "triplets" on the double bass drums that lock into both the cross rhythm and Tony's and Geezer's groove (in a 2:1 ratio to the former, 3:1 to the latter). This section is short, as Ozzy sings four short vocal phrases, and it goes back to the postverse riff.

They drop back into half-time feel, but that would be 65 bpm. Instead of going all the way down to 58 as it was, they settle a hair faster at 60, keeping the energy up. Just before the fourth verse begins, strings play a pickup note and then leap up an octave and hold the note for three seconds. They do that four times behind the verse. Some accounts say it was a string quartet; other accounts, a larger group. If it was a quartet (two violins, a viola, and a cello), it is likely they did several overdubbed "passes" to make the ensemble sound larger. This part is quite simple and could be easily mistaken for a Mellotron. However, when the strings back up the second guitar solo (4:30–end) it is clear that it is a string section. They play a four-second-long, five-note motif consisting of four short notes and then one long one. Listen for the crunch of the bow on the strings for the four short, staccato notes. Their motif, or riff if you will, is as every bit heavy metal as is Apocalyptica decades later. The motif is repeated until the end, where it fades out on the fourteenth time. Bill said it was his idea to put strings here; "I could hear the strings," he said.[35]

Tony's second solo is very similar to the guitar solo on "Supernaut" (1:41–2:21). Both solos feature unison bends, trills (5:06–5:08, 2:01–2:02 in "Supernaut"), and the same three-note figure from 4:55 to 5:01 (2:12–2:16 in "Supernaut"). They are both fine examples of his personal style.

"Cornucopia" is quite the cornucopia of riffs; there are seven different riffs/sections, an astounding number for a song less than four minutes in duration. There are multiple tempo and feel changes, and it changes key for the sixty-eight-second-long middle part, which itself has three sections. The intro riff, which never comes back in its entirety, is especially sinister and dark. Recall "Black Sabbath" with its evil-sounding tritone interval; this riff is based on two different tritones, taking the *"diabolus in musica"* to another level. It is slow (72 bpm) and requires detuning the strings to play its lowest note. Although the riff is slow, Bill uses the double bass drums from 0:12 to 0:14, giving the music a barrage of low drums. On the fourth iteration of the riff, they "tag" the last four chords three times (a convention probably coming out of their blues band roots). Riff 2 begins at 0:32 in a faster tempo (142 bpm) and a shuffle-like feel; Bill plays similar groove on the end of "Sabbath, Bloody Sabbath" from their next album. After Ozzy's verse, there is a brief extension (0:53–0:56) and a postverse guitar melody that never returns (0:56–1:03, riff/section 3). Riff 2 returns for another verse and then skips the postverse and leads directly into a chorus (1:23, section 4). The extension from thirty seconds earlier becomes the first half of the chorus riff. The chorus is slightly less than half time (about 68 bpm) and without the swing/shuffle feel. To close this part of the song, they return to the intro riff but use only the "tagged" chord bit at the end (1:37). At 1:44, they change keys, tempo, and feel. This interlude/transition section (section 5) could be felt in a slow "two" at 43 bpm, or medium "three" or "six" at 129 bpm. At 1:48, Bill plays a cymbal roll and then a tam-tam at 1:50, 1:55, and 2:00. The tempo picks up at 2:06 back to a shuffle feel (this time at 148 bpm) for riff 6, first played by Tony, but Bill and Geezer soon join in. Riff 7 starts at 2:19, and Ozzy joins in for a verse at 2:26. Riffs 3 and 7 never return, making their place in the song unique. This middle part closes with riff 6 (2:39–2:52). At 2:52, they go directly back to the original key and use half of a chorus (section 4) without vocals as a transition. At 2:59, the guitar in the right channel plays a chord as if continuing for the rest of the chorus but stops. The chord clashes with the guitar in the left channel that plays the "tagged" chords from the end of riff 1. From 3:07 until the end, the song progresses as it did from 1:07 to 1:43 (verse, chorus, and end of riff 1).

"Laguna Sunrise," according to Tony was "about the beach and the sea,"[36] inspired by a sunrise at Laguna Beach, located about sixty miles south of LA. He and Spock Wall were up all night, and Tony came up with the idea on an acoustic guitar. Spock, also a guitarist, wrote down drafts for the string orchestra part, and they later hired a professional orchestrator to properly notate and arrange the parts. The piece begins with a twelve-string acoustic guitar strumming the harmony in the left channel and an acoustic guitar in the right channel playing the melody. The melody consists of a twelve-second phrase played twice and a five-second extension. This extension is a motif derived from the main melody played twice; it is played over a chord that leads the ear back to the beginning. The string orchestra enters on that extension (0:25). The section is repeated at 0:30. A "B" section comes in at 1:00 and gracefully uses harmony from outside the key, taking the music somewhere. The tempo is faster in this section (90 bpm instead of 80), helping to move the music along—a very orchestral thing to do. Although this section is half the length (five bars instead of ten), the duration is even shorter because of the faster tempo. The "A" section returns at 1:13 and is played twice more at 1:43 and 2:12. Notice the moving violin line starting at 2:15. If you listen closely, the strings don't always play stagnant, long notes but instead move around very discerningly. Although the end of the A section leads the ear back to the beginning chord, at 2:41 the extension motif is repeated and ends there. In some respects it sounds incomplete, but regarding the mood and other aspects, the ending is perfect.

"St. Vitus' Dance" sounds lo-fi compared to the other tracks, giving it an "indie-rock" quality. Geezer is fairly low in the mix and has little definition, and the hi-hat is especially quiet (yet the crash cymbals are loud). Comparing the left and right channels, it sounds as if the rhythm tracks were recorded in mono and made to sound stereo by putting a slight reverb/delay in the left channel. It makes it sound as if the drums are placed slightly to the right. A tambourine is placed mostly in the left channel, giving it a more stereo sound. The main riff has a Cajun flavor to it for the way that it uses bends, open strings, and accents on unusual beats (nearly turning the beat around)—all features of Cajun music. Even Geezer's bass line is like a typical Cajun bass line. However unintentional, the similarities are there. I call it the "main riff" because it is heard before and after every section of the song. Metal takes over at 0:13 when they enter a half-time feel to play the verse riff. It sounds darker here because of the power chords and since it went from a major key to a minor key. After a verse from Ozzy, the main riff, tambourine, and major key return at 0:32, but it goes back to the darker, slower minor-key riff at 0:45, and Ozzy sings another verse. The main riff returns at 1:04, and they do something clever at 1:17 to make the bridge section even heavier than the verse. When they went from major to minor at 0:13 and 0:45, they kept the same bass note (C major to C minor). When they go to the bridge, they go down (C major down to A minor). What this does is make the riff even lower, thus heavier. The riff for the bridge is based on the verse riff, so it sounds *like* the verse riff, only heavier. Moreover, it requires a note so low that one has to tune down the guitars to play it. The choice of key changes is quite conservative, so the key changes go pretty much unnoticed because they sound so natural and organic. Thus, they allow the verse and bridge riffs to exhibit darkness and heaviness without them sounding jarring and out of place. The bridge is the climactic point of the song for its heaviness and for Ozzy's vocals. Although the guitars are playing lower, Ozzy's primary melody notes are a step higher. The reverb on his voice in this section is a nice effect and fills out the sound. The main riff returns at 1:36, and they go back in half time for another verse. The song ends with the fifth appearance of the main riff.

The intro riff for "Under the Sun/Every Day Comes and Goes" is an example of the sum being greater than its parts. Tony's part is evil sounding partly due to the use of the "flat 5" (like the tritone discussed earlier), its first three notes like "Cornucopia." Geezer's part is dark when played on its own but maybe not as evil sounding as Tony's. When put together, it creates one of Sabbath's heaviest riffs ever because, aside the first note, Geezer plays a harmony part to Tony's riff. Harmonies used in frequencies that low create a very muddy sound, so most bass players avoid doing so in that range. But that's what makes this riff so special. Moreover, some of the notes are so low that the guitars must be tuned down three half steps in order to play them, giving it an even heavier sound. The tempo being very slow (45 bpm) also contributes to the riff's sinister quality. At 0:32, the main riff comes in at nearly triple the speed (130 bpm). Bill and Geezer stop at 1:10 for Tony to play a brief solo lick that incorporates some exotic notes outside the key. The main riff returns for a verse from Ozzy, and they stop for Tony's solo lick again.

The next part of the song known as "Every Day Comes and Goes," registered as a separate title in ASCAP but not listed on certain releases, begins at 1:56 in a new key and a new tempo. It is one of the fastest tempos in any Sabbath song: 230 bpm, more than five times as fast as the intro! After a verse from Ozzy, Bill plays a brief drum solo, and the riff is played a key higher. After another verse and drum solo, the key goes up again for a guitar solo heard in the right channel. Listen for Tony-isms such as the unison bends and slides panning across the left and right channels at 3:03. The key changes in "Every Day Comes and Goes" are used to add excitement; notice the key goes up yet again at 2:54 in the middle of the solo. The key goes up one last time at 3:11 when it returns to the main riff of "Under the Sun." To connect Tony's solo lick at 3:48 with the new, outro riff at 3:57, there are sounds of a tam-tam ringing. The sound is played backward (tape reverse) and forward (normal tape direction) at the same time, so the tam-tam blends with itself. At 4:11 two guitars come out of the texture of the outro riff to play a duet, but it sounds like only one because they play the same thing for the first thirteen seconds. The duet ends at 4:56, but Tony teases the listener, as it sounds like another solo will begin at 5:09. Instead, he simplifies the outro riff at 5:15. The outro riff is played slower at 5:25 and even slower at 5:35. Bill includes some double bass drum work at 5:40 as it drags to the end for the final chord at 5:48.

LIVE AT LAST AND PAST LIVES

To hear what the band sounded like live around this time, check out *Live at Last*, released in 1980 but recorded in 1973. It contains songs from the first four albums such as "Children of the Grave," "Cornucopia," "Paranoid," "Snowblind," "Sweet Leaf," "Tomorrow's Dream," "War Pigs," and "Wicked World." It also includes an earlier version of "Killing Yourself to Live," which appeared on their next album. Within the eighteen-minute version of "Wicked World" you will find parts from

"Into the Void," "Supernaut," a live-only work-in-progress song known as "Sometimes I'm Happy," an extended guitar solo, and even some jazz (swing-style drums, walking bass, etc.). *Live at Last* is CD one of *Past Lives* (2002). The second disc of *Past Lives* includes performances from 1970 and 1975.

3

PROG SABBATH

A string orchestra, chamber choir, harp, piano, harpsichord, organ, synthesizers, Mellotron, timpani, and a glockenspiel. Multisectional songs, some over eight minutes. A guest appearance by Rick Wakeman of Yes. A keyboardist on tour. This description sounds like a progressive rock band, but if you add that to heavy metal, you get Black Sabbath as they progressed musically in 1973–1975. They used instruments such as flute, bongos, claves, congas, a shaker, a tam-tam, and a vibraslap. Regarding their use of different instruments, Tony said, "I did things like that to get a different sound into our music."[1] On the production side, they used tape-speed manipulation and tape reversal for additional interesting sounds.

Regarding the experimental aesthetic, Tony Iommi viewed their next album *Sabbath, Bloody Sabbath* (*SBS*; 1973/1974) as a continuation from *Vol. 4*. He said, "Compared to the previous records, [*SBS*] has more class about it, more arrangements, . . . and it's more adventurous. It was a leap forward."[2] Thus, if he thought *Master of Reality* (*MoR*) to *Vol. 4* was a "complete change," having "jumped an album,"[3] and from *Vol. 4* to *SBS* was a "leap forward," then the band had come quite far from *MoR* to *SBS*. Ozzy Osbourne had the same perspective, saying that *SBS* was "stage two" of a "new trip" that began with *Vol. 4*.[4] Tony said in 1973, "We played a much more jazz-influenced music before we hit our present formula."[5]

What inspired them to continue the experimental qualities of *Vol. 4* and take them to another level? In the time between the recording of

Vol. 4 and *SBS* there was the performance with the legendary progressive rock (prog) trio Emerson, Lake and Palmer and fourteen performances with Badger, a prog band that included Tony Kaye, the keyboardist that had been in Yes before Rick. But more significantly perhaps were the fourteen dates with Gentle Giant, one of the more quirky and experimental prog bands of the time. It is likely that the nearly thirty performances alongside prog bands had influenced, or at least inspired, Sabbath to continue in that musical direction when writing material for *SBS*. Tony, at that time, said, "I think that with the passage of time, we've improved as musicians."[6]

The musical growth and experimentation aside, there was an extramusical aspect to these two albums: anger toward the management. Two songs from *SBS* and two songs from *Sabotage* deal with this theme. Geezer Butler said in a 1974 interview that "Sabbath, Bloody Sabbath" showed their "attitude towards the ol' music business—the business side of it."[7] "You can hear the frustration [with management and lawyers] on *Sabotage*," said Ozzy.[8]

In late April 1973, they returned to LA—to the same house actually—to write material for their fifth album. Tony said he had "writer's block"[9] and only a couple of songs (based on live recordings, one of them would have been "Killing Yourself to Live"), but not much more than that, so they returned to the UK to try writing there instead. They rented Clearwell Castle, in southwestern England near the border of Wales, to continue working. On August 2, Tony said there was one more song to record and some of the lyrics and vocals yet to write, so the bulk of the writing and recording must have been done between May and July. According to Geezer in 1974, they spent six months working on the album (for Sabbath in 1973, that was a long time) and that it was the first album they had produced and mixed completely by themselves.

SABBATH, BLOODY SABBATH

The album opens with the title track named after the 1972 "Bloody Sunday" event in Northern Ireland, but it was actually about the management problems they had, their dislike of the press (the British press, in particular), and their attitude toward the music business. Tony offers a menacing riff to start the song. Bill Ward and Geezer soon join in, adding to the heaviness of the main riff. Bill does not play a typical rock beat but instead plays to the riff. Geezer milks the penultimate note of the riff by holding it out slightly longer than Tony and bending it, giving it his personal touch. Ozzy sings in his high register for the verse, always higher than the guitar, leaving plenty of sonic space. Some accuse Ozzy of following the guitar riff in his melodies (e.g., "Iron Man"), as if it is a bad thing to keep it simple and focused. This is an example of how Ozzy goes in contrary motion to the riff, enhancing the riff by giving it another dimension. Notice how, in the second half of the riff, Ozzy's melody descends, but the riff ascends: "have to learn" goes down as the three guitar chords go up (0:17).

For the chorus, Ozzy comes down to his middle register, Tony plays acoustic guitars and electric guitar without distortion, and Bill plays lighter, giving the music a mellower vibe. Some of the types of chords Tony uses in this section are more common to jazz and folk-pop, contrasting it with the heavy metal power chords used in the verse. Moreover, Ozzy's melody for "on your own" is jazz-like in how his notes relate to Tony's chords. In this section, Tony plays some nice guitar fills after the first three vocal phrases. After the fourth, where Ozzy sings the highest, the band comes in heavy again.

The main riff returns, and a second guitar plays the melody of the riff higher, but still lower than where Ozzy sings. In the second verse, the words "hands of doom" recall the song "Hand of Doom" from *Paranoid* but in a different context (or similar context, as "hands of doom could take your mind away" could be interpreted as a drug reference). Geezer changes his bass line a bit at the end of the riff at 1:44 just after Ozzy sings "mind away." He plays that same variation during Tony's solo at 2:43–2:46. The band extends the second chorus (2:21), and as the music intensifies, Ozzy sings even higher for the words "you bastards," leading it to the guitar solo.

The solo is actually two guitars, one in each channel, playing almost exactly the same thing. The first phrase is played twice (2:25–2:38) with the left guitar an octave lower. The third and fourth phrases (2:39 and 2:46) are variations of the first, and the left guitar is now as high as the right guitar. The left guitar holds out the very last note throughout the whole phrase, but the right cuts out a half second earlier (2:53). If it weren't for these small differences, it would sound like one guitar split into two channels.

The band concludes this part of the song by going on to a bridge section and never bringing back material from the first three minutes. Notice in the second half of each time through the melody (3:04–3:07 and 3:11–3:14) that Geezer and Tony play in harmony by not always playing the same notes as each other. Then (at 3:15), a long, held chord allows Bill the space to play a fill to take it to the next section. Notice the swing-like rhythms of his fill that foreshadow the outro of the song (4:50–end).

At 3:18 you will hear one of Sabbath's heaviest riffs ever, heavy thanks to the palm-muting of the strings, the thick distortion, and the very low register (so low in fact one must tune the guitar down three half steps in order to play it). As Geezer and Tony enter the abyss, Ozzy goes to the stratosphere by singing the highest notes of the song. These are no higher than the verse's high notes, but it seems like it because the guitars are so low and he slides up the note at the start of the phrase. Sabbath's music is multidimensional. Other metal bands might play an entire song in the low register. But Sabbath saved this low register for over three minutes into the song, making it sound heavier by standing out in contrast with the other sections, especially the chorus. To add color to the heaviness and high vocals, there is a shaker throughout, a tambourine plays at the beginning of each iteration of the riff, and some clave hits can be heard before Ozzy comes in. The tambourine is also used in the previous bridge section (3:00–3:14). When this section returns (4:06), there is no tambourine, but the shaker and clave do come back.

At 3:52, Tony plays a new riff, a sort of postverse riff if you will, and Bill and Geezer stop momentarily to join back in for the big hits. The same held-out chord from 3:14 is played again at 4:02 for Bill to play another fill to take it back for another verse. After Ozzy's final verse, they repeat this postverse section again (4:40), but on the held-out chord (4:50) they change the groove or feel of the song. The feel, not unlike "Children of the Grave" from *Master of Reality*, was hinted at during Bill's fill at 3:14 in the song. Geezer joins in with the new groove, and then Tony at 4:57 for a new riff. Over this groove is a long pick slide on the guitar and overdubbed drum fills. As in "Children of the Grave" with the overdubbed timbale parts, we hear two Bills. Once the groove is established, a second guitar solo begins (5:10) but is quite short, and by 5:28 there are more pick slides and other noise from the guitar as the song fades out.

The opening riff to "A National Acrobat" was written by Geezer, and as Tony explained, was probably the first one Geezer wrote that appeared in a Black Sabbath song (not considering the main riff to "Black Sabbath," whose lineage appears to be Gustav Holst to Geezer Butler to Tony Iommi). Geezer as author of the riff makes sense because it is a single-line riff requiring no chords, and bassists usually play one note at a time. Other single-line Sabbath riffs from this era include "Supernaut," "Electric Funeral," and "Black Sabbath." Listen for Geezer's inflection/ornamentation at about two-thirds the way through the riff (e.g., 0:04, 0:11, etc.). It's these little things—the bends, the hammer-ons, and the slides—that set Geezer apart from most bass players. Also, notice Tony's harmonized version of the riff melody played much higher (0:13–0:26, 0:33–0:39, etc.); he used this same approach on "Supernaut" as well. Under Ozzy's vocals in the verse, Tony plays four heavy chords, the first of which is especially heavy due to the detuning of the guitar strings (0:27, 0:41, 1:28, and 1:42). In the second half of the verse, the chords are different and Ozzy harmonizes with himself in the left channel (0:54–1:02 and 1:08–1:15). The lyrics, as explained by Geezer, are about sperm that don't make it to the egg. At 2:16, Tony introduces a new riff, never returning to the first one. This wah-drenched new riff uses the so-called Hendrix chord (2:20, 2:26, etc.), supported by a funk drumbeat (listen how Bill delays the snare drum a la the so-called James Brown beat: cf. "Cold Sweat"). After two verses over the new riff, Tony plays a guitar duet (3:34–3:59): the one in the left channel focused on slow bends and long tones, and the one in the right channel busier. After the third verse from Ozzy, it is an instrumental until the end. At 4:52, they go into a double-time feel and change to a major tonality, making the song sound as if it is opening up. After a riff change and key change, Geezer drops out to give it a stop-time feel as Bill and Tony continue (5:35–5:48). Notice here the bongos and cowbell in the right channel and the congas in the left. The added percussion and Bill's use of the bell of the ride cymbal give it a Latin-rock flavor (compare this to Santana, for example). The song ends with a final explosion from the full band: busy bass ascent, two guitars (left and right channels) ascending, and accented snare drum rolls, all culminating on the final climax of a single note.

The next track on the album is an instrumental work titled "Fluff," named after Alan "Fluff" Freeman, a BBC DJ who played their instrumental piece "Laguna Sunrise" for the opening of his show. It is not "fluff," as in album filler, but a fine composition worth a closer listen. It begins with a lone guitar outlining just two chords, and a second guitar introduces the melody at 0:11. At 0:34, the harmony changes and another guitar enters picking at twice the pace of the first, adding momentum. When the tension in the music resolves at 0:56, Geezer enters on long tones and the piano enters (played by Tony), taking the role of the third guitar by outlining the chord in a fairly quick, but delicate, manner. A fourth guitar, one drenched in reverb, answers the melody with its own (1:03–1:06, 1:08–1:11, and 1:14–1:16). At 1:19, when the harmony changes as it did at 0:34, a harpsichord is added, also played by Tony. At 1:42, the fast activity stops and the texture thins and focuses on the melody of the bridge section. At 2:05, there is a slight departure from the key, but Geezer and Tony navigate their way back, and by 2:28 it focuses and releases at 2:33 for the return of the main melody. The harpsichord drops out, leaving only bass, piano, and guitars, but it returns at 2:57 for the buildup. At 3:20, the focus is on the melody again with the absence of the fast guitar and harpsichord. It builds again starting at 3:43 but drops like a sigh at 4:06 via three little notes on the guitar and one from Geezer.

The first two minutes of "Sabbra Cadabra" have a medium-fast shuffle groove, and it really swings. Tony starts alone in the left channel; then at 0:12, the bass, drums, and a second guitar join. Geezer's bass line descends at first, but when the guitar solo starts at 0:24, his bass line ascends and changes twice as quickly. And at the second half of the solo (0:31), he jumps to a higher register, all this adding tension that gets released at the start of a new riff at 0:36. Based on the opening riff, a guitar plays a high melody in the left channel with a warbled effect before the verse begins. This melody comes back at 1:17 and 1:46 but harmonized in the right channel. Ozzy sings love song lyrics atypical for Sabbath (they even had "Lovely Lady" as a working title for this song). At 1:58, they drop the tempo more than half (164 to 77 beats per minute [bpm]) for a new section. At 2:04, you hear Rick's Minimoog synthesizers, one in each channel. After Ozzy's effect-laden verse, Bill comes into a beat that is slightly faster (81 bpm) and heavier. Listen to Geezer's fast ascending lines and funky, syncopated descending lines in this section, and when it comes back at 3:41. At 2:53, the tempo picks up a bit more (84 bpm), and the piano, cowbell, and tambourine help to drive it. At 3:05, the tempo drops back to 77 bpm, and the "lovely lady" section returns for more Minimoog and another verse. From 3:53 until the end, the band jams on the repeated groove, including Ozzy, whose vocals are highly obscured by effects. Pay special attention to Geezer throughout this jam, 5:13–5:20 in particular, for he plays some nice fills.

The piano is credited to Tony and Rick, but the bluesy licks are very much in Rick's style, so it is likely he played most—if not all—the piano parts on this track. Rick was at Morgan Studios during the same time Sabbath was, as he was working on Yes's four-song, yet eighty-one-minute, album *Tales from Topographic Oceans*. If you are not familiar with his work from that period, check out that album, as well as *Fragile* (1971), *Close to the Edge* (1972), and his solo albums such as *The Six Wives of Henry VIII* (1973). According to a review in *Melody Maker* of a performance near the beginning of the *Sabbath, Bloody Sabbath* tour, Tony plugged in to an ARP synthesizer during a twenty-five-minute version of "Sabbra Cadabra."[10] The extended version of that song in live performance is consistent with other reviews, but this is the only piece of literature I have read that mentions Tony using a synthesizer onstage.

According to Geezer, "Killing Yourself to Live" was about the rigors of the road and, like "Sabbath, Bloody Sabbath," about the management problems. It was written before the rest of the album, with an earlier version from the *Vol. 4* tour appearing on *Live at Last* and *Past Lives*. The earlier version uses almost exactly the same music but with significantly different lyrics. The earlier lyrics were not about the rigors of the road and did not include the words "killing yourself to live"; thus, the newer lyrics reflect on their experiences on the tour that they had completed. The song is in three parts (0:00–2:44, 2:45–4:07, and 4:07–end), the second titled "You Think that I'm Crazy," and the third "I Don't Know If I'm Up or Down" for publishing purposes. In fact, these were registered as separate titles (not as alternate titles) with the American Society of Composers, Authors and Publishers (ASCAP), meaning that, for publishing purposes, they are treated as separate songs. After a thirty-second intro, it settles into a verse riff with an eerie effect on the guitar in the left channel. The message is clear: "You work away your life, and what do they give? You're only killing yourself to live." That line sets up the chorus, which is quite heavy with its half-time feel. At the end of the second chorus (1:43), Ozzy goes higher for "killing," adding emphasis to the song's title. After a guitar duet, Ozzy sings a third verse, but over the chorus riff, to close part one.

Part two starts with a new riff, still in the slower, half-time feel but a bit faster (about 76 bpm). Bill builds it up to 2:58, and at 3:00 and 3:06, Ozzy and/or Tony (both are credited) add some nice brassy synth sounds. At 3:10, the riff changes, and when Bill and Geezer stop, the melody is played by Tony in the right channel and sung by Ozzy in the left. They really match each other's phrasing well on this part. An instrumental section takes the song into part three, for a medium-fast shuffle/boogie (starts at 174 bpm, climbs to 184) at 4:07. After two more verses, Tony plays a guitar duet (one in each channel) over Geezer's walking blues bass line and Bill's swinging—yet still rocking—drumming; their days of a blues band clearly show here. Bill's double bass drums bring Tony back to the main riff. Tony closes the song with a final riff, relaxing the tempo slightly from 184 bpm to 176, with Bill and Geezer providing big hits to end it.

The keyboard-driven "Who Are You?" was written by Ozzy on his ARP 2600 with lyrics about someone who is "confused about everything and didn't know who to trust."[11] It opens with the synth played by Ozzy in the left channel, and then a second one is added on the right doubling the melody with a third playing a low note that fades in. Tony said Ozzy played the main theme, but Geezer played the "filler bits,"[12] which could include that third synth. When Bill and Ozzy enter for the verse, Geezer comes in doubling the synth melody on bass guitar. For the second verse (1:18–1:54), Ozzy harmonizes with himself in the right channel. The middle instrumental section begins at 2:02 with a synth melody in the left channel probably played by Geezer. He is also credited with Mellotron, and it sounds as if the strings tape set was used in this section to fill up the sound. The harmony part in the right channel sounds like a synth, but it is guitar with effects (hear the slide down the frets at 2:25). Also in this section is some nice piano work from Tony, including some tasty figures in the high register from 2:22 to 2:25. The instrumental section closes with some nice orchestral percussion from Bill: rolls on the snare drum, timpani, and suspended cymbal and the bolero rhythm on the snare drum hinting at Ravel's orchestral work

Bolero. The song goes back to the main riff and then a final verse, again harmonized by a second Ozzy. After some of the layers of synth sounds dissipate (4:03–end), there is a resonance of what appears to be a tam-tam. If you rewind to 3:43, it sounds as if the tam-tam was struck there, but it is hard to hear as the complex set of overtones mixes so nicely with the layers of synth effects.

Like "A National Acrobat," "Looking for Today" features a single-line riff. This allows Tony to harmonize it later in the song (1:30 and 3:10, left channel). The chorus is smoother and more relaxed than the verse, not unlike the verse/chorus relationship in "Sabbath, Bloody Sabbath." Instead of distorted guitars, the chords are played by a strummed acoustic guitar and sustained organ chords, both played by Tony. He also adds some flute, one with some flurries and stabs, and another less audible one playing longer lines. There is also a vibraslap (0:52, 0:59, 2:09, and 2:17), the percussion instrument heard in the intro of Ozzy's "Crazy Train." The electric guitar is added at the end of the chorus during the buildup (1:11 and 2:28). Notice Bill's train-like snare drum pattern for the verses, similar to what he plays for "Johnny Blade" on *Never Say Die!* During the second and third verses there are handclaps in the left channel, which are either tongue-in-cheek or ironic. According to Geezer, the song is about "up-and-coming bands who thought they were brilliant and lasted for like a week"[13] —one-hit wonders, if you will. Is the use of handclaps poking fun at pop music, or is it ironic that they used them in a song about pop music? After the second chorus, the song has a refrain repeating the song title, "Looking for Today." Is this another pop music technique used as pastiche? After another verse it skips the chorus and goes directly to another refrain at 3:42. The guitar solo starts at 3:57, but by 4:06, it becomes more of a guitar/drum duet with all of the overdubbed drum fills.

The album closer, "Spiral Architect," has a majestic sound thanks to clever songwriting, a powerful performance, and an artful use of a string orchestra. The orchestra arrangements were done by Wil Malone (credited as "Will Malone" on the album), who also did choir and horn arrangements for Sabbath on their sixth and eighth studio albums. Tony says in an August 2, 1973 interview, before the album was complete, that there are two tracks with strings, a "Moog one" and a guitar feature.[14] Assuming he was referring to "Who Are You?" and "Fluff," it is unknown what the other song with strings was.

The introduction, played twice by a solo guitar, begins sad and pensive, but it becomes hopeful. The electric guitar, acoustic guitar, and hi-hat take that hopefulness and turn it into a bright, driving pattern. At 0:52, the full band enters in a Who-like fashion boosting the energy to another level. Bill's drums sound huge—like cannons—thanks to his heavy hitting and reverb. The riff ends with a closing motif (1:05–1:08) that momentarily changes up the rhythm and harmony. Over the motif, Tony plays a melodic line, Geezer plays three long notes and then a moving line, and Bill accents the chords throughout. They repeat the riff, but shortened, and after the closing motif, Bill plays a simple fill to dissipate the energy and set up the half-time feel.

The verse begins at 1:22 in the new, slower tempo. The DNA- and creation-themed lyrics were written by Geezer over a period of three months, with Bill contributing some (including the title). The harmony has a bittersweet quality about it: the major chord continues the hopefulness from before, but the second chord, an unexpected minor, gives it sadness. The lyrics reflect the mixed emotion: "giving piece of mind" with "sadness fills the superman, even fathers cry." The string orchestra magnifies the bittersweetness of the verse when they enter for the chorus (1:50–2:03). The harmonies here are both beautiful and sad, but hope wins out when it resolves at 2:04 for the return of the main riff. The lyrics for this brief section, written by Bill, end with "and know that it is good," reflecting the positive character of the music.

Ozzy continues the vocal line over the main riff with "you know that I should," and the full band comes with the Who-like hits. After the closing motif, Bill settles it back down into half time for another verse and chorus. Notice in the choruses (1:50–2:03 and 2:51–3:05) a second, higher Ozzy harmonizing with himself. Also notice that although the chords change in the chorus, Geezer stays primarily on one note, thus grounding it, allowing the strings to soar above, and bringing out the dissonant crunch of the third and fourth chords (1:53–1:56, 2:00–2:03, 2:54–2:57, and 3:01–3:04).

As before, Ozzy sings "you know that I should," and the full band comes with the Who-like hits. Instead of going into the closing motif at 3:18 to take it back for another verse, they extend this section to feature the string orchestra. At first the strings play only long tones, but the violins play a fast, rhythmic descending figure at 3:36 and again at 3:39.

Then, the full string orchestra plays four gorgeous chords before the band plays the closing motif to close the instrumental section.

When Ozzy returns for a third verse, the strings play a secondary melody in and around his vocal line. Because of this part especially, the use of the string orchestra in this song is not a mere novelty, as it contributes on many levels. After another chorus, it goes back to the main riff. After Ozzy sings "you know that I should," he goes higher and repeats the line four times. Each time he repeats the line, the band plays their two big hits. The strings are holding the last chord in anticipation of the closing motif. Instead of Tony playing his line during the closing motif, the violins play an ascending scale. The violins apply their last three notes to the little rhythmic idea from 3:36/3:39. Meanwhile, the violas and cellos go with Bill and Geezer's accented notes. Everyone comes together to hit the final chord at 5:05, and a few seconds later applause is added (this was not a live performance). At 5:21, the conductor shapes the cutoff nicely with a slight crescendo at the very end. At 5:15, acoustic guitar, bass, and drums reenter playing the chorus for a curtain call fadeout; without Ozzy's melody and the orchestra's chords, it is almost unrecognizable as the chorus.

SABOTAGE

In January 1975, the band went to Ozzy's country home in Ranton, Staffordshire (thirty-five miles northwest of Birmingham) to work up material for a new album. After a couple of weeks, they relocated to Weobley, Herefordshire (sixty miles southwest of Birmingham) to continue rehearsing. In February and March, they recorded the new material in London at Morgan Studios, where they had done *Sabbath, Bloody Sabbath*.

It had been a year and a half since *SBS* was released, long enough for Brian Harrigan of the *Melody Maker* to ask Geezer if their upcoming 1975 tour was their comeback. "A comeback?" he fired back, "We hadn't ever left."[15] Sabbath's next album *Sabotage* (1975) continued in the progressive tradition heard on their last two albums by using a variety of sounds and rhythms, long forms, and dissonance. At that time, Tony did not view *Sabotage* as taking the progressive approach to another level but more of a continuation of what they did on *Vol. 4* and

SBS: "We could have gone on into more technical things and fulfill a lot [of which] the band is capable of achieving, and which we don't necessarily do on stage either. But we decided we had reached the limit as far as we wanted to go."[16] Ozzy in 1975 said they were "stronger now than ever we were as musicians."[17] According to another 1975 interview, the band felt there was "more sophistication" on *Sabotage* than on their previous albums.[18] Regarding sophisticated rock music, the band met Frank Zappa in the time between *SBS* and *Sabotage*, around the time his albums *Apostrophe (')* and *One Size Fits All* were released, the latter being the Mothers' most prog rock. Bill once said, "The songs [on *Sabotage*] are a little bit unpredictable. We try to make it a bit unusual for the listener,"[19] something one could easily say about Zappa's music. As discussed in the introduction, Sabbath looked up to Zappa, especially Geezer who cited the Mothers as his second favorite band.

The album starts with "Hole in the Sky," a song about pollution, explains Geezer, who uses a menacing, distorted bass tone that cuts through. Bill describes the medium-shuffle feel of the song as "behind the beat." And because of that, it is "kind of tricky" because "you've got to drive it hard but you've got to keep relaxed."[20] The second riff (0:24 and 0:58) is similar to—and a logical outgrowth of—the first. After two verses, Tony has a third riff for the chorus. This four-second-long riff is based on a one-second-long rhythmic idea played four times, but with the chords changing on the third and fourth times. Bill applies that rhythmic idea to an Afro-Cuban-like feel in the toms and cymbal by having two levels of groove at once: one in "two" at about 120 bpm; the other in "three" at about 180 bpm. After another verse and chorus, Tony plays a guitar duet (one in each channel) where sometimes the guitars play the same thing, and other times the same rhythm but in harmony. After a fourth verse, they recall the second riff (3:28) and end with an abrupt cutoff of the main riff played three and a half times.

"Don't Start (Too Late)" is a forty-nine-second miniature that serves as an interlude between tracks 1 and 3. The volume of the track is very soft (about 15 percent of the volume of "Hole in the Sky"), making the distorted guitar at the start of next track sound even louder (especially if you turn up the volume in order to hear this track!). To have a close listen of all that is happening in the music, boost the volume about 700 percent. There seems to be a freer treatment of dissonance (i.e., clashing notes and chords) on *Sabotage* than on earlier albums, and on this piece in particular. For instance, the guitars from 0:03–0:07 and 0:10–0:13 are dissonant against each other and might remind the listener of Gentle Giant's music in that respect. Recall that Gentle Giant opened for them for several dates in 1972. It also has a Spanish quality due to some of the chords and scales (collection of notes) used.

After the softness of "Don't Start (Too Late)," the opening riff "Symptom of the Universe" hits hard. It is about five times as loud, and when Geezer and Bill enter, it's even louder. The huge difference in volume is very effective, surprising the unsuspecting listener. This riff is among the heaviest Tony has ever written. Like the main riff from the song "Black Sabbath," this riff features the interval of the tritone. There are other similarities between those two famous riffs. Both riffs are based on only two notes, and if they hadn't tuned down their guitars three half steps on "Symptom," it would be the same two notes. Both riffs use one note in the first half and the other note in the other half. The biggest difference is the speed, where "Symptom" is about two and a half times faster. Thus, if one were to play the riff from "Symptom" without tuning down and at 37 percent the speed, it would fit with the "Black Sabbath" riff quite nicely. Another difference is that in "Black Sabbath," the notes ring out, but here, the notes are palm-muted in a heavy metal fashion. When Geezer enters, he turns the two-note into a three-note riff by playing the other note from Tony's power chord (e.g., 0:15, 0:20, etc.) in the second half of the riff. The three-note riff Geezer plays here is closer to Holst's "Mars" melody that was the impetus for the "Black Sabbath" riff. Geezer is good at playing notes other than the primary one of the chord to add interest to his bass lines.

The second riff (0:22–0:33) consists of three held-out chords over which Bill plays what in essence is a drum solo. The main riff returns for the verse, and Ozzy's melody seems strange at first. It is primarily a two-note melody, and although the second note matches Tony and Geezer, the first one doesn't. He leaps up to a third note for the word "love" (0:57), making it basically a three-note melody. Like the first note, it doesn't match the riff. However, those three notes are the same as the three chords from the second riff, making them not so out of place after all by combining the ideas from the two very different riffs. After the verse, Ozzy screams "yeah" over the second riff. It's not enough to constitute a "chorus" but more of a postverse riff.

After a second verse and postverse, Tony introduces a third riff in a new key (1:58). Bill and Geezer mostly lay out: Bill keeps time on the hi-hat, and Geezer hits a few notes. When Geezer does play here, he does it dramatically by hitting hard and sliding down from the note. After the second time through the riff, the bass guitar and bass drum play two short hits in the middle of each (2:05, 2:07, 2:10, etc.), adding variety to the section.

It returns to the original key for another postverse and goes through the sequence of main riff, verse, postverse once more. They play the third section once more, as before, in the new key. Instead of going back to the first two riffs, they close this part of the song by never returning to any of it. They utilize the new key of the third riff by naturally moving from it to a new, but closely related, key for a new riff (3:35). The rhythm and feel, however, is very different, making the change seem abrupt. They retain the feel for the guitar solo (3:49), the fifth section of the song. Tony said this song "has been described as the first progressive metal song and I won't disagree with that . . . it does have a lot of changes to it."[21]

At 4:12, the feel abruptly changes again, but this time into a half-time, funky drumbeat not unlike "Behind the Wall of Sleep" from the first album. Notice here the pitch of the sustained guitar chord slowly rising via manipulating the tape speed. Also notice the building sound that suddenly gets "sucked up" at 4:23; that is a tam-tam but with the tape played in reverse.

From 4:23 to the end, they play a two-chord vamp (compare to Santana's "Oye Como Va" or Frank Zappa's "Variations on the Carlos Santana Secret Chord Progression"). The Latin-rock fusion sound is furthered with the addition of the claves at 4:26 and bongos at 4:33. With the chord progression and scale used, it has a connection to jazz (Tony uses this scale [Dorian] often when alluding to jazz). Referring to this part of the song, Bill says "we actually show up with jazz parts."[22]

Geezer enters at 4:29 with a nice, smooth bass line, and Ozzy enters at 4:34 for a verse. The vocal melody, chords, and feel are similar to various incarnations of "Sometimes I'm Happy," a song they only performed live. It never developed into a full song, thus never recorded in the studio, but they continued to rework the material and play it live. The end of "Symptom" and parts of "Nightmare" from *The Eternal Idol*

(1987) are probably the closest that material came into fruition, but only in similarities.

Although Ozzy said "Megalomania" was about schizophrenia,[23] Bill said it was about greed or coveting and that it and "The Writ" are "intertwined"[24] for their common lyrical themes. Geezer said that it, like "Killing Yourself to Live," was written about their management and people in the music industry in general. It is in two parts; the second part (3:23–end) dates back to at least November 1974 because they played an earlier version of it on tour in Australia. The working title was "Adolph" up until at least the time of final mixing, a late decision—and a good one—to use a title sans Hitler reference. The song begins with mysterious, ominous chords in the guitar (left channel) and organ (right), bass, light drums (e.g., cross-stick on snare drum rim), over-dubbed cymbal rolls, and a short melancholic guitar melody (0:07). Ozzy's repeated vocal "I hide" fades in on a tape loop before the verse begins. The other effect on the voice is eerie (Ozzy said in 1975 that, from some of the effects used, the listener can tell he had seen *The Exorcist* several times). The effect is made possible by running the tape backward and adding reverb, and when played normally, the voice sounds as if it's being sucked in ("reverse reverb"). When the band kicks in loudly at 0:47, it recalls the song "Black Sabbath" with its alternation of soft and loud sections. A new chord enters at 1:03, and it steps up like in a blues progression at 1:19. As expected, that chord resolves with a return to the beginning. When this section comes back around again at 3:07, it doesn't resolve but instead uses Beatles-esque chord progressions and piano to transition from part one to part two of the song.

A chord is held, a cowbell establishes a new tempo, and a new riff begins (3:23), played slightly differently by the two guitars in the left and right channels. When Ozzy's vocals follow the guitar riff in the second half of the third verse (4:04), his voice part is doubled much lower. With it being just below his vocal range and the tone quality sounding unnatural, it is likely that the low part was recorded using an octave pedal as an effect. At 4:29, when Ozzy slowly brings his note back up on the word "now," the guitar in the right channel slowly goes down: Tony goes lower than his lowest note, even though he tunes down, so it would have been tape-speed manipulation, as it does not sound like a "whammy" bar lowering the pitch. After another verse, the chorus returns with different lyrics but still with tambourine (5:29).

After a guitar duet (one in each channel), there is another chorus, a verse, and yet another chorus. At 7:52, Ozzy screams a very high note to bring it to the final (mostly) instrumental jam; the voice is used for texture, not for lyric purposes. A Mellotron (the strings tape set) plays a rising four-note figure eight times from 8:09 to 9:01 (notice the wrong note at 8:31 that is fixed at 8:32). At 8:48, Tony doubles the Mellotron line on guitar, and then a second guitar harmonizes that line becoming a solo from 9:01 to 9:21. Also at 8:48 there seems to be an edit point, a "punch," where Bill stops and then comes back in for a ten-second drum solo on all toms. At 9:01 Bill is back in with the drumbeat, Geezer is in the high register, and the Mellotron holds out the note as the solo guitar begins. By 9:07, the Mellotron is out and Tony's rhythm guitar is back to the riff. At nearly ten minutes in duration, "Megalomania" is Sabbath's longest stand-alone song.

The intro section to "The Thrill of It All" has an unusual groove. It is similar to "War Pigs" in that it has a "three" feel with swinging rhythms within each beat, but it is deceivingly not in "three." Although it could be counted in a slow "four" at 59 bpm, the feel is more like three plus three plus two at 118 bpm in which it sounds as if it's in a moderate "three" but with the last beat shortened to "two." Some drummers would play a basic rock beat in "four," but Bill plays to the riff and exploits this unevenness to create an interesting drum part. When Geezer enters at 0:06, he starts at his very lowest note and comes up to match Tony's riff. The note is so low that it requires detuning the instrument three half steps (like most of the album) in order to play it. At 0:33, the tempo jumps to 128 bpm for a new feel, and what sounds like a simple change of harmony is actually setting up a key change. Listen for Bill's double bass drum here (0:40–0:44, 0:48–0:51, and 0:55–0:58). At 1:03, the tempo drops to slightly more than half time (68 bpm) for a new, heavy riff. During the verses there are handclaps; only Sabbath can make handclaps sound menacing.

A brief interlude pushes the tempo up to 74 bpm and leads to the next section (2:59), which is even faster (about 133 bpm) and in a major key instead of minor. The change to major and faster tempo gives the music excitement and hope. A synthesizer plays a melody twice, and then Ozzy comes in for another verse (3:13). At 3:28 the synthesizer returns (this time louder in the mix) and Ozzy alternates between his high and medium registers on "oh yeah." After another verse (3:56), the guitar plays a variation of the synth melody and Ozzy does the "oh yeah" alternation again. At 4:11, surprisingly, they go back to the section from 0:33, but because they are slightly faster in tempo (133 instead of 128), it has a heightened sensation. Instead of going back into the slow, heavy riff after the return of this section, they go back to the synth melody at 4:25, another verse at 4:39, and harmonized version of the synth melody in the postverse at 4:54. At 5:08, Tony plays a very melodic solo, similar to that of Brian May for instance. However, Queen was fairly new at the time: A *Night at the Opera* had yet to be made, for example. This solo and solo section is along the lines of Boston or Styx (e.g., compare this to the guitar solo of "Come Sail Away"), but of course this is before *Boston* (1976) and *The Grand Illusion* (1977). Hearing this solo at the end of "Thrill of It All" makes all the more sense, as by the time these bands (and Foreigner as well) came around, the style resonated with Tony.

Requiring a choir, piano, harp, and glockenspiel in addition to the band, "Supertzar" has never been performed live, but the recording is used for many of Sabbath's concerts. Tony wrote it at home using a guitar, harp, and Mellotron, the latter to get the choir sounds. Like the wordless Mellotron choir tapes, the choir sang only the "ah" syllable, the arrangement by Wil Malone. The piece begins with the harp pluck-ing a low string, the basses holding out the same note at the bottom of their range, and Tony's riff. The meter is nine, a highly unusual meter for music, one that is more commonly associated with progressive rock (e.g., the "Apocalypse in 9/8" section from Genesis's 1972 song "Sup-per's Ready") than heavy metal. At 0:06 a piano is added to the held low notes, and a harmonized version of the riff is played by a second guitar. The tenors from the choir enter at 0:13 following the guitar riff, and two snare drums fade in playing a marching rhythm. The B section starts at 0:26 in a more relaxed manner for various reasons: strummed acoustic instead of distorted guitar, brighter tone with the glockenspiel and the women in the choir, major chords instead of minor, and a meter in four. The suspended cymbal rolls help to give it an orchestral sound even though there are no strings, winds, or brass. The A section returns at 0:38, and a two-note harp figure is added (0:44, 0:51, etc.). At 0:51, the women add a countermelody that pairs nicely with Tony's riff.

After another B section (1:05–1:17), the C section starts with a new riff accentuated by a few harp plucks. The riff emphasizes a note outside of the key, giving it a slightly darker character. At 1:21, the choir ascends and gets louder, accompanied by a harp glissando and suspended cymbal roll (again, making it sound "orchestral"). When the A section returns at 1:29, Geezer joins the harp for the low, sustained note, and there are now two countermelodies sung by the women (the altos and sopranos). The B section at 1:55 sounds richer with the sopranos, especially their high note at 2:01 (their highest yet) that starts a downward cascade. The C section returns at 2:08, and that "dark" note from the riff helps the harmony move for the D section (2:20–2:45). The sopranos sing an even higher note, followed by a lovely melody doubled by the harp. The guitar plays a simple riff, and the harp plays a few other passages, including a big glissando at 2:45 to take it back to the C section at 2:46. Then, at 2:56, the harp glissando and suspended cymbal roll take it back to the final A section. Here, at 2:48, Geezer and Bill return. The countermelody from 0:51 also returns but is sung an octave higher by the sopranos, and by 3:02, they reach their highest note of the piece. I am hard-pressed to call it a "song" or other vocal genre (anthem, cantata, etc.) as there are no words, so "piece" will suffice. As the riff repeats, a tambourine is added and plays every seven seconds (3:04, 3:11, etc.). There are plenty of very musical aspects to listen for in this oft-overlooked piece of music.

"Am I Going Insane (Radio)" is not a radio edit, nor does it imply that Sabbath had disdain for commercial success, as one author assumed. It is an instance of British rhyming slang: "mental" rhymes with "rental," which is short for "radio rental" (a service that was provided by the UK company Radio Rentals), with "radio" and "rental" used interchangeably for "mental." The song opens with a melody played by guitar in the right channel and by synthesizer in the left. The synth is very smooth with the notes sliding from one to the next (portamento), giving it a glossy texture. At 0:15, Ozzy's paranoia-themed lyrics are sung in his medium-low register as if soft-spoken and careful—as if his thoughts are to himself internally or spoken softly to himself. He could sing this melody an octave higher with ease, but that would change the mood and character of the voice. Geezer and the synth play a pattern that oscillates fairly quickly between two notes. The pattern shifts up slightly at 0:19 and back down at 0:22 with harmonies that are Spanish-like. Ozzy said, in a pre-politically correct 1975, the song "sounds Mexican, like Guacamole Joe and his Tequilas,"[25] and I suspect he is referring to this chord progression. Bill and Tony play sparsely here, with only the occasional drum and guitar fill. To keep the energy throughout, there is added percussion in the right channel. The other uses of added percussion in the song are nice, such as the tambourine in the left channel at 0:44, the overdubbed bass drum (or large floor tom) played with sticks (0:51–0:58, 1:06–1:12, 1:50–1:57, and 2:04–2:11), and the hi-hat bouncing from channel to channel (2:16–2:36). Ozzy's harmony part to his melody in the chorus (0:44 and 1:41) is one of his best and most effective. It's higher than the melody, helping it cut through, and it outlines the overall harmony nicely. On the repeated word "insane," the melody (main Ozzy) goes down, but the harmony (background Ozzy) goes up, the contrary motion giving it a nice shape. He also does that in the second verse on "to see" (1:37–1:39). The guitar duet at 2:10 has an exotic flavor for its note choice and pedal effect; the two guitars harmonize and play simple melodies in favor of fast blues licks. Here, the tambourine stops and the snare drum takes over its role until 2:38, when the guitar duet continues over a half-length chorus. It sounds like a single guitar with the signal split, but it's actually two playing the same thing (aside from a missing note in the left guitar at 2:43). The solo ends with the "insane" motif from Ozzy's vocal melody. After another verse and chorus, sounds of laughter begin, a recording of one of Geezer's friends, "a complete nutter" as he described him.[26]

Layers of laughter take over as the song fades. At 3:11, there is a disturbing cry, as if someone is being tortured or going "mental," or "radio," if you will. It is a recording of a baby crying but slowed down, and therefore it sounds lower too. Ozzy revealed in a 1975 interview that he discovered this idea when he played back a recording of his daughter Jessica crying, but the tape speed was slow. Although it has been said that it is her on the recording, the interview implies that it was not her—that he only got the idea from recording her years prior. Moreover, she would have been three years old by the time they recorded *Sabotage*, and the recording is clearly a baby. Unless they used that original tape, it is probably some other baby (and not his son Louis either, as he was born after the album was recorded). Mike Butcher, an engineer on *Sabotage*, recalled in 2012 that the recording came from an unmarked cassette found at the studio.

The laughter and crying continues over onto the final track of the album, "The Writ." For thirty-nine seconds, it is Geezer alone playing only two different notes, very patiently about seven seconds on each. He said he used wah-wah and flanger effects, which gave it a "really ethereal sound." The band comes in suddenly at 0:41 at about five times as loud, so it has a similar startling effect as "Symptom" coming out of "Don't Start." Tony's guitar tone is wicked; it starts to feed back on the fifth harmonic (0:42–0:44, 0:45–0:47, etc.). Ozzy sings in his highest range, moving between bluesy notes and Tony's feedbacking harmonic. The anger in his voice is evident: not only is it high and loud, but also his delivery is assertive. Ozzy wrote most of the lyrics and said "all of the anger I felt toward [former manager Patrick] Meehan came pouring out."[27] A writ is a legal document, so the song's title references the legal troubles they were having. Recall that, in reference to the lyrics, Bill said this song and "Megalomania" were "intertwined" thematically. After a chorus, it goes back to the beginning with the addition of three tape-reversed cymbals (2:16–2:25). During the second verse there is a backwards hi-hat in the right channel and a shaker. After a shortened chorus, it goes into a bridge section, where as in "Megalomania," the vocals are doubled much lower, but this time probably using tape-speed manipulation. None of this material comes back, so the first part comes to a close here, giving it a verse-chorus-verse-chorus-bridge (or A-B-A-B-C) form.

A transition section at 4:25 connects it to the second part of the song (4:32–end). Part two has a well-structured palindromic arch form: D-E-F-E-F-E-D. The intro/outro riff (D) at 4:32 establishes a new key and tempo (about 75 percent faster) to distinguish it from part one. The E section, whose first three chords are similar to "Never Say Die" (same key, even), has the qualities of a chorus, but the lyrics aren't the same each time. At 5:00, they extend the last chord with Ozzy going up the chord one note at a time in rock 'n' roll manner (e.g., like the Beatles' version of "Twist and Shout"). The F section (5:08) is like a verse, and here the music relaxes greatly. Even with drums absent, the tempo feels as if it's in half time. Distorted guitars are replaced with acoustic guitar, harpsichord, and the occasional glockenspiel. The chord progression is the same as in "Never Say Die" (but in a different key), but Geezer stays on the same note as he did in "Spiral Architect." The chorus (E) returns at 5:57 but with different lyrics, and Ozzy interrupts himself with four iterations of "I know" before another verse. The final chorus (7:06) uses lyrics from the second chorus (5:57) at first, but new lyrics follow. The riff at the beginning of this second part (D, 4:32) returns at 7:28 to close the song. This intro/outro riff acts as bookends to this arch-form second part.

SABOTAGE TOUR

Although Tony said they "could have gone on into more technical things,"[28] they did go "into more technical things" after 1975 (see chapter 4) and found ways to do them onstage. With the use of keyboards and strings on their last three albums, Sabbath hired keyboardist Gerald "Jezz" Woodroffe for the 1975 tour to re-create some of those sounds and textures for live performances. Before that tour, Sabbath only occasionally used keyboards in live performance: a synth was used on "Sabbra Cadabra" (likely played by Ozzy) on at least two shows in 1974, and piano and Mellotron (played by Tony and Geezer, respectively) were used on "Changes" on a few concerts in 1973. Tony, in 1975, said that Jezz played on only three songs for that tour, including Mellotron on "Spiral Architect" and organ and string synthesizer on "Megalomania." The third must have been "Sabbra Cadabra," where a synthesizer and electric piano can be heard on 1975 bootlegs. Jezz said his four Moog synthesizers were the "key to doing the Sabotage songs" and that he also used Ozzy's ARP 2600 for "Am I Going Insane."[29] Pictures from the next tour reveal that he had a Wurlitzer electric piano, a Clavinet, and a Korg 800 DV (aka MaxiKorg). It is quite possible that he did not have any Moogs and used "Moog" as a generic term for synthesizer in the same way some use "Fender bass" for electric bass, "Kleenex" for tissue, and so forth. Sabbath did not attempt to re-create "Supertzar" in concert with a live choir, harp, and glockenspiel but instead played the studio recording before the band entered on stage. Jezz would also play the backing guitar riffs on a Fender Rhodes through a fuzzbox so that Tony's riffs would be present during the guitar solos.

4

JAZZ SABBATH AND OZZY'S DEPARTURE

The band was "stretching it too far"[1] musically, thought Ozzy Osbourne, and by 1979 he was out of the band. Ozzy was referring to the jazz horn section on the song "Breakout" from *Never Say Die!* (1978). Bill Ward, however, thought it was "fucking great," calling it "an interesting sound collage that is the wackiest thing Sabbath had done or would ever do."[2] Geezer Butler said that Tony Iommi suggested they have a saxophone solo on that song because Ozzy was not around to record vocals, and when Ozzy did arrive and heard it, he walked out. This is just one example of the lack of productivity in the band in the late seventies that led the band to fire Ozzy. It was not the first time that Ozzy was not in the band, however. Ozzy left the band in 1977 and was temporarily replaced by Dave Walker (of Fleetwood Mac and Savoy Brown), but he returned within days of the *Never Say Die!* recording sessions.

Ozzy has stated that Tony, in the late 1970s, was striving to sound like Queen and Foreigner, and that Bill and Geezer were "into" those bands as well.[3] The listener might hear elements of "prog lite" or "Ameriprog" (e.g., Kansas, Styx, etc.) on their two albums from the late seventies (*Technical Ecstasy* and *Never Say Die!*), and perhaps they were influenced by bands such as Kansas by sharing the bill on the *Sabotage* tour, or with Boston and Journey on the *Technical Ecstasy* tour. Ozzy said in 1979, "We were influencing bands at one time, and the bands we were once influencing are now influencing [us]."[4]

In Spring 1976, Sabbath went to Wales and then to Ridge Farm Studios, just south of London, to write new material for what would become *Technical Ecstasy*. At the end of May, they went to Miami, Florida, to continue working and to record at Criteria Studios. Like *Vol. 4*, *Sabbath, Bloody Sabbath*, and *Sabotage*, it contained elements of progressive rock (prog). Recall from chapter 3 that Sabbath hired Jezz Woodroffe to play keyboards on the *Sabotage* tour. Before joining Sabbath, Jezz was working with a jazz fusion group (although his wife's blog states the group was called "Mabutu" and Mick Wall's 2015 book says "Matibu," Jezz told me "Mobutu"). He was present when Tony wrote material for *Technical Ecstasy*, allowing Tony to try out ideas while Jezz supplied chords as accompaniment. Not surprisingly, then, keyboards played a more prominent role on that album than previous ones.

It was not only the heavier use of keyboards on *Technical Ecstasy* that makes it sound closer to progressive rock; it was also the more elaborate transitional sections used in the songs, such as the instrumental transitions in "Backstreet Kids" (e.g., 1:46–2:00, 2:30–2:43, and 3:03–3:05). In October 1975 during the *Sabotage* tour, Ozzy said that Sabbath would do a concept album for their next release. During the final week of the tour (January 1976), he said they were thinking about doing a rock opera based on "Iron Man." As concept albums and rock operas are often associated with progressive rock, the fact that Sabbath had considered writing one for their seventh studio album suggests they were thinking along those lines. *Technical Ecstasy* is not a prog album, nor is it a jazz-rock fusion album, but it is notable that those elements are present.

TECHNICAL ECSTASY

Technical Ecstasy opens with "Backstreet Kids," a fairly straightforward rock number. The first half of the song alternates between the main riff (used behind the verses) and a secondary riff (used behind the post-verses) felt in half time. From 1:46 to 2:00 is a prog-sounding instrumental transition. Here, Jezz plays some fast synthesizer runs similar to the keyboard work of Ameriprog/prog-lite bands such as Kansas and Styx. During the bridge section (2:00–2:28), Bill plays two tom hits instead of the usual snare drum hit on beat "four." That, with the playing on the bell of the cymbal, gives the bridge a quasi-Latin feel. The transition returns from 2:29 to 2:42 and again features Jezz's synthesizer work. Tony's solo goes from 2:43 until the return to the main riff at 3:05. Behind his solo is Jezz playing mostly long tones; pay special attention to the last keyboard lick (3:03–3:05) and how, through his fast lines, he maneuvers his way back to the original key. Ozzy returns for a third verse, but Bill provides some extra interest, like the syncopated bass drum hits from 3:16 to 3:18, for instance. The song abruptly ends with the postverse, which is quite effective given how that riff is constructed.

The second track, "You Won't Change Me," starts with sound effects and synth sounds a la Pink Floyd. The band enters with a slow, sinister riff that is ambiguous about the key. It is truly an intro riff, as it never comes back, but bits of it do play a part in the bridge section later. The last note of the intro riff sets up the organ to establish the key. The band exclaims with two big hits, and once the verse begins, Bill answers each big chord with two tom hits. After a chorus, the organ part returns, but this time Bill colors it with ride cymbal. After the second verse and chorus, they abruptly change key and go into the bridge section (3:06). Notice the first three notes of the guitar/bass part (3:06–3:11) are the same as the first three notes of the intro riff (0:22–0:25), connecting these sections on some level. Continuing the bridge section with a guitar solo, they add two chords (4:08–4:10) to smoothly bring it back to the original key and bring back the organ. During the third verse (4:18–4:45), notice how Tony's long note turns into feedback as it is held through the first half of the verse and pans to the left channel. For the second half, he plays guitar fills around Ozzy's vocal melodies. As before, there is another chorus, followed by a bridge, a second guitar solo, and the two extra chords to get back to the organ part that ends the song.

The first and the most obvious point to make about "It's Alright" is that Bill is singing instead of Ozzy, the first time he sang on a Sabbath track. In the days before Sabbath, Bill actually sang in the band the Rest. The other point is that the structure of the song is especially simple: verses, middle instrumental section, and more verses. The same twenty-four or twenty-five seconds of music is repeated four times before the middle section, but there are small changes along the way for interest. Verse 1 has vocals, piano, organ, and bass, and then drums and percussion enter for verse 2. Lyrics change for the three verses, and falsetto "oooh's" are used in place of a fourth verse. There was great care taken by Tony for the solo in the middle instrumental section (1:38–2:25). Two guitar parts are panned to the two channels. As one plays in a high register, the other plays the same thing but lower. They switch positions (high/low) several times, and then have just one guitar in the center at 1:50. At 2:13, they both play high, then at 2:17 the left guitar bends a note, then the right guitar mimics it, and they are together again. Verse 4 (2:25) adds acoustic guitar, playing melodies to complement Bill's vocal part. In verse 5 (2:48), the guitar becomes more active and the keyboard becomes more prevalent (especially from 3:02 to 3:07). As the chord progression is heard for a seventh time at 3:12, the increasingly active guitar part becomes a solo. The solo continues during the eighth iteration of the chord progression as the song fades out.

"Gypsy" is structured as if it were two different songs combined into one. For the first three minutes, each section moves on to the next without looking back, and the material from the first one minute and fifty seconds never returns. The intro is played by shaker, hi-hats, and tom with some bass drum and cymbal hits, and then the guitar, bass, and organ enter with a riff vaguely reminiscent of the postverse riff in "Sweet Leaf." The riff continues for the verse and then a rock groove for the chorus. Instead of a second verse and chorus, it goes to a bridge section in a new key (1:33–1:50). That bridge leads into the second part of the song, as if it were starting a different song altogether but with similar lyrical content. The organ plays a repeated chord, and the song has entered a new key, one far removed from the original. Ozzy sings a verse and a chorus, so by 2:42 in the song there have been five different sections of music without returning to any of them. At 3:05, it returns to the repeated keyboard chord of 1:50, but this instrumental break is extended to feature Bill's drum fills. Ozzy sings a shortened verse and another chorus. This chorus has background vocals on "aaaaahh" and guitar fills. A guitar solo grows out of those fills and the song ends. This chorus and solo sections anticipate the solo sections in "Lonely Is the Word" a few years later by using the same two-chord progression.

The opening track of side two, "All Moving Parts (Stand Still)," includes fine work by Bill, Geezer, Jezz, Ozzy, and Tony. Before pointing out specific contributions by each musician, it would be helpful to listen to how the various sections of the song are organized and how they relate to one another. The song itself may be experienced as having two main parts, with the first part coming back (3:12–end). Within each part are multiple sections that are different but related.

Part one consists of an intro riff, a verse riff that is almost the same as the intro riff, and a postverse. It starts at a moderately slow tempo of 80 beats per minute (bpm) but speeds up slightly to 84. The postverse feels short: it consists of only one phrase lasting only eleven seconds. It has the characteristics of a prechorus, but it does not lead to a chorus, as it goes back to the intro riff (0:46). After a second verse, it goes to an extended version of the postverse. Notice how the chord goes up twice (1:21–1:29), comes back down (1:27–1:35), and then goes back up but only halfway (1:33–1:38). By going only halfway, it allows them to smoothly go to a new key for part two.

Part two (1:39–3:11) is much faster, nearly twice as fast (it jumps from 84 bpm to 150). It consists of two different riffs and a keyboard solo. The first of these two riffs (riff 3) speeds up slightly to 154 bpm and provides a backdrop for Ozzy's "I like choking toys" verse. The second riff is slightly faster, 160 bpm, which is exactly twice the opening tempo of 80. I refer to this riff as the "chromatic" riff because they use many notes outside of the key. It is played three times (not an even four as one might expect), and it slows back down slightly to return to riff 3 for another verse from Ozzy. The chromatic riff returns, and again it is played at 160 bpm. It is evident that they did not play to a steady "click track" and that they intended to play these riffs at these tempos. The last section of part two is a keyboard solo in a new key, the third for this song. It is about the same tempo of riff 3, 156 bpm.

Part one returns, but it is shortened (the postverse is only played once). The tempo drops in half to 78 bpm, but it speeds up slightly back to the original 80, and by the end, 84. It is in the original key, but the change of key from the keyboard solo into the intro riff is subtle and natural. Tony plays a solo over the intro riff, Ozzy sings a final verse and postverse, and there is a second guitar solo over the intro verse riff.

Ozzy's melody for the verse of part one is in a limited range, leaving him room to be more expressive in other sections. The first postverse only lasts one phrase, with only one rhyme, and he goes a bit higher for the words "yes he's" (0:42). The second postverse is extended by seven seconds, so it has three rhymes. He goes one step higher for the words "very strange" (1:34–1:37). This gradual ascension builds tension and leads to part two quite logically. During the two extended postverses, notice Ozzy's harmony parts (1:21–1:27 and 3:50–3:52) that are a bit higher than his melody, giving those moments a nice color, especially with his inflection on the word "guessing" at 3:52. The lyrics, according to Geezer, were Thatcher inspired and about a woman who has to dress as a man to become president, for U.S. society is too "misogynistic."[5] It was written just after Margaret Thatcher became the first woman to lead a major political party in the UK but three years before she became prime minister and forty-one years before Hillary Clinton nearly became the first woman president of the United States.

The song opens with a short solo by Tony over the intro riff, and after backing up Ozzy with some nice funk-inspired chords and rhythms, he plays another short solo between the postverse and second verse (0:46–0:57). He also doubles Ozzy's melody, incorporating some nice pinch harmonics (e.g., on the word "radiation," 1:13). For part two, Tony plays a unison riff with Geezer ten times backing up Ozzy before going into the "chromatic riff." This riff is not blues derived like the others but has ten different notes. That is unusual for Sabbath, as they usually stick to five, six, or seven. This induces an unsettling and unstable effect because it does not lend itself to any one key. Also, the riff is played three times, not the usual two or four. After the keyboard solo at the return of part two, Tony plays another brief solo to take it to another verse from Ozzy. His full-length solo happens at the end, starting at 4:04. It starts in the right channel but over time pans to the center and eventually to the left. If you listen to the opposite channel (i.e., starting in the left and panning to the right), you will hear a second guitar that is drenched in reverb and played in reverse (tape effect).

Although the intro riff and verse riff are similar, Geezer has a different bass line to distinguish the two sections. Notice how punchy the bass is in the verses, giving it a funk sound (think Larry Graham or Bootsy Collins, for instance). It's not common for Geezer to lay down the "fonk," but it works with Bill's drumbeat and Jezz's Clavinet work (cf. Stevie Wonder's "Superstition"). After the first postverse, he plays a big slide to bring it back to the intro riff (0:46). He really drives the band through the second postverse to increase the energy for part two. The energy is ramped up, especially during the keyboard solo where he occasionally uses a galloping rhythm (sometimes called the "heavy metal gallop"). As he tends to do during Tony's solos, Geezer cuts loose during the last minute of the song. A couple of interesting bass fills happen at 4:21 and 4:24, for instance.

Jezz adds to the funkiness of the rhythm section with the use of the Clavinet, which is most prevalent during the verses. His synth solo is brief (2:59–3:11) but effective. Instead of trying to fit as many notes as possible in a twelve-second solo, Jezz instead plays a simple blues-based melody. This section introduces a new key, which helps to make it sound fresh. The way he descends from 3:10 to 3:12 makes the transition back to the original smooth and natural.

"Rock 'n' Roll Doctor," as the title suggests, harkens back to early rock 'n' roll, with very much an American sound. The lyrics are uncharacteristic for Sabbath (e.g., "gotta see my rock 'n' roll doctor"), and Geezer attributes some or all of them to Ozzy. The song begins with a big tam-tam hit, and a slow, plodding groove on the toms under Tony's riff. This material does not return, and it heads into a rock 'n' roll groove. Aside from the prog-leaning middle section, it is a straightforward rock song. At 0:20, notice the clanking cowbell on every beat not unlike the infamous "more cowbell" *Saturday Night Live* sketch starring Christopher Walken and Will Ferrell. At 0:23, Bill plays the snare drum on all the beats and locks in his bass drum with Geezer. Once the verse begins, it goes into a straight rock feel with some honky-tonk piano from Jezz. From 1:44 to 2:07, they juxtapose prog-like music against the rock 'n' roll. This section features a guitar solo, drum fills, and synthesizer throughout. The dissonant crunch of the synth at 2:06 closes out this section, and they return to the original material. At 2:48, they vary the main riff, and it has a Led Zeppelin-esque character about it. Ozzy's voice, although still in a high register, is particularly gravelly.

"She's Gone" begins with a string orchestra, arranged by Mike Lewis. By 1976, Mike was already a veteran with more than a hundred arranging credits to his name, including sessions at the same studio in Miami. The mood changes at 0:11 when the harmony in the strings changes from major to minor. Here, the acoustic guitar enters and the strings fade out. When Ozzy enters at 0:49, the strings return in a medium and low range, and Jezz plays some harpsichord. For the second verse (1:33), higher strings are added. Ozzy's "ooh, my baby" closes the vocal section, and the strings take over with their own melody. The passage from 2:37 to 2:46 is beautiful, as the strings play three consecu-

tive major chords, each one higher than the last. This ascension is up-
lifting, giving a sense of hope to this sad song. But when the chord
resolves at 2:47, it is minor again, recalling the sad character. Here,
Geezer finally enters and provides a very melodic bass line for the third
verse from Ozzy. The strings return at 2:56, continuing through Ozzy's
fourth verse. At 4:34, the three hopeful chords from before emerge
(2:37–2:46), and as before, it resolves melancholically on the last chord
to end the song.

Unlike the rest of the album, "Dirty Women" has appeared in the
band's set lists in more recent years. It is also the longest on the album
and has a lot going on musically. Jezz takes claim to writing the song
although he was not credited on the album. If the music was written in
rehearsals in the UK, the lyrics surely were written later when the band
was in Miami: Geezer said they would see prostitutes on their way to
the studio, providing lyrical inspiration.

The song is in three parts (0:00–1:25, 1:26–3:56, and 3:57–end) that
never look back. In other words, once they go on to the next part, they
do not bring back earlier material. It keeps the song moving forward
and keeps everything sounding fresh. Within each part, however, they
bring back riffs and different sections so the music still makes sense and
is not scattered.

Part one begins with the main riff played on guitar and organ at a
moderate tempo (110 bpm), and the riff continues for the first half of
the verse (two vocal phrases). The second half of the verse (0:26–0:38)
changes and is over a different harmony. To add intensity for the second part, the band plays slightly faster (116 bpm), Ozzy sings in a higher
register, and harmonized guitars (one in the left channel, the other in
the right) climb up the scale. After the verse, it drops back in intensity
(and in speed to 112 bpm) and goes back to the main riff. After a second
verse, it returns to the main riff one last time to close part one.

Part two starts with an interlude, so it does not sound as if it is in a
new part until the new, heavy riff begins at 1:55 (one of the reasons
being that it is suddenly faster, 120 bpm). However, the interlude
comes back at 2:26 so it sounds as if it belongs to part two. Also, the
interlude is in a new key, and it never goes back to the original, so it
sounds like the song has moved somewhere different. From 1:25 to
1:38, Tony plays a melody three times, altering it each time for the
change of each chord and carefully navigating the change of key. The

chord at 1:38 establishes the new key, but if you notice the second half of the verses of part one (0:26–0:38 and 1:05–1:16), it is the same harmony. This relationship between the second half of the verse and the last six and a half minutes of the song makes it seem like a logical place to go.

The new, heavy riff (1:55) in the new tempo is a backdrop for a guitar solo. When the solo begins, it sounds as if there is a delay with the signal split between the two channels. There is a bit of sleight of hand: that is actually two guitars playing the same thing, and that becomes apparent at 2:03 when they start to play different notes from each other. They come back together at 2:11 by playing the same thing, but they split again at 2:15. When the interlude returns at 2:26, they keep the faster tempo instead of going back to where it was at 1:25. In fact, at 2:55, they go even faster for the next riff (129 bpm). This riff has two interesting characteristics. The first is that it is very syncopated, almost a jazz-fusion or Latin quality, which is creatively exaggerated by Bill's drumming. The other is that it borrows one note from another key, which gives it a darker color. When Tony and Jezz play the first half of the riff (2:55–2:56), they shift everything down exactly without regard to the key. By not adjusting to stay in the same key, that third note of the riff (at 2:57) ends up being out of the key, giving that moment of the riff a unique character. They play the riff four times, so you can hear the "odd" note at 2:57, 3:01, 3:04, and 3:08. Also, compare this riff to the main riff from Judas Priest's "Breaking the Law" (1980); although played in a different key, the first half is the same and the second half is similar. After the riff, the organ takes over the texture to close this section. They return to the heavy riff from 1:55, and it becomes the accompaniment for Ozzy's gravelly "Oh, dirty women, they don't mess around" verse.

At the 3:57 mark, other bands might end the song and fade out, but Sabbath drops into a half-time feel (61 bpm) for part three and continues for more than three additional minutes. For the remainder of the song, they repeat the same chord progression. The chords are reminiscent of the Beatles, especially the chord changes from "Dear Prudence" and "Lucy in the Sky with Diamonds." To keep it interesting, there are many variations they put on the music, which I will address.

Before Ozzy sings his last verse, one guitar plays the chord pattern, and a second and third guitar panned left and right. They play a sort of question and answer game. The left guitar starts with a single note (3:57), and the right guitar answers with the same note but lower (3:59). The left guitar plays a lick (4:00), and the right answers with the same lick but lower (4:02). When the verse starts, they reverse roles: the right plays first and higher, and the left answers and plays lower. At 4:13, it goes back to the left playing first and higher, and the right answering and lower. They reverse their roles again at 4:21, but behind the fourth vocal phrase at 4:29 the left guitar takes over and plays throughout. This leads into the guitar solo that lasts until the end when it fades out. At 6:33, a second guitar solo is added, and the two guitars are panned left and right again. A third guitar solo is added at 6:52, and possibly a fourth solo starting at 6:55 as the song fades. As the song fades, it intensifies, contrary to what many fade-out songs do, with a cacophony of Tonys.

Bill and Geezer also add variation throughout part three. Once the vocals start, Geezer goes into the higher register on every fourth phrase (4:30–4:36, 5:02–5:08, and 5:32–5:38). When Geezer goes higher at 5:02–5:08, Bill builds it up as if he will get more intense, but he saves it for one more phrase to go double time (122 bpm) at 5:16. When Geezer goes higher at 5:32, Bill launches into double bass drums for two phrases (5:32–6:01) and speeds up the tempo slightly to 126 bpm. Listen to how fast those bass drums are: they are played by alternating the two feet. This is notable because fast double bass drum patterns have since become nearly ubiquitous in metal drumming, but Bill used them sparingly and effectively. At 6:02, Bill returns to the one bass drum but keeps the faster tempo, and in the second phrase (6:10–6:15), Geezer goes to the higher register to play a simple two-note melody that is strikingly similar to the two-note melody of the Beatles' "Dear Prudence." Bill takes it back to the half-time feel, but the intensity is greater than the start of part three. After two phrases, he brings down the volume a bit and moves the right hand to the hi-hat. This allows for Tony's duet of guitar solos to be heard (6:33). At 6:47, Bill builds up as if he will go back to double time but instead keeps it slow but plays the bass drum quickly, four to a beat, for one more phrase. At 6:56, he launches back into double time, and Geezer, instead of his usual walk-down bass line, stays on the same high note for the last sixteen seconds of the song. As the song fades out, the band does a slight slowdown in the last part of the phrase, but it is barely audible by that point.

NEVER SAY DIE!

Some time in 1977 after the *Technical Ecstasy* tour, Ozzy left the band. When they reformed with Dave Walker, Jezz was no longer involved. Jezz mentioned in two interviews during the *Sabotage* tour that he was working on a solo album titled *The Ascent of Man*, but he did not release a solo album until 1980, titled *Opposite Directions*. Sabbath hired Don Airey to play keyboards for their next album, *Never Say Die!* but they did not employ a keyboardist for the tour. Although Jezz is classically trained and had been with a jazz fusion band before joining Sabbath, his contributions to *Technical Ecstasy* do not sound as closely connected to classical and jazz as do keyboardist Don's performance on *Never Say Die!*. Don had been with Colosseum II, a jazz-rock/prog outfit that had a few albums out before his brief time with Sabbath.

With Ozzy back on board for the new album, they went to Toronto to record *Never Say Die!*. Ozzy was not keen on the material they wrote with Dave, so they wrote new material and reworked existing material. "Junior's Eyes" was written when Dave was in the band, and according to Mick Wall's 2015 book, "Over to You" and "Swinging the Chain" were as well. Because Ozzy refused to sing "Swinging the Chain" and "Breakout," Bill sang the former, and the latter became an instrumental. It was written and recorded in the beginning of 1978, and it is very cold in Toronto that time of year. Perhaps that coldness affected their songwriting and performance and made its way onto tape, but regardless, there are some spectacular performances on this album.

Never Say Die! starts out with the song "Never Say Die," a fast (about 193 bpm) shuffle boogie, one of their fastest songs to date. Like the tempo and feel, the chords for the intro and verse are bright. By using all major chords, even the second chord, which would have normally been minor if it kept to the key, gives it a bright sound, even though Ozzy uses some blues inflections. When the chorus hits (0:40, 1:34, and 2:50), they color it by using some chords from the minor key, giving it a slightly darker sound. Here, listen how Tony plays a low melody between Ozzy's vocal lines (0:42, 0:47, etc.), and then it climbs as Ozzy sings, "Don't you ever, don't ever say die" (0:55, 1:49, and 3:05). At the very end of the second and third choruses, Geezer goes very high to build intensity into the next section (1:54 and 3:12). The character of the song changes at the bridge (2:09–2:30) with its mellower vibe and darker tone. At first it sounds as if it may have changed key, but as it goes through, they are just using minor chords as they did in the chorus to contrast the brightness of the verses. After a guitar solo, the song ends with seven big hits and "never say die" sung in a very low register, a full octave lower than any other vocal parts in the entire song.

"Johnny Blade" starts with a thirty-five-second solo from Don on a Yamaha CS-80 synthesizer (compare it to his intro to "Mr. Crowley" from Ozzy's first solo album, *Blizzard of Ozz*). The classical influence is strong here (nineteenth century especially, due to all the chromatic notes), putting the intro very much into prog territory. Listen for Don's blazing-fast prog-sounding descending licks at 2:19 and 2:26 and his prog-like synth lines that alternate with Ozzy from 4:33 to 4:57. Geezer said that he used a fretless Rickenbacker on "one part"[6] of the song, which is notable because fretless basses are commonly associated with jazz fusion; and Rickenbackers, with prog. Bill enters with a driving train-like snare drum pattern with occasional bass drum hits, and Don plays some blues-inflected synth lines a la Rick Wakeman. When Tony enters, Don plays in a higher register, and Geezer locks in with Bill's bass drum hits.

At only 1.6 seconds long, one of Sabbath's shortest riffs starts at 0:48. A verse, at twenty-six seconds long, has the riff played sixteen times; its repetitiveness is what makes it effective. The prechorus (1:19–1:30) is blues derived, and when one expects the last chord of the blues form, they instead change key for the chorus (which is more of a refrain, as it is only six seconds long and Ozzy sings "Johnny Blade" only twice). Instead of going back to the original key, they stay a step higher and Ozzy is singing even higher, adding intensity to it all. They go up a key again for the second chorus/refrain and double the length. After a short connector with a descending riff and drum fills throughout, they drop into a heavy riff in half-time feel at 2:34 for more verses. A nice touch of added instruments is that there is a guiro on the word "spider" (2:51) and again at 2:53, and there are harmonized funk-style guitars panned left and right starting at 3:27. Don's prog-like synth lines and Bill's fast drum fills alternate with Ozzy from 4:33 to 4:57, and then Bill and Tony are featured at 4:58. At 5:09, they double the tempo, back to the original but slightly faster. Here, Tony plays a wonderfully crafted solo, and even foreshadows a motif from "A Hard Road" at 6:07–6:09. At 6:23, the band plays a tag for a tight, strong ending. This "Johnny Blade" character, by the way, was partly based on Bill's brother.

Without any silence between tracks, "Junior's Eyes" begins with Bill and Geezer playing moderately softly. With no Tony at the outset, it is noticeably softer than the end of "Johnny Blade," but it fades in over time and Tony enters. Bill and Geezer are very tight here, and Geezer's intricate line is super clear thanks to his clear execution and equalization with higher frequencies that allow for such definition. Although on certain notes it sounds as if this clarity also comes from using a pick, Geezer said he never uses a pick in the studio. Geezer said he saw Jack Bruce (Cream) use his fingers and said to himself, "That's the way you play bass."[7] From 0:20 to 0:31 you will hear what is probably a piano played with the tape reversed, a huge fade-in made possible by the studio trick to create an unnatural crescendo. Although the music was written in the days with Dave on vocals, the lyrics were written about Ozzy's father, who had recently passed away. A beautifully sad moment in this song occurs with a little word painting when, at 0:46, Ozzy ascends to a high note for the word "sky" on the line "his hands reached out to the sky." Ozzy also navigates through the chord changes of the chorus with a lovely melody by mixing major and minor scales. In the second chorus, Tony plays a nice melody in long tones around Ozzy's vocal line that reaches a very high note at 3:08 and comes back down to close the chorus. Bill's twice-as-fast hi-hat pattern along with tambourine announces the instrumental section. Tony's solo is very melodic, opting for long notes instead of fast lines. Although this section is loud and heavy, there is an added acoustic guitar (3:31–4:09). They return to the original groove for another verse, and Tony's various guitars through a wah-wah effect color it nicely. The final chorus includes nice melodic lines from Tony around the vocal melody. The song ends with held-out chords with plenty of space for Bill to play drum fills. To hear an earlier version of the song and to hear what Sabbath sounded like with Dave on vocals, check out the recording broadcast on BBC Midlands' *Look! Hear!* on January 6, 1978.

Like "Never Say Die," "A Hard Road" is another shuffle-feel song but this one much slower at 126 bpm. After the second chorus (1:59) and after the guitar solo (3:17), there are postchorus sections ("why make the hard road") with a guitar melody recalling a motif from 6:07–6:09 in the "Johnny Blade" solo. During the guitar solo, you will hear two backward cymbal hits (tape reverse effect) at 2:40 and 2:44. During the fourth chorus (4:43), they add background vocals for a chorus hook, including the first and maybe only time Tony would sing on a Sabbath album (perhaps he sang backups on "Shock Wave" as well). This is an example of the influence of the "arena rock" and "corporate rock" bands.

"Shock Wave" is a great track that, unlike most of the songs from *Never Say Die!*, made its way onto the touring set list for 1978–1979 but only briefly. There are six sections, with the first two never coming back. Geezer is aggressive on this song, especially in the first section (he really cuts through at 0:37, for instance). The third section (1:15) is really a transition that sets up the new key that finally arrives at the fourth section (1:33). Geezer is aggressive again in this fourth section. Here, he creates a very melodic bass line by playing different notes from Tony's chord. That may be the Paul McCartney influence, but paired with the rhythmic aggressiveness and bright bass tone, it sounds more like Geddy Lee of Rush. Bill recalls the guys from Rush being at the studio actually, which would have been in late April between their *Farewell to Kings* and *Archives* tours. At 1:58, when Ozzy finishes the vocal melody, the overdubbed Ozzys complete the chord: you'll hear the two other Ozzys added one at a time. The fifth section, starting at 2:01, contains three parts (2:01–2:15, 2:16–2:29, and 2:30–2:41), each with a different melody and all in a new key. The sixth section goes to half time, and Tony solos on top of a descending blues riff. At 3:17, it returns to the third part of the fifth section but without Ozzy, and Tony plays a melody different than what Ozzy sang before. It abruptly changes key by going back to the third section (3:17) for more soloing but with Tony's rhythm guitar playing Ozzy's melody in the background. This retransition leads to the fourth section (3:46), and Ozzy is back in. But instead of going to the fifth section again, it goes directly to the sixth for the half-time blues riff. Instead of a solo, there are background vocals "ooh-ooh" and then a final verse. Echoes of the late seventies "corporate rock" sound are most evident in Tony's guitar in the third section (1:18, 3:32) and in the "ooh-ooh's" at the end. Although there may be influence from bands such as Boston, Foreigner, Journey, Kansas, Queen, and Styx, the song is still distinctly Sabbath.

If there is one song that exemplifies the eclecticism of *Never Say Die!* it would be "Air Dance." As part of the musical fabric you will find elements of jazz, Latin, hard rock, and prog. Bill described it as "almost like a modern jazz quartet,"[8] although Don contributes so much to the song that it would be a quintet including Ozzy. The instrumental performances by Bill, Don, Geezer, and Tony are stellar on this track.

During the *Technical Ecstasy* tour, Sabbath played two performances with the jazz-rock prog band Caravan and with the world-fusion group Shakti, a band that included fusion guitarist John McLaughlin, known for his work with Mahavishnu Orchestra. In a 2013 interview, Don cites classical music as a "huge" influence, naming several classical composers and pianists, jazz musicians, rock keyboardists, and Jan Hammer's work with Mahavishnu Orchestra.[9]

The song opens with a harmonized melody played by the guitars in a minor key. The drums here are simple, with the standard snare drum hits on "two" and "four," but the ride cymbal pattern offers some interest. Bill is very solid and simple here to provide a foundation, or in other words, a consistent beat to which the melody plays against (much of the melody is syncopated). Although Bill often reacts to this kind of rhythmic activity by accenting along with it, he keeps his parts simple here.

At 0:33, the groove changes significantly when Bill and Geezer provide a Latin-jazz feel. Notice how the snare drum comes in slightly later than in a standard rock feel, played consistently on the "and" of beat "two." Geezer's rhythm and note choice for the bass line is fairly typical for Latin jazz. The accents, the feel, the bass line, and the tempo (111 bpm) give the music a bossa nova feel. Compare it, for example, to most recordings of the Latin-jazz standard "Blue Bossa."

The verse begins at 0:41, and Don provides piano fills that musically navigate in and around Ozzy's vocal melody. At the end of the fourth vocal phrase (0:56), he plays a simple melody right before Ozzy sings "a distant dreamer." The scale choice here is slightly different from the intro (only one note different), giving the music more of a jazz flavor. This scale, called Dorian, is commonly associated with jazz. Tony on occasion uses this scale for the passages that sound influenced by jazz guitarists (for example, recall the solo from "Planet Caravan"). However, Don's piano parts have more of a classical sensibility than jazz. At 1:09, during the seventh vocal phrase, listen to Don's fast cascading piano fills. Here he plays fast three-note figures (they outline chords, actually) that descend down the scale. Visually, this piano passage always makes me think of a cascading waterfall.

The next section, a postverse, begins with harmonized guitar melodies alternating with Ozzy's vocal lines. Tony's lines recall the original key, not the jazz-like Dorian sound of the verse. He also uses bluesy inflections, giving the music more interest. At the end of the verse, notice Don's piano line: it ends with a note outside of the key to complement Tony's "blue" note, thus seamlessly connecting the two sections (1:17). Don also plays organ through this section, but it is fairly quiet in the mix. This postverse is six bars long (twelve seconds), and after the two harmonized guitar lines, it ends with a two-bar (four-second) guitar lick, and then Ozzy finishes with "she danced the night away." From 1:29 to 2:25, it repeats the material from 0:33 to 1:29 but with new lyrics. Tony plays a tasty guitar fill before the second verse starts, and Don again plays some nice figures behind Ozzy's vocals.

At 2:25, the music changes considerably: the key changes abruptly and the drums drop out. Ozzy repeats the word "away," Tony plays a couple of clean (i.e., without effects) guitar fills, Geezer plays a smooth bass line implying two different chords, and Bill plays some cymbal rolls. Don plays a repeated pattern on the piano, but notice there is one note that changes every four or so seconds. That changing note may imply an impending second key change, keeping the music ambiguous. He also plays some textural synth parts throughout this section. At 2:42, Tony begins a guitar solo, still clean, and the jazz influence is clear. At 2:59, a synth doubles the guitar melody and the two chords are played in reverse order. With the reversal, the piano pattern stops (as it would no longer work) and Don plays chords instead. At 3:15 the chord changes, confirming that second key change, and Tony and Don play the melody together. The chord changes again at 3:19 and 3:23, so it is evident the key is changing, leaving the listeners unsure of where they are and where they may be heading.

But a big buildup from 3:24 to 3:32 makes it clear that they have traveled to yet another new key. Here, a new riff is played, and the song is at its heaviest yet—the only real "hard rock" section of the song. The riff is only heard four times, and then the band recalls the first four bars of the postverse. The organ is again quiet in the mix, but because it holds out a bit longer than the last snare drum hit, you can hear it clearly, but briefly, at 3:54.

The feel changes yet again, but it is a faster version of the Latin-jazz feel from before (0:33–2:25). Although the drums, bass, guitar, and piano set up the new feel, it is Bill and Geezer driving it. With the faster tempo (183–186 bpm instead of 111) and the more active and aggressive rhythms, it has a Latin-rock-jazz fusion feel about it. The guitar/synthesizer duet begins at 4:00, and the style here is very much jazz-rock fusion; compare this to, say, John McLaughlin and Jan Hammer. The synth follows the guitar so closely that on first listen it sounds as if the synth is an effect on the guitar, or as if a guitar synth was used (that was new technology at the time). At first it sounds as if the guitar signal was split and run through a guitar synth or pedal effect to get the synth sound, but at 4:21 you will hear Tony play a three-note figure (the highest of the solo) by himself, which is then repeated with Don joining him at 4:22. That brief moment where the guitar is not doubled by the synth makes it clear that it is not simply an effect on the guitar but played by Don. By digitally slowing down the track without changing the pitch, it is clearer that the synth part is not an effect but performed separately. Considering the complexity of the guitar solo, it is quite an impressive feat that Don doubles the solo so meticulously.

From 4:26 to 4:36 there are a few brass notes that help the transition to the next section and help change back to the original key. Although this may be a synthesizer, it is likely that the brass used on "Breakout" played a few notes here as well. From 4:36 until the end there is a repeated pattern in the synth that is very much in the vein of progressive rock. Here, Bill's drums accent Don's pattern, and the guitar/synth duet continues, although with several long tones. The vocals never return, making the second half of the song purely instrumental.

The intro to "Over to You" has very much a Boston or Foreigner sound about it (cf. "Feels Like the First Time"), but the verse is very Sabbath-like. In the prechorus (1:01–1:41), Tony and Bill lay it down, Ozzy has a nice vocal line (written by Bill, actually), and Geezer and Don provide some interesting work. Listen how Geezer plays very melodically and uses the whole range of the bass: low notes (1:05, etc.) and very high ones (1:26 and 1:33). He even plays two notes at the same time at 1:32. Don plays some nice piano passages behind Ozzy throughout, such as the fast figures (1:11–1:14), a long chromatic scale (1:15–1:19), and others. The chorus (1:42) has a funky groove about it with Tony's higher-register chords, Geezer's bass line, the tambourine, and Bill's drumbeat with the open hi-hat just before the snare drum and cymbal immediately after. After another verse, prechorus, and chorus (3:39), it goes back to the very beginning with the rock organ and then a final verse.

"Breakout" is different from other Sabbath tracks, most noticeably for the use of a saxophone solo and a jazz horn section. Although Bill called it the "wackiest" thing they had ever done, I believe "FX" from *Vol. 4* earns that distinction. After all, rock bands with horns were not entirely unusual for the 1970s, and Tony had been interested in groups such as Chicago and Blood, Sweat & Tears. The riff for the song is a four-note motif (horns ascend, Geezer descends), followed by a big, loud, long chord. Notice how this simple, short, four-note motif develops into something more over the course of the song. After the horns have played it seven times, there is a five-note descending melody (1:03–1:06). It is played again but a step higher (1:12–1:15). By 1:20, it has grown into a five-second-long melody played four times, all with a slight swing to the rhythm. It changes at 1:53, and each time it gets bigger, the fourth time (2:18) with high trumpets. Credit this fine arrangement to Wil Malone (credited as "Will Malone" on the album), the same one who did the arrangements for the orchestra on "Spiral Architect" and the choir on "Supertzar." It ends on a held-out chord with a collective improvisation, but a saxophone had been soloing for nearly two minutes by this point. Notice the pitch slowly rise over the last ten seconds via tape-speed manipulation; the effect is unnerving and makes the release into the next song a relief.

The blues roots are obvious on "Swinging the Chain," the last song on the album, with the shuffle-like feel, bluesy vocal melodies, the blues chord progression in the chorus, and the use of harmonica. Although Ozzy played harmonica on "The Wizard" from the first album, those duties were covered by John Elstar. John has harmonica credits on a few other albums (Kim Fowley, Mama's Boys, and the Pretty Things); he often seems to be confused with vocalist Jon Elstar (of Highway, which opened for Sabbath in 1973). Ozzy did not sing either; instead Bill sang and wrote the lyrics. Notice how high Bill sings at 2:26 and 2:30—this ranks among the very highest of all Sabbath singers!

TOUR AND BREAKUP

Black Sabbath began their tour in mid-May 1978, the album not released until over four months later. The 1978 tour would be the last with this lineup for many years to come. To get a sense of what Sabbath sounded and looked like live at this time, check out the *Never Say Die* DVD. Of the ten songs, it contains "Never Say Die" and two from their previous album, "Dirty Women" and "Rock 'n' Roll Doctor." Geezer's use of a Rickenbacker on the video has misled many to believe that was his touring bass and what he played on the album, but it was merely the case that he had forgotten his usual one. Ozzy's voice sounds gravelly, and he struggles to hit high notes. In his defense, Geezer and Tony did not tune down for "Children of the Grave," "Snowblind," and "Symptom of the Universe" as they did in the studio, effectively placing the songs at the top of Ozzy's vocal range. He alters the vocal melodies to accommodate. If the listener does not notice that the songs are played in a higher key, the blame is usually placed on Ozzy for not hitting the high notes. Whether that is fair is debatable.

Sabbath completed their tour in December, and in March, they went to Los Angeles to write material for another album. According to Tony, "Ozzy wasn't into it."[10] Ozzy was fired from Sabbath by the end of April, and they recruited Ronnie James Dio to replace him for the next album, *Heaven and Hell*.

5

ENTER RONNIE JAMES DIO

Some assume that when a lead singer leaves a band, subsequent albums are completely different. That would certainly be true if the singer is the primary songwriter, but that is not the case for many bands. A listener that only pays attention to the vocals and not the entire band would likely think that. Certainly *Heaven and Hell* is a much different album than the previous eight, but there are plenty of stylistic elements that remain. Tony Iommi was always the primary composer of the music, so there is continuity in that regard. Performance-wise, Bill Ward, Geezer Butler, and Tony are present, and like the previous several albums, there is the occasional use of keyboards. Moreover, some of the material was worked up during the few months Ozzy Osbourne was still in the band. Geezer and Tony have said that they have recordings of "Children of the Sea" and "Die Young" with Ozzy singing, but that is probably only true for the former, as Tony said in 2008 that they wrote "Die Young" in Miami. Ronnie James Dio said that "Die Young" was written in Miami as a collaboration with him and Tony as a "germ of an idea" that they took "to fruition,"[1] so perhaps only some material was kept from the earlier writing sessions. However, bassist Craig Gruber lays claim to writing the fast sections of "Die Young," so perhaps the only music left over from the Ozzy demo was the slow, soft middle section (or Geezer and Tony confused it with another song). According to Martin Popoff's 2006 book, there are "skeletal incarnations" of "Lady Evil" and "Heaven and Hell" from that time as well.[2] Sometime in mid-1979 after he left the band, Ozzy predicted what Sabbath's next album would sound like: "They'll probably sound very much like Foreigner. I couldn't stand where they were going musically. . . The year before it was Queen; now it's Foreigner."[3]

Ronnie James Dio, who was six to seven years their senior, joined the band with years of recording, performing, and songwriting experience. Ronnie has album credits dating back to 1958. Have a listen to the albums he did with Elf (1972–1975) and Rainbow (1975–1978) to contextualize his contributions to Sabbath as a singer and songwriter. The blues-influenced hard rock on these albums is but one commonality with Sabbath's music. Listening to his early and midsixties recordings will give insight to his softer vocal style (e.g., "Children of the Sea," "Die Young," etc.) and will reveal excellent vocal versatility, intonation, and technique. For instance, his 1963 recording includes "I Left My Heart in San Francisco," a song made famous by Tony Bennett one year prior. In a 1980 interview, Ronnie cited Paul McCartney, Stevie Wonder, and Paul Rodgers as his main three influences, and added Paul Simon for his work as songwriter and lyricist. In other interviews he named Sam Cooke, Mario Lanza, Otis Redding, and Jackie Wilson as influences. This myriad of influences and experiences shows Ronnie's breadth as a vocalist.

Commenting on Ronnie's contributions to the songwriting, Tony said, "Some of the things we had already written before Ronnie came. . . . We had riffs but no vocal stuff. . . . He came up with a few other ideas to add to the songs."[4] He said that having Ronnie in the band "created a different way of writing. . . . Ozzy would sing a lot on riffs, [whereas] Ronnie would sing on chords."[5] Thus, they were able to incorporate more chord progressions into their songs instead of using riffs throughout. Tony also said that Ronnie would give suggestions for chords, something Ozzy wouldn't do.

Ronnie's primary songwriting contributions were the vocal melodies and lyrics. Geezer relinquished his lyric writing duties to Ronnie, which he called a "relief" because he was "sick of writing lyrics at the time."[6] The lyric that starts the bridge of "Neon Knights" ("circles and rings, dragons and kings") is a good example of the difference between Ronnie's lyric writing and Geezer's. Lyrical content aside, Ozzy and Ronnie are stylistically very different, although they both show influence from the blues. For one, Ronnie will sometimes use a wide vibrato and at other times a straight tone. He will alter the timbre of his voice by using falsetto or the growl for which he is probably best known. Although the highest notes that Ronnie sings are not as high as Ozzy's, he usually sings in a slightly higher register than Ozzy usually does. In other words, Ronnie's usual register would be medium-high or high for Ozzy. With very few exceptions, the only times he sings in Ozzy's medium-low or low registers is when performing their older songs in concert (e.g., "Black Sabbath," "War Pigs," etc.).

Geezer had left the band for a time, so at times Ronnie had to fill in on bass during the songwriting sessions (Ronnie played bass in Elf until the midseventies). In mid-July 1979, they brought in Geoff Nicholls, the guitarist/keyboard player for the Birmingham-based metal band Quartz, to play bass temporarily. Quartz, formerly known as Bandy Legs, opened up for Sabbath on tour in 1975. To hear Geoff's musical background, have a listen to the singles from Bandy Legs (or "Bandylegs" on some releases) and Quartz's eponymous album that Tony played flute on and produced. There are musical similarities between Quartz and Sabbath; compare the main riff of "Wildfire" to the heavy riff of "Megalomania," for instance. Geoff played a role in the songwriting on *Heaven and Hell* although he was not credited. For instance, the slow, galloping bass line to "Heaven and Hell" was derived from the Quartz song "Mainline Riders," and Geoff said he wrote the chord progression for the solo section in "Neon Knights." There are likely other moments on the album to which Geoff contributed in some way or another. Bill said, "[Geoff] needs to be credited. He was very much a big part at that point."[7]

On Ronnie's recommendation, they brought in Craig Gruber on bass temporarily, as they worked together in Elf and Rainbow in the midseventies. Ronnie said that Craig "didn't fit in,"[8] and Geoff concurred, saying he "wasn't able to fit into the unit."[9] That fall, Geoff said they "met up with Geezer in Miami, played him the stuff, and he loved it."[10] With the exception of "Neon Knights," which was done later, the album's songs were likely fully formed by that point. Although Tony said they removed Craig's bass lines before showing Geezer what they had recorded, Geezer said he did hear them. Geezer kept the existing "Heaven and Hell" bass line, so there are likely other bass lines written by Craig, Geoff, or Ronnie that he kept but probably only if the bass lines were integral to the song or if he especially liked them. Geezer said, "I didn't want to listen to the bass that was on there so that I [wouldn't] copy it." "Although," he continued, "there [were] some good parts—[pause]—that I 'nicked,'" he laughed.[11] It would be unnecessary to attribute bass lines that follow Tony's riff to Craig, Geoff, or Ronnie, but if Geezer were present earlier along in the songwriting process, perhaps he would have come up with something different. Listening to the album, there are Geezer-isms in the bass parts that give the songs his personal stamp. Thus, even if the genesis of the bass lines came from someone else, he does enough elaborations to make them his own.

With Craig on bass, Geoff moved to rhythm guitar and keyboards. Recall that Sabbath's songs have overdubbed guitar parts, so having a second guitar would have made live performances sound more like the albums. Also recall that Jezz was hired not only to re-create the keyboard and orchestral textures but also to thicken up the sound during the guitar solos by playing Tony's riffs on a keyboard through distortion. Rather than approximating the sound of a guitar on a keyboard, the idea here was to use an actual guitar. With Ronnie calling the composite guitar sound "mushy,"[12] this idea was scrapped temporarily, and Geoff's primary performing and recording duties became keyboards. Geoff still contributed to the songwriting, albeit uncredited; Graham Wright called him "Tony's right-hand man, on the music side."[13] Paul Clark, Sabbath's tour manager around this time, said, "Though [Geoff] never got the credit for it, he definitely helped write some of that stuff on *Heaven and Hell*. Him and Tony in L.A."[14]

The band left LA for Miami, and according to Geoff and Tony, they arrived during a hurricane, so it must have been at the beginning of September 1979, when Hurricane David hit Florida. The band lived in Barry Gibb's (of the Bee Gees) home, where they continued to write the album and prepare for recording sessions at Criteria Studios (where they had done *Technical Ecstasy* a few years prior). According to David Tangye and Wright, Geezer rejoined two weeks into the recording sessions, and according to Geoff, the band recorded until Christmas. They enlisted Martin Birch, whom Ronnie had worked with on the Rainbow albums, to produce the album. Geoff and Tony said that the band decided the album needed a faster song to contrast the slow and mid-tempo songs. That is an interesting observation because "Wishing Well" is fast by Sabbath standards (145 beats per minute [bpm]), the middle section of "Heaven and Hell" is quite fast (207 bpm), and "Die Young" is the fastest on the album (212 bpm). Another reason that likely played

ENTER RONNIE JAMES DIO

into the decision to add another song is that the album was only thirty-six minutes long at that point. Thus, in early January, the band went to Jersey (Channel Islands) to write and then to Studios Ferber in Paris to write and record what would become "Neon Knights." From there, they went to Townhouse Studios in London for overdubs and to mix the album.

HEAVEN AND HELL

The album starts with their newest song "Neon Knights," which is indeed fast (about 186–194 bpm). It is about the same tempo as the opening track on their last album, "Never Say Die" (about 193 bpm), but with a much different rhythmic feel (straight instead of swung). These two and "Die Young" were Sabbath's fastest songs at the time, as the only faster tempos Sabbath played in the seventies occurred in middle sections of songs—not for an entire song. Commenting on their general lack of fast tempos, Tony said, "I find that writing fast songs is difficult."[15] Ronnie said, "Fast songs . . . are the hardest things on Earth to write."[16] Geoff called the song "probably the only real band writing effort on that entire album because Geezer was involved at that stage."[17] However, Ronnie said that Bill was not present when the band was writing in Jersey. Geoff lays claim to coming up with the chords for the solo section (1:58–2:43), which makes sense because this section is based not on riffs but on different harmonies and chords. Also, the way those harmonies relate to one another is different than earlier Sabbath songs, something I had noticed before reading Geoff's clarification.[18] Leading up to the solo is a bridge in two parts (1:08–1:28, 1:28–1:58) that establishes a new key at 1:48 on the words "neon knights." The solo abruptly returns to the first key but with different harmonies; thus, it sounds new, yet it makes the return to the main riff seamless (2:43).

The next track, "Children of the Sea," opens with two acoustic guitars in an almost folky/quasi-classical style. Some of Geezer's finest moments in this song are in the intro and the fast lick at 2:16. Ronnie uses his clear, straight tone for the first verse (0:14) but applies a hard-rock tone for later sections. Tony says he has a recording of an earlier version of the song with Ozzy and that it was "changed around with Ronnie's involvement. . . . The way he'd approach things was a lot more operatic."[19] The key changes for the heavy second verse (0:40) and again for the middle instrumental part (3:07–3:50). The keyboard here is a Mellotron with choir tapes, but the reason it doesn't sound like the standard Mellotron choir is that Sabbath had tapes custom made for them. The custom tapes (which also included strings, percussion, and sound effects) were recently discovered in an abandoned Mellotron storage facility in Birmingham. After the guitar solo, the last chord is held (3:44) and the Mellotron finishes this part connecting it to the intro material (3:50). The key change back to the original is subtle because it comes out of the held chord. The fourth verse (4:04) is the same as the first but with slight changes to the melody. There is an added synthesizer sound and bell tree or wind chimes (4:07 and 4:21) for more color. The final verse (5:02) repeats "look out" five times, a little rhythmic motif that serves to end the song.

The acoustic intro, melodic use of the bass guitar, and the Mellotron sounds recall the progressive rock (prog) elements heard on their earlier albums. However, most of the rest of the album heads away from the seventies-era prog style and is closer to NWOBHM (new wave of British heavy metal) in style and intent. Bill said, "Musically, it's a blues-based song. Tony and I just played blues behind it because that's basically what it is."[20] I'm not sure what he means because the song is closer to folk, pop, classical, and prog rock than it is to blues. The main riff (0:40) has a bluesiness about it, almost as if it were inspired by slide guitar playing. Bill's fill getting into that riff (0:38) has a slight swing, so maybe that's what he means. Or perhaps he or the interviewer confused it with "Lonely Is the Word," which has more of a blues connection.

"Lady Evil" has a classic rock feel and sound but not like seventies Sabbath, especially with lyrics such as "Lady Evil, she's a magical, mystical woman." However, the key changing up a step in the solo (2:24 and again at 2:47) is classic Sabbath (e.g., "After Forever," etc.). The section from 2:39 to 2:57 is very similar to the intro of "Rock 'n' Roll Doctor." Both have a tom-driven drum part, the same type of key change halfway through, similar bass lines, and they both go to a "rock and roll" feel after. A new riff, played only once, closes the instrumental section to take it back for another verse. The ending is the same as the end of "Johnny Blade."

The title track, "Heaven and Hell," begins with the main riff played at a moderately slow tempo (89 bpm). The bass follows the guitar part, and Bill's hi-hat foreshadows the rhythm of the verse bass line. At 0:22, the intensity and volume decrease, and the tempo drops slightly (to 86 bpm). Here, Geezer plays the bass part from the verses of Quartz's "Mainline Riders." This was Geoff's contribution when he was on bass duties, but because it became an important part to the song, Geezer kept it. He has commented that he would have come up with something different. The biggest difference between the Sabbath and the Quartz riffs is the brief four-note idea that Geezer inserts (e.g., 0:43). That four-note idea comes from the end of the main riff (0:23), but Geezer has used it enough in other songs that it has become a signature of his playing. This provides a calm backdrop for the verse in which Ronnie sings in the top part of his range. At 0:55, a brief section with the song's title in the lyrics functions like a prechorus. It sets up the next riff (1:01), which is essentially a heavy variation of the verse's bass line riff. Geezer plays the same pattern, but Tony adds different notes and a higher chord (1:02 and 1:08) just as before the second verse of "War Pigs."

It comes down again for a second verse but with added harmonized guitar parts (1:17). Notice the guitars fade in, there is minimal distortion and no pick sound, and the notes are smooth and connected. It sounds as if he used an e-bow on two or three guitar overdubs to achieve this sound (cf. Steve Hackett's e-bow work in Genesis). Live, these parts were played with fingers (no pick) and synth, or just guitar with controlled feedback. After the verse, the "prechorus" bit is repeated three times before the "heaven and hell" refrain. Here (1:55), the main riff returns and Tony plays a solo under Ronnie's vocals. The solo is not flashy but instead melodic and even harmonizes the end of the main riff (2:02–2:05 and 2:13–2:15). At 2:05, Ronnie introduces a vocal motif ("fool, fool") that will return later in the song.

The bridge (2:17) features some nice harmonies outlined by vocals, guitar, and bass. Ronnie's lead vocal navigates through them, and two background Ronnies (on "ahh") supply part of the chord. On Tony's third, fourth, and fifth chords (2:22–2:30), Geezer plays notes other than the main one/"root" of the chord to provide additional sonic variety, showing the Paul McCartney/Beatles influence.

The riff from 1:01 returns and is used to accompany the third verse. When the "prechorus" returns at 3:10, it is heard only once as with its first appearance. This time, however, there is no "heaven and hell" refrain or heavy verse riff. The music instead becomes subdued, and a guitar solo begins at 3:18. For the first note, Tony releases a bend over three seconds giving it the same crying, sad sound as the opening of "Wheels of Confusion." If "Heaven and Hell" weren't detuned a half step, it would be the same pitch. The simple bass and drum part allow much space for Tony, and he holds the first note for five seconds. A delay is set at about 682 milliseconds so it repeats every beat at about 88 bpm. It repeats six times, and each one gets softer as if it's echoing and traveling away. This adds another dimension to the music—depth—to the binaural sound of left and right channels. Having the multiple repetitions creates a thicker sound as it makes it seem like there are several guitars.

The solo begins very patiently, as there is just the bent note and echoed crunchy note for the first eleven seconds—a fine use of temporal space. A second guitar, placed mostly in the right channel, plays two slowly released bends (3:30–3:35 and 3:40–3:45) with a soundscape/atmospheric approach. At 3:45, the lead guitar uses the delay effect to create harmony by treating it like a canon, allowing the repetitions to harmonize with itself. At 4:01, two chords take it to the bridge (4:03), but only the first half is used. The background/"ahh" vocals return but not the lead vocal because the guitar solo continues.

At 4:16, the tempo goes to more than double time (90 to 202 bpm), and by 5:50, the band has sped up to 207 bpm. Bill uses the "train" snare drum pattern (cf. "Looking for Today" and "Johnny Blade") with an overdubbed backbeat and, at 4:22, overdubbed tom hits. Although the rhythm guitar changes chords, Geezer stays in order to complement Bill's part. When Bill goes into a fast rock beat (4:35), Geezer elects to remain, alternating the same two notes.

A verse begins at 4:44, and because of the new tempo, the vocal delivery is much different. The riff at 4:54 is truncated to start another verse at 4:59. The lyrics here (e.g., "they'll tell you black is really white," etc.) are the clearest examples of the song being a "story of contradictions," as Ronnie described it.[21] He brings back the "fool, fool" motif and places it in a different musical context. He and Tony exchange brief phrases: short guitar solo licks alternate with vocal lines. Geezer's bass line does not follow the roots of Tony's chords but instead slowly ascends to create a smooth melodic line. He also plays some excellent bass fills on the last chord of the riff (4:53, 5:07, 5:21, and 5:30).

Tony's lines between Ronnie's vocal phrases become a solo at 5:32 that ends with a final chord at 5:50. As it fades, two nylon string acoustic guitars come in. By 6:14 they are spread into two channels: the melody in the right, and the finger-picked chords in the left. The fingerstyle recalls "Orchid," and the music evokes early music (centuries before the Classical era) in the way that "Embryo" does. This part is not done in concert and is replaced by a held-out chord, a return to the main riff, or other material.

"Wishing Well" has elements of their old and new style. For one, the song is fast, unlike so many other earlier Sabbath songs. The chorus (0:40) and bridge (1:30) sections have pop-like chord progressions instead of riffs, perhaps with influence or input from Geoff or Ronnie. Conversely, the acoustic guitar strumming at 2:07 recalls Sabbath's midseventies sound and texture. Bill plays a bit differently on *Heaven and Hell*—a bit simpler and more straightforward ("Heaven and Hell," "Lady Evil," etc.)—and I wonder if that was a personal choice or a suggestion from a band member or the producer. He was also going through personal battles and claims he doesn't remember recording the album. However, the drumming on this song is definitely in his usual style, as it is busier than the other songs on the album (e.g., 0:29, "mini fills" in the middle of phrases).

Geoff starts "Die Young," one of the few Sabbath songs that begin with synthesizers. He oscillates between two chords every three and a half seconds, holding one note and moving the other two back and forth. He sustains a low note throughout the entire forty-eight-second introduction, holding it all together. This gives the intro a simple, slow-moving texture, allowing much space for Tony's solo (0:14–0:48). Atmospheric synthesizers supporting a guitar solo creates a rare texture for Sabbath but common to prog rock, so it gives an aura of prog-ness in contrast to their norm. Starting at 0:04, a second synth fades in and out of the texture, moving left to center. This synth has a "bubbly" sound created by an arpeggiator that goes up and down the chord, sounding one note at a time in rapid succession. In a casual hearing, it may sound as if Geoff is playing the pattern, but it is so fast that it wouldn't be able to be played by a human. The notes change every fifty-four milliseconds (thirty-seven notes in the span of two seconds), giving it a mechanical, "bubbly" sound.

After Tony's guitar melody, four additional guitars enter: two in the left channel and two in the right. The first two (left and right, 0:27) play in harmony, and the next two play the same two notes 1.5 seconds later. It sounds as if the notes bounce from one channel to the other because the guitar in the right channel answers the note from the guitar in the left, and vice versa. Over the course of thirteen seconds, they climb to the apex and it echoes every 1.25 seconds, implying a very slow tempo of 48 bpm.

The main riff enters suddenly at a very fast tempo of 212 bpm, about four and a half times as fast (0:48). It was Sabbath's fastest song to date, aside from middle sections of earlier songs. At 1:06, the riff is extended because the chord is held and Bill plays a long fill as Tony finishes his solo. The verse riffs (1:08–1:12, 1:12–1:15, 1:16–1:21, and 1:21–1:25) are based on the main riff, so each sounds like a logical outgrowth of the former. The riffs in the second verse are like the ones in the first but with slight variation (e.g., 1:42 with added bass fill). There are five versions of the riff in these two brief verses. Other Sabbath songs might simply have the same riff played four times, but their songwriting skills have matured over the first ten years of the band's existence. Moreover, they omit the extension from 1:06 when going from the solo into the second verse, so it seems to propel the energy because it comes sooner than expected. This material was likely written by Craig but reworked by the band through the rehearsal and recording process.

The bridge (1:53) is the song's first climax, as it includes Ronnie's highest note and some very busy bass work. To close the first fast part, Bill, Geezer, and Tony play a quick seven-note line (1:59) and give five big chord hits (2:01), out of which a slower, softer middle part emerges. Tony says that when they were writing it, Ronnie said to him, "You can't do that . . . you can't change that drastic[ally] to something that quiet."[22] Of course, drastic changes in volume are an important element in Sabbath's music, and Ronnie was still getting used to how Sabbath constructed their songs. Without drums, a half-time feel is implied here. It is slightly less than half speed (about 96–97 bpm), giving it an even more relaxed feeling. As the main guitar fades, another guitar plays a moving line with an e-bow (2:04–2:08, fades out by 2:12). Two guitars with a clean tone, one that sounds like a piano, play a fast pattern to provide the harmony. From 2:08 to 2:13, synth strings play an ascending line like the Mellotron string part in "Megalomania."

All this sets up Ronnie's third verse, where he sings with a soft falsetto timbre (2:13). It sounds high, but it's actually slightly lower than the verse. At 2:21, Geezer takes on a melodic role by playing a bass fill and then playing the two-note "die young" motif (2:23 and 2:26). It's also a part of Tony's pattern, so all three doing it makes it cohesive, yet each part remains mostly independent. The music takes an interesting turn at 2:30 when they all drop lower for the second "die young," spicing up the harmony. The chords relate to one another almost like a jazz chord progression. They contain four or five different notes, so they are very harmonically rich, especially when compared to a power chord. A bit of word painting occurs at 2:34 when the band abruptly stops when Ronnie sings "stopped."

Immediately following the break, an elaborate instrumental section makes up the second half of the middle part. There are vocals, but they are treated instrumentally using the vowel sound "ah." It is slightly faster (100 bpm), but even if felt in double time (200), it is still not as fast as the first part (212). It basically splits the difference between them (96 and 106), incorporating the feeling of both. The focus is a single line riff played by Bill, Geezer, and Tony. Bill not only "plays to the riff"; he plays exactly with it in a tightly orchestrated fashion. In other words, he's not improvising around the rhythms as he normally would but instead plays a worked-out drum part precisely with them. It's more than a riff, as it develops instead of repeating. It is based on a three-note motif (2:40) that is repeated higher (2:42) and lower (2:43). Then, two hits (2:44) connect it back to the main motif (2:45) for the second iteration of the "riff." Instead of repeating it verbatim, they change the two hits from 2:44 to a three-note moving line (2:48–2:49). These small variations of minimal material make for an interesting and tightly composed/coherent musical phrase. They repeat all that at 2:50, but there are interjections from the guitar. A closing phrase is introduced at 2:59, and the harmony changes, as does Geoff's keyboards. At 3:01, Tony plays an ascending line doubled and harmonized by Ronnie whilst Geezer plays a descending line. This contrary motion creates dissonant harmonies and a classical-like texture. The climax of that line ends on a very dissonant chord, arguably the most dissonant harmony they have ever used (3:02). Here, Geezer plays two notes at once as Ronnie's background vocal hovers around a third note in a very wide vibrato. Although lower in the mix, Geoff's synth adds to the complexity of the sonority. Notice when the synth arpeggiator returns (2:35–3:05), there are two layers this time, giving it a thicker sound. With the complexity of the guitars and drums, the synths act as a textural pad by keeping it smooth, filling in the spaces, and holding it together. The cleverly worked out unison drums/bass/guitar passages, the synthesizer pads, contrary motion in the bass, and the type of dissonance used take the music into prog territory. Although there are some prog-like moments in "Children of the Sea" and "Heaven and Hell," "Die Young" is the song from *Heaven and Hell* that most closely resembles their seventies-prog leanings, however infrequent these moments are in their catalog. Most of the song is straightforward rock, but it's the intro and this middle part that make the song stand out in that respect.

With a sudden shift to the main tempo, syncopated hits from Bill, Geezer, and Tony take it back to the main riff supporting a guitar solo. There is no extension as at 1:06, so it heads directly into a recall of the first verse. Ronnie alters the melody slightly, for example, the higher note on "help" (3:18) and different melody on the third "you run" (3:31). During this "you run" phrase, the tempo picks up from 208 to 212 bpm, giving it that final push to the bridge. Geezer is especially busy in the bridge, making it more intense (3:33). Skipping the closing riff from 1:59, it goes directly into a chorus-like section (3:40) that repeats the song's title. It repeats the three chords from the verse riff (1:08–1:12), and overdubbed vocals harmonize the word "young" (3:42, 3:47, and 3:52). Geezer remains busy, and Tony plays a guitar solo that is not mixed too loudly in order to leave room for the vocals. After Ronnie sings "die young" five times successively, the guitar solo takes over and the song fades.

"Walk Away" has a hard-rock/pop-rock style and sound to it, a result of the direction that Ozzy did not like the band heading—the one he predicted would "probably sound like Foreigner." It is evident in the guitar tone and the predilection for major sonorities. Only the middle riff (2:42–3:13) has a darker, bluesier sound. The main riff is very similar to Kiss's "Lick It Up" (1983) in regard to chords and rhythm. Even the "oh" background vocals (1:21) match the chorus from "Lick It Up."

The album closes with the slow (about 55–56 bpm) and expansive "Lonely is the Word." Bill's drummer-as-percussionist approach can be heard in the first section as he avoids playing a typical rock beat and focuses on drum hits with very little use of cymbals. When a rock beat comes in, it only lasts five seconds for a truncated chorus (0:51). The chorus has the most blues influence of any section for the chords used and Ronnie's vocal melody. The longer second chorus (1:39) heads to the guitar solo. A background guitar lead plays long tones with bends, but the lead has minimal distortion and is played with fingers instead of pick and in octaves a la Wes Montgomery. The harmonic structure for the solo is simple, for it oscillates between only two chords, each lasting for about four to five seconds, recalling the end of "Gypsy" and antici- pating a similar three-chord progression at the end of "Over and Over" one year later. The solo is interrupted by four loud, descending bluesy hits (2:31) that set up the second part of the solo that features fast licks and has much greater intensity. The four hits return at 3:10 but are played twice. It is the same notes and rhythm as part of the verse riff to Spinal Tap's "Heavy Duty" (1981 and 1984), which also does it once first and then twice later. When Ronnie returns for the chorus, the guitar solo continues behind him. The third part of the guitar solo begins after the chorus at 3:48. As the solo never truly ceases, it is essentially one four-minute-and-twenty-second-long solo. At 4:06, the chords change twice as fast (now every two and a half seconds), and Geoff's four-note synth melody is repeated twenty-three times as the song fades. Near the end of the fade-out, at 5:29, notice Bill's huge, fast fill during Tony's final phrase of the solo.

MOB RULES

Struggling with alcoholism and other personal issues, Bill quit the band in the middle of the 1980 tour and was replaced by Vinny Appice. Although stylistically Vinny is different from Bill, what he did worked well for Sabbath. Vinny said, "Bill didn't play 4/4 [meter] or a beat through a lot of the songs. He did when necessary, and then he played a lot of tom and percussion kind of parts. . . . So when I came in, I was a little bit more straight forward."[23] "I had to follow what Bill Ward was doing and capture that vibe of the old stuff, which is really weird, you know, [it] speeds up/slows down."[24] Also, Bill has more of a swing feel (certainly the jazz influence), and Vinny comes from a rock background. An example of the swing versus straight rhythm feel is in the fast section of "Black Sabbath" on *Live Evil* when Vinny plays "straight eighths" on the hi-hat with his left foot against the swing rhythms in the other parts. Geezer describes Vinny as "more direct," "less complicated," and "less swingy" than Bill.[25] To get a sense of his background, listen to Derringer's studio and live albums (1976/1977) and Axis's *It's a Circus World* (1978); the drum intro to Axis's "Bandits of Rock" is pure Vinny. Neither is as heavy as Sabbath, but both could be classified as hard rock.

During a break in the tour, the band went to Startling Studios to work on music for the animated film *Heavy Metal*. Startling was located just west of London in the former home of John Lennon and Yoko Ono and, at the time, owned by Ringo Starr. Vinny said the writing and recording sessions took place over a few days a couple of weeks after John was murdered, thus dating it just before Christmas 1980. "E5150" and "The Mob Rules" were recorded at Startling for the movie, but the latter was rerecorded for *Mob Rules* at the Record Plant in LA, where the band did *Vol. 4* nearly a decade earlier. Most of "E5150" was kept from the Startling sessions, but some guitar overdubs were likely recorded at the Record Plant, where they recorded the remainder of the album. Tony said they wrote the rest of the album in a rehearsal room northwest of LA in the San Fernando Valley but that he and Geoff would work ideas out in a rented house in nearby Toluca Lake and that he and Ronnie would work on ideas in his hotel room on Sunset Boulevard (a few miles south). They found it to be more productive at times to work in pairs instead of the entire band in the room at once. Ronnie said they wrote "Slipping Away" at a studio in England called Goldrock Road and that they mixed the album there as well, but I have found no information about a studio under this name.

Like *Never Say Die!* and *Heaven and Hell*, *Mob Rules* begins with a fast (181 bpm) song, "Turn Up the Night." One of the interesting things about this song is how the band shortens and extends phrases to fit Ronnie's vocal parts. For instance, notice how the first verse could end at 0:33 with "story told," but an extra chord is added for almost three seconds (or eight beats) to support "so get a good hold." On the second and third verses, the fourth phrase is skipped and it goes directly into the "extra" chord but for twice as long (five seconds, sixteen beats). These extensions support "so let it all go" and "so get a good hold," the former at the top of his vocal range. They also play with the length of the chorus. At first it is seven seconds (an asymmetrical five bars of four beats each), but at 2:44 they add two seconds (eight beats). The chorus is repeated at 2:53, and the extension is doubled to four seconds (sixteen beats). The extensions create seven- and nine-bar choruses, and the repeated choruses that follow are all eight-bar phrases as if to balance the asymmetry. Even the bridge uses an extension: notice how the "climb" at 1:43 lasts six seconds in order to include "spark to burn." The "climb" returns at 2:07 to close the guitar solo, extending Tony's last phrase.

"Voodoo" is a midtempo rock song driven by Vinny's simple rock beat and Geezer's driving bass. Although there are many really cool bass fills (e.g., 0:18, 0:23, etc.), he primarily stays on the same note during the main riff. Listen for Geoff's keyboards in the choruses (1:09 and 2:02), as he is absent or buried for most of the album. Like "Turn Up the Night," "Voodoo" has extended phrases. Notice the brief extensions at the end of the first and fourth verses (0:38 and 3:19). The chorus is an uneven length (six and a half bars), with the word "voodoo" (1:18 and 2:11) lasting only two beats (half a bar) followed by a two-bar break. It seems the riffs were constructed in tandem with the lyrics, as opposed to the Ozzy era where the music was written first.

At nearly eight minutes, "The Sign of the Southern Cross" is the album's most expansive and slowly developing song. Dynamically, it ranges from the soft acoustic introduction to the loud, dramatic chords later in the song. Ronnie says, "That's the one everybody mentions when you talk about the album."[26]

It begins with two acoustic guitars, one in each channel. At 0:09, two additional guitars enter in harmony with each other. The second pair is much drier in sound, for they do not ring as long as the first pair. Geezer enters near the end of the phrase (0:19). The first verse begins at 0:25, and only Geezer and the first two guitars continue to accompany Ronnie. He sings with a clear tone, in much contrast to his growl-laden heavy metal voice. He stays mostly in his lower register, and the line "then how I can know" (0:30) is the lowest he sings on these two studio albums. He shows great vocal facility: listen to the ornamentation on his vocal melody (0:35–0:38 and 0:51–0:55). He goes into falsetto at 0:59 for the two vocal parts; they are very high but not any higher than he normally does. Thus, the use of falsetto is to achieve a different timbre, and not in order to hit notes out of his vocal range, which is why many singers use falsetto. In this passage, Geezer plays quickly and very melodically. Being at the top of the range of his bass, the tone matches well with Ronnie's vocal parts.

A tam-tam sent through a phaser and/or flanger effect (1:12) and Vinny's drum fill (1:15) take it the main body of the song (1:17–end). The guitar and bass play the main riff twice, and Ronnie sings two short vocal phrases. Another layer of sound continues the phase/flange effect from the tam-tam. At 1:34, the energy subsides as Tony's chord is held out, Vinny moves from the ride cymbal to the semi-open hi-hat, and Geezer's effect-laden bass creates an aural soundscape. Vinny makes it more subdued for the start of the verse (1:42) by closing the hi-hat. His drum part is very simple: for the most part, the bass drum and snare drum alternate, one hit each per beat. There are some slight variations for interest, such as the two bass-drum hits that go along with Ronnie's "somewhere" at 1:46. Geezer's part is also simple in the verses, with an occasional four-note figure (1:50, etc.). It is like "Heaven and Hell" in that respect, which in fact, uses the same four-note figure. Ronnie's voice is dramatic, moving between a clean tone and a growl. At 2:05, he puts a growl on "a certain song," and his aggressive vocal sets up three dramatic hits by the band (2:06), bringing Tony back into the texture.

The chorus riff (2:15–2:21) has an interesting asymmetry about it. The first part of it only lasts two beats, just long enough to last through Ronnie's "sign of the southern cross." The second part holds out the chord for four beats. Shortening the first bit gives it a forward momentum. The riff is played twice, and they return to the main riff at 2:27. As before, there are a couple of short vocal phrases, the energy subsides a bit (2:44), and another verse begins.

Instead of waiting for Ronnie's third vocal phrase to do the three dramatic hits, on the second verse, it happens after the first one, set up by his aggressive delivery of "forgotten psalms" (3:00). A new lick is used at the end of the second phrase (3:08), and the three dramatic hits return at 3:16. This increased activity leads into the second chorus (3:25). The heightened energy sets up Geezer and Vinny's fill at 3:29 and for Ronnie to sing even higher at 3:33. Ronnie goes even higher at the bridge (3:37), which is the climax of this forty-five-second gradual crescendo. The bridge riff is played four times, but on the fourth time, Tony plays it higher and Geezer and Vinny stop momentarily.

The listener expects the main riff to return at 3:55, but instead they give only the held-out chord to start the middle instrumental section.

By not playing the main riff here, it is absent for two and a half minutes, making its return at 5:03 all the more effective. At 4:04, a guitar chord fades in followed by two "War Pigs"–like chord hits at 4:08. Those hits echo once every beat, alternating between the left and right channels. At 4:09, another guitar holds out a high note. This eight-second musical gesture is done five times. On the fourth time, Vinny moves from the ride cymbal to the hi-hat, making it sound more subdued. The bridge riff returns at 4:45, but Tony plays a guitar solo in place of Ronnie's vocal parts. To bring it back to the main riff, Vinny plays the snare drum twenty-four times in the span of only two seconds (5:01–5:03). He uses this rhythmic idea on other songs, and I call it "Vinny's fast twenty-four triplet lick." The lick can be heard again at 6:27–6:29 but on toms instead of the snare.

The third verse progresses like the second, with the dramatic and the lick from 3:08. It builds into the final chorus (6:00), which leads back to the main riff (6:12). The main riff is repeated until the end with some vocal phrases, but they are not arranged like verses. Ronnie approaches it like an instrumentalist would, as if improvising ideas without concern for constructing a verse structure. Compare this with the end of "Sweet Leaf" where Ozzy sings vocal phrases that aren't organized in verses. A second guitar solo begins at 6:53, but it is not mixed very loudly, so it doesn't become the main focus of the music here but more a part of the texture. The music begins to fade at 7:24 at which point a high-pitched squeal fades in. The high sustained sound connects to the next track, "E5150."

The title of the fourth track, "E5150," is listed on many websites and books as "E5150," and some people pronounce it as "E fifty-one fifty." But on the album, notice that the *1* is an *I*, printed as a Roman numeral, so if anything "E, five, one, fifty" would be more accurate. I point this out because the *I* shouldn't be overlooked since it is the hint to the meaning of the work's title: using Roman numerals, 5 may be written as V and 50 as *L*. Thus, "E5150" spells out "EVIL." The official title registered with the American Society of Composers, Authors and Publishers (ASCAP) is "E FIVE ONE FIVE NIL," and the use of *nil* for *0* makes it sound quite British, as if it were from the score of a football match. The music appears in the movie *Heavy Metal* uncredited, and it is not included in the soundtrack. The piece starts about nine seconds in at about 57:30 into the movie but with only the high-pitched squeal (the midrange guitar sounds on the album aren't used until about thirteen seconds in). The music is the same for the most part, revealing it was mostly done at Startling and not completely redone at the Record Plant as "The Mob Rules" had been. Notice the "scoops" (e.g., 1:00) and Geezer's oscillation between two notes are the same in both versions. One key difference is the added slowed-down vocal part (0:37–0:44) in the album version. It comes from "Voodoo" (1:43–1:47), although it sounds as if it comes from a different take. It is played at about 75 percent speed, so if you play it at about 135 percent speed (or at 45 RPM instead of 33 1/3 RPM on a turntable), you will hear Ronnie sing, "Fade into shadow, you'll burn. Your fortune," with the last syllable cut off. The other key difference is the added guitar part starting at 2:25. In the original (movie) version, there is no guitar at this point, and instead Geoff's keyboards play for eighteen seconds before "The Mob Rules" begins. On the album, the keyboards don't come in for eighteen more seconds and are only heard for nine (2:43–2:52).

"The Mob Rules" was written and recorded at Startling for the movie soundtrack but was rerecorded for the album. The song structure is the same in both versions, and the two performances are very similar. Some of the drum fills are the same in both versions revealing that Vinny is not improvising but had worked out the fills prior and then reproduced them for the later version. This is another stylistic difference between Bill and Vinny: Bill is more improvisatory and reactionary in approach, and Vinny plays in a more composed-out fashion. Some of the fills are different, however, especially from the third verse on. Ronnie's performance is also similar; one notable difference is after "you're all fools," he adds "the mob rules" for the album version (2:38). Notice the "heavy metal gallop" behind the guitar solo (1:21–1:58), a rhythm associated with NWOBHM, particularly with Iron Maiden (so much that sometimes it's referred to as the "Iron Maiden gallop"). Also notice Tony's use of the "whammy" bar (which he uses very sparingly throughout his career) on the word "fools," diving down at 0:39 and 2:09, scooping down and up at 1:19, and slowly ascending from 2:23 to 2:27 just before the second solo starts. The key change for the guitar solo (1:21) is subtle and smooth, and could easily go unnoticed. The return to the original key coming out of the solo is also subtle: they alter the prechorus slightly (compare 0:29 and 1:58), and Geezer changes his part to suggest staying in the new key. The return to the original key is solidified when verse 3 begins at 2:11. By making the key change slight and subtle, it doesn't disturb the flow of this relatively short song.

It is interesting to listen to "E5150" and "The Mob Rules" in context of *Mob Rules*, but hearing it in their original context (within the movie *Heavy Metal*) provides a different experience. Legendary film composer Elmer Bernstein (who already had thirty years of film credits) did the movie's score, and Sabbath's music is juxtaposed with traditional movie music, providing a strange aural experience. The shift is immediate: Bernstein's music abruptly stops followed by "E5150," and his music returns as a truncated "Mob Rules" finishes. Overall, *Heavy Metal* is a strange musical phenomenon with this style of movie music juxtaposed with rock music—these two styles are never fused. Of any of the bands' contributions to the movie's soundtrack, "E5150" is the closest to Bernstein's but only for its atmospheric nature and lack of a drumbeat. Also, much of the soundtrack would not be classified as heavy metal, reminding the listener that Black Sabbath is truly a heavy band.

"Country Girl" is a good example to compare Ronnie with Geezer and Vinny with Bill. Lyrically, it's a departure from what Geezer had written for Sabbath (e.g., "fell in love with a country girl"). Geezer had approached the love song genre from a variety of perspectives (e.g., "N.I.B.," "Sweet Leaf," and "Planet Caravan"). Vinny is much more of a straightforward rock drummer than Bill, playing fairly simple rock beats that are elaborated upon when the music calls for it. Bill, as discussed in the first four chapters, plays "off the riff," avoiding drumbeats and patterns for the most part. I suspect Bill would have approached playing the main riff (0:06–0:13) much differently. Here, Vinny plays very simply and sparsely, alternating between bass drum and snare drum, one per beat (bass, snare, bass, snare, etc.). Bill would have likely played busier, especially in the second half of the riff where Geezer and Tony play the four held-out notes. There are moments in the song were Vinny plays busier; for example, the closing section of the soft part (2:08–2:22) has some very interesting drum work. Notice the drum fill at 3:19–3:22; it is another variation of the "twenty-four-note fast triplet lick" heard on "The Sign of the Southern Cross" and on later albums such as *Dehumanizer* and *The Devil You Know*.

"Slipping Away" has a simple structure, containing only verse and chorus sections. The intent seems to be less about the songwriting aspect and more about being a vehicle for featuring the band instrumentally. Vinny's approach is quite different here (in fact, similar to Bill's in that he plays to the riff); for instance, notice the delayed snare drum hit in his groove (0:07, 0:10, etc.). Ronnie said that Tony said, "Let's make this a bit funkier,"[27] which may explain the difference in feel. At 1:45, they create a new riff by reordering the three chords from the chorus, but essentially it's the chorus section without vocals. Here, Geezer and Tony stop in the middle of each riff to allow Vinny to play drum fills, like four "mini-solos" (1:47, 1:53, 1:59, and 2:05). Because drum fills are most often played at the end of a phrase or riff, by placing these drum breaks in the middle of the riff the focus is on Vinny. The main riff returns at 2:11, and instead of a guitar solo as what might be expected, Geezer and Tony alternate brief two-bar (six-second) solos. The blues influence on these four six-second solos is evident. To come to the fore, the volume of Geezer's solos is cranked; his tone is distorted and menacing.

"Falling Off the Edge of the World" begins with a slow (about 69 bpm) passage for guitar and what sounds like an uncredited electric violin. The pulse is very elastic here for expressive purposes. If felt in "four," the last beat is stretched out to about twice as long (0:03, 0:07, etc.), so it's almost a slow "five." When Ronnie enters, the last beat is stretched, but not as much, so it's like four and a half beats (0:21, etc.). It's in strict time by 0:51, so it's no longer stretched, but at 1:06 the guitar, bass, and keys pay three extra notes to close this section. At 1:07, it sounds as if the key has changed, but the synth slowly decreases its pitch to the original key from 1:14 to 1:22. This transitional instrumental section (1:07–2:19) is unusual for its placement, as usually Sabbath puts instrumental sections at the beginning, later in the middle, or at the end of a song. Vinny's overdubbed drum starting at 1:30 is very low, and it was likely recorded at a higher speed in order to sound lower and bigger. At first it sounds like a part of his drum set, but there is cymbal and another drum playing along with it. There is also an overdubbed tam-tam hit at 1:46, making this section especially dramatic. From 2:02 to 2:06 there is a crash cymbal and an electric piano playing a chord seven times and played in reverse leading up to the fast section. Here the tempo nearly triples, from about 57 to 150 bpm, and it stays at this faster pace for the remainder of the song. Ronnie uses a gentler timbre in his voice in the first section, but here he adds his rock growl to his tone. He sings in the same register as before, but the change in timbre makes his voice sound much different.

The album ends with the slow and heavy "Over and Over." The feel is like the beginning of "War Pigs," in that it could be felt not only in a moderate "three" (about 90 bpm) but also in a very slow "four" (about 30 bpm) because of Vinny's snare drum backbeat. Throughout the song—even during the guitar solos—the sound is thick because of the sustained rhythm guitars and keyboards. Geezer leads the build from 3:31 to 3:37 for the start of the second guitar solo. The remainder of the song is instrumental, aside from some background vocals on the refrain (4:16 onward). The climax of the instrumental is 4:39 to 4:47 when Geezer, Tony, and Vinny really cut loose.

LIVE EVIL AND OTHER CONCERTS

There are several audio recordings from 1980 to 1982 that are worth checking out to hear this early Ronnie era of Sabbath. There are several recordings with Bill, and the ones from August 31, 1980, and later are with Vinny on drums. The October 17, 1980, performance was filmed, known as *Black and Blue*, which is excellent for seeing what the shows were like. Recordings from three concerts between December 31, 1981, and January 2, 1982, were released on CD as *Live at Hammersmith Odeon* in 2007. There is a bootleg video of the January 2 show.

Their 1982/1983 release *Live Evil* was Sabbath's first band-approved live album, a fine document taken from four spring 1982 performances from the *Mob Rules* tour. There is extant video footage from one of those concerts (Dallas, May 12) and perhaps more somewhere. In 1994, Ronnie called it an "untrue" album, claiming that Geezer and/or Tony replayed their parts in the studio—perhaps a fabrication out of anger toward them.[28] *Live Evil* contains Ozzy-era songs, so one can use it to compare the stylistic differences between Ozzy and Ronnie. Rather than attempting to re-create Ozzy's vocal parts, Ronnie took artistic liberties to make them his own, yet he stayed true to the melodic framework. There is a moment in "Black Sabbath" (2:42) where he sings lower than the original, demonstrating the extent of his vocal range. "Heaven and Hell" was extended to a twenty-three-minute medley that includes additional verses, an extended guitar solo, "The Sign of the

Southern Cross," and "Paranoid," and culminates in a reprise of "Heaven and Hell." An extended "Voodoo" has additional lyrics and bluesy improvised passages. This was nothing new for Sabbath, as they would open up songs when performing live with Ozzy in the seventies. This was not new for Ronnie either; listen to Rainbow's *On Stage* (1977) to hear Ronnie sing in this way.

On live recordings, *Live Evil* and elsewhere, Geoff's keyboards can be heard behind the guitar solos and at other moments in the songs. Like Jezz Woodroffe, he was hidden offstage but could be heard, albeit low in the mix. Geoff's background vocals are audible on some live recordings (e.g., "Neon Knights" on the November 18, 1980, concert in Tokyo) but were likely edited out for *Live Evil*. There were arguments about the mix on *Live Evil* that eventually led to Ronnie and Vinny leaving the band.

6

STONEHENGE AND THE REVOLVING DOOR OF MUSICIANS

With Ronnie James Dio gone, Sabbath auditioned several singers. Their manager, Don Arden, suggested Deep Purple alum Ian Gillan. Don arranged for Geezer Butler and Tony Iommi to meet with Ian at a bar in Woodstock, Oxfordshire. Heavy drinking ensued, and they decided to join forces to record an album. Having never played together and not knowing how they would jell as a band, Tony called it "putting it together on paper."[1] He said that Ian was officially in the band by February 1983. Geezer invited Bill Ward to rejoin the band, but he was in detox and needed to stay in LA until his health improved. Meanwhile, in Light and Sound Design studios in Birmingham, Geoff Nicholls, Geezer, and Tony began writing material for the new album, using Malcolm Cope of Quartz as a temporary drummer. Soon thereafter, Ian came in, but he would not sing because of nodules (nodes) on his vocal cords (essentially calluses on the vocal folds). Thus, they were writing songs without knowing how the vocal parts would go. Malcolm described the writing process as "mostly jamming," with riffs and ideas being brought in and then constructing and "mapping out" the songs. He also said that Geoff would present material to Tony outside of rehearsals and have keyboards set up during the "jamming" rehearsals.[2]

Penned by Ian, the lyrics on this album, *Born Again*, are quite different from Geezer's and Ronnie's. Gone were the political, drug, sci-fi, black magic, and neomedieval themes of the earlier albums. A song titled "Digital Bitch," for instance, would seem out of place for Ozzy

Osbourne or Ronnie. Songs such as "Disturbing the Priest" and "Trashed" are about events that happened during the recording sessions. Ian's usual register is similar to Ronnie's, which is slightly higher than Ozzy's. Notice that in every song except "Keep It Warm," Ian starts the verse in the same register, comparable in register to the "oh no" that opens "Neon Knights." The biggest difference is that Ian's melodies will leap around and change registers often. Whereas Ronnie might stay within a certain range for a song, Ian would extend it twice as wide. Ian has a rich low register, but the most defining feature is his high, head voice screaming. His upper register stretches from Ozzy's and Ronnie's highest notes to well above (e.g., "Born Again," "Digital Bitch," "Disturbing the Priest," "Hot Line," and "Trashed"). To better understand Ian's vocal style, check out his work from 1969 to 1982: this includes albums with Deep Purple, his solo project Gillan, and his solo jazz/rock fusion group, the Ian Gillan Band.

Malcolm said he played the drum parts "straight" in order to leave room for Bill to interpret the music in his own style. In other words, he avoided playing anything "too specific" that might influence Bill's musical choices or the songs themselves. Although he said Bill came in and changed the parts to "suit his own style," we agreed that Bill didn't play in his usual improvisatory, reactionary style on many parts of *Born Again* but instead played more straightforward in approach.[3] For that, the drumming here is closer in style to his work on *Heaven and Hell* than on the seventies albums. Perhaps it was a result of entering late into the process in the same way it affected Geezer's work on *Heaven and Hell*. Maybe he was influenced by what Malcolm had played. It could have been a conscious choice, the producer's preference, or other factors such as the fact that he was battling to remain sober. Bill said he was "pretty shaky, learning how to be in the world without a drink" and that "living in the new world was difficult." He said he "felt pretty good" about his drum work, but because of how it was produced, there was "a lot of hidden work" that didn't "necessarily come through" because it "turned out to be a bit washy." He says, "The drums need to be far, far drier than what they are. They're way too wet," calling it "an '80s sound."[4]

The "wetness" to which Bill referred is the reverb heard on the album, which is most prevalent on the snare drum. The band and fans have complained about the sonic quality of the album, particularly the mix. Tony called the sound "dreadful." Ian described it as muffled and demonstrated the overall sound by placing his hand over his mouth. A newer release has the equalizer bringing out higher frequencies in order to make it sound less muddy, but it is still not entirely clear. A mixdown of how the album stood on June 26, 1983, was released as a bootleg called *The Manor Tapes*. Although there are moments on the bootleg that are clearer than the official release, the album was incomplete at that point, missing some vocals, keyboards, and flute, and the track "The Dark."

BORN AGAIN

The opening track "Trashed" is about an experience Ian had when they were working on the album. After the initial writing sessions, the band went to live and work at the Manor Studios in Shipton-on-Cherwell, not too far from Woodstock, where they had met up earlier. Ian took Bill's car and raced it around the narrow go-kart track next to the house/studio. The canal of the "canal turn" referenced in the lyrics is the River Cherwell (part of the Oxford Canal at this point), which is only about forty or so feet from the track. Ian, drunk, rolled and crashed the car, coming to a stop "precariously close" to the canal, as Geoff described it.[5] Malcolm, who was still present at the time assisting Bill, helped Ian get out of the car.

Giving the feeling of a racing car, the song is fast (about 176 bpm) but not as fast as "Die Young" or "Neon Knights." The music was written before the crash had happened, so the use of a fast tempo was not a reaction to the incident. Moreover, Ian said he did not hear the music to "Trashed" until the day after the crash, thus he wrote the lyrics to go with the music. Ian is first heard on *Born Again* with his distinctive scream at the very top of his range (0:15). He leaps down to start the intro verse (0:20), but because the first note was so high, he is still in a high register. He goes into his medium-low register for the bridge sections (1:42–2:05 and 2:53–3:15), showing his versatility. Bill plays some nice tom work in these sections (1:54–2:04 and 3:04–3:14) that may remind the listener of his fills in "Symptom of the Universe," but for the most part he plays in a fairly straightforward way on this song.

"Stonehenge" is presented on the album like an introduction to "Disturbing the Priest," so they are paired together in this book. Extant recordings from the tour show that it was not presented as such, and "Disturbing the Priest" began with the four descending chords (0:00). "Stonehenge" was used at least once on that tour (on the Worcester, Massachusetts, concert) but as part of the intro to "Iron Man." Geoff said the piece was his concept, having recently visited Stonehenge. He described it as an "ethereal idea" intended for Tony to play over.[6] However, Bill and Geezer contributed enough to the musical fabric that the band decided not to add guitar.

As heard on the *Manor Tapes*, "Stonehenge" was originally much longer. After the intro section, there were two alternating sections. With its intro-A-B-A-B-A-outro structure, it felt like a complete piece. In the album version, it goes directly to the outro after the first A section (1:34). Because of its brevity and lack of a contrasting section, it feels like a miniature or a character piece, or perhaps it doesn't feel like an independent piece at all. "Stonehenge" is placed immediately before "Disturbing the Priest" without any silence separating the tracks, so it feels like an extended introduction.

The primary part of the texture is Geoff's keyboards, but Geezer's bass through his pedals creates the greatest variety of sounds. The delay and other effects on Geezer's bass should remind the listener of "E5150." For instance, the scoop-like sounds in the outro in "Stonehenge" (1:37, 1:43, etc.) are the same effect as on "E5150" (e.g., 1:00). Bill plays a metal plate or anvil dipped in water to alter its pitch. It is difficult to hear it clearly on the recording, but Geoff's custom Mellotron tapes include isolated samples of it (and many other sounds from *Born Again*). For the album track, it sounds as if the anvil hits were played at various tape speeds, sometimes with delay added (e.g., 0:09, 0:23, 1:46, etc.). Bill also plays timpani and suspended cymbal, the same two percussion instruments used on "Who Are You?" again giving it an orchestral sound.

Geoff starts the piece, his two pairs of tritones (0:00–0:10 and 0:10–0:21) giving it an evil sound. Geezer enters at 0:08, his bass so laden with effects it is almost unrecognizable as a bass (unless the listener is familiar with "E5150"). Geoff's four-note pattern is repeated at 0:21, and Bill and Geezer continue with anvil and bass.

The next section begins at 0:44 with a new chord progression and fuller keyboards, adding the Mellotron choir to the layers of synth. Geezer plays a bittersweet note, both beautiful and sad, over Geoff's new chord at 0:52. Bill's timpani enters at 0:54, his two oscillating notes anticipating the chord at 0:58. Bill's suspended cymbal roll and Geoff's majestic major harmony make this point feel like an arrival, and Geoff's description of "ethereal" seems apt. Another major chord follows, Geezer plays another crying note (1:04), and Bill's timpani and cymbal return to take it back through the progression once more. A high-pitched wind-like sound and a heartbeat are added to this repeated section (1:11–1:33). Comparing to the heartbeat sound on Geoff's custom Mellotron tapes (which sounds as if they used a bass drum), the heartbeat sound on the album is faster and from a different sound source and was likely added later. The whistling wind-like noise was sampled on Geoff's custom Mellotron sound-effects tapes, so it seems they had plans to include "Stonehenge" in live performance.

Instead of going to a contrasting section as heard on the *Manor Tapes*, they skip ahead to the outro section (1:33–end). The track fades with sounds of keyboards, bass with effects, anvil hits, and heartbeat with a reversed cymbal roll at 1:55. Before fading out completely, "Disturbing the Priest" begins abruptly with four descending chords. Ian screams in his high register, scooping up to the top of his range (0:01).

For the intro/outro verse of "Disturbing the Priest" (0:13 and 4:34), Ian borrowed the vocal melody from the title track of his 1977 solo album *Scarabus*. Comparing the opening verses of the two songs, the notes, rhythm, delivery, and phrasing are nearly identical. The songs start in the same key, making the similarities stand out even more. Although the Ian Gillan Band was a jazz-rock fusion project, the beginning of "Scarabus" sounds like early Rush. Although *Born Again* is a metal album, the vocal parts in the first verse of "Scarabus" have a clear connection to "Disturbing the Priest."

The lyrics were inspired by an experience the band had with the vicar from the Church of Holy Cross, which is located adjacent to the manor house/studio. Tony said he set up in a building in the back of the house, trying for a different guitar sound, and the local residents complained. The church is situated only about a hundred feet from where he would have been playing. On a separate occasion, Ian said they were in the studio in "loud playback mode with the door open."[7] The studio was a bit further from the church but still only about two hundred feet away. The vicar came over to the studio and politely informed them that the sound was disturbing the choir rehearsals. Ian apologized and agreed not to disturb any future choir rehearsals. Laughing about the situation inspired the song's title, "Disturbing the Priest," as a play on words of the term "disturbing the peace." Although the evil-sounding laughs and lyrics such as "Do we mind disturbing the priest? Not at all, not at all, not in the least" have a sinister implication, Ian said that "it was out of nothing but respect for the fact that they were having choir practice."[8]

The intro/outro riff (0:03 and 4:24) is nearly atonal due to the relationship between Geoff's two Mellotron choir chords (0:04 and 0:06) and Tony's high notes (0:03 and 0:05). The disagreement in key gives it an evil sound. However, Ian's vocal melody confirms the key—thus stabilizing the music—when he enters (0:13). The first note of his vocal melody is the same as the first note of the opening verses of "Trashed" and "Zero the Hero." He also begins the songs "Born Again," "Digital Bitch," and "Hot Line" in the same register, so it seems Ian has a preference for singing in this register. Notice how Bill doesn't play a rock beat in this section; instead, his snare drum and bass drum fill in the spaces between the hits with Geezer, Geoff, and Tony. This is some of Bill's most interesting and creative drumming.

The next section begins (0:35) with characteristics of a prechorus, but instead of leading into a chorus, this transitional section links the unsettled intro into a softer, mellower verse section (0:56). Bill's approach is much more straightforward here, yet he still "plays to the riff" in the first half of each iteration of the riff. Geezer plays some impressive lines, and his tone is distorted and penetrating. Ian sings in his medium register for most of this transitional verse, but he leaps up to his high, screaming register for the third line (0:47). Showing his technical prowess, he effortlessly returns to his medium register in the middle of the vocal line (0:49).

The energy begins to dissipate at 0:56 as the music becomes softer and simpler. The bass and drums are simple, as in the "Heaven and Hell" verses. Two guitars are split in the left and right channels, providing creepy textural sounds. Entering at 1:06, Tony on a third guitar plays higher textural sounds using a slide for smooth, connected lines. Bill's metal plate/anvil sounds at 1:01, and you can hear its high pitches bent from being dipped in water at 1:03. Ian sings in his medium-low register with a second vocal track from Ian in his low register, the combination of the two giving it a darker, creepier character. He sings the second half of the verse (1:28) in his medium-high register, giving it a more aggressive quality.

Tony's two chords at 1:49 interrupt the verse and anticipate the chorus (1:51). By having the riff start at the end of the verse, it provides a clever setup, or "pickup," to the chorus. It also sets up a slightly faster tempo for the chorus (96 bpm, instead of 90 as before). At 2:10 and 2:20, Ian screams in the high register for which he is probably most famous (cf. "Child in Time" from Deep Purple's *In Rock* [1970]). It is harmonized by a second, even higher, vocal part, but it is not very present in the mix; the higher background vocal is easier to hear on the *Manor Tapes*.

After another verse and chorus, it returns to the transitional section from 0:35. Here (3:42), it functions as a postchorus. The vocal and instrumental parts are the same as before, but at 4:02 they repeat the riff four more times, effectively doubling the length of this section. This extension allows Ian to showcase his high, screaming register (4:08–4:24). At 4:19, Geezer and Tony play a new chord that acts like a retransition, taking it back to the four chords of the very beginning (0:00) at 4:21.

The intro riff returns at 4:24 as the outro riff, and the intro verse (0:13) returns as the outro verse (4:34). The vocal parts are mostly the same except for a few small details: Ian descends for "all the while," he rests to skip "don't be fooled," and he stretches out "eyes" as the riff repeats. During the rest (4:50), it sounds as if a faint scratch/guide vocal track bleeds in the words "don't be." At 4:58, on "eyes," Ian scoops up into his high, screaming register. In an improvisatory manner, he works his way up to the top of his range (e.g., 5:10), the same high note at the beginning of the song and in "Trashed." The riff repeats, Ian sings and laughs, and the song fades. For a Sabbath song nearly six minutes long, it is notable that there is no guitar solo.

"The Dark" is essentially the introduction to "Zero the Hero," rather than a stand-alone piece. Geoff called it "Geezer's thing,"[9] as it consists of bass and sound effects, likely produced by the pedals Geezer used on "Stonehenge" and "E5I50." The sound effects were sampled onto Geoff's custom Mellotron tapes and used in concert (see Chicago performance). After several seconds of sound effects, Geezer's four-note pattern begins at 0:09 and is repeated at 0:20. The last note of his pattern is changed (0:28), he hits a final note at 0:31, and the main to "Zero the Hero" starts to fade in at 0:32. Although the duration of "The Dark" is listed as 0:48 on the LP and the timing on most CDs listed it as 0:45, the song starts at the end of "The Dark" track. The riff changes after about fourteen seconds, the point at which the CD release begins the next track.

"Zero the Hero" is a moderately slow, heavy rock song (about 81 bpm). Bill says about the tempo, "I love that pace, a 'Heaven and Hell' feel, a really solid pace, doomy, laid-back. It's just enough where it can sound really heavy, like 'Into the Void' or 'The Writ.'"[10] For comparison, "Heaven and Hell" is about 88 bpm, "Into the Void" is about 75, and "The Writ" is about 73. The drums are fairly low in the mix, but if you listen carefully, you can hear some of Bill's intricate playing, such as the nice triplet ghost-note work on the snare drum at 0:00–0:24 and 4:22–4:48 (it is far more audible on the *Manor Tapes*). Tony picks up on Bill's triplet rhythm and incorporates it into his solo at 4:26.

Over the riff just before verses 1 and 2, there is a flanger effect just before the snare drum hits (0:32, 0:35, etc.). Geoff was once quoted as saying he did the "powerful choirs" in "Zero the Hero" and the "swirling drum fills" in "Disturbing the Priest."[11] It seems he confused the two songs, as there are Mellotron choirs in "Disturbing the Priest," and what I suspect he called the "swirling drum fills" are those flanged sounds just before Bill's snare drum hits in "Zero the Hero." The effect can be heard on Geoff's custom Mellotron tapes.

Ian's vocal melody in the verses stays on the same note throughout. Thus, the focus is on the rhythm and the lyrics instead of the melody; in that sense—and only in that sense—it is stylistically similar to rap music. The death metal band Cannibal Corpse, whose vocal style favors rhythm and lyrics over melody, picked up on this stylistic trait and recorded a cover of "Zero the Hero" in 1993. There are some harmonized vocal parts to offer some variety to the monotone melody (e.g., 1:12, 2:21, etc.). Ian's melody in the chorus has more motion, but overall, he stays in a very limited range—which is very unlike the other songs on *Born Again*.

To add interest as the song comes to a close, there is an overdubbed snare drum part that repeats the five-note rhythm of the song title starting at 6:14 and a backward piano from 6:30 to 6:32. These are included on Geoff's custom tapes, so they were likely used in live concert. Also, there are some bongos or high-pitched congas in the left channel (6:20), right channel (6:24), and elsewhere. There are two guitar solos in the fade-out (one in each channel), and a third solo begins in the center at 7:21.

Ian has not publically identified the muse for "Digital Bitch," but he says, "Neither she, nor her father, had anything to do with computers."[12] The "computer"/"looter" was simply a convenient rhyme. Many people have assumed it was Sharon Arden (later Osbourne) and her father Don Arden, Sabbath's manager at the time, but that is an unsubstantiated theory. The verse vocals are in Ian's medium-high register, but he drops much lower for the chorus. In fact, the lowest note of the verses is higher than the highest note of the chorus. To complement the lower-register singing, the bass guitar and bass drum is heavier. Tony plays some nice solos in the song: with the use of the whammy bar, the opening solo (0:11) has an Eddie Van Halen quality about it, a style that Tony would return to occasionally. Geezer plays quite busily in the second verse, but it is muddy and hard to hear. Bill plays in a very straightforward way for most of this up-tempo song, like Vinny Appice for that matter. The one exception is the bridge (1:56–2:06), where he avoids playing a rock beat yet still keeps it very simple. This section recalls the chord progression from the chorus from "Spiral Architect" (1:50, 2:51, and 4:27).

The song "Born Again" demonstrates Ian's wide vocal range. He begins the verse (0:53) in his medium-high register and gradually descends to his low register (1:19), and he effortlessly leaps back up again (1:26–1:28). He saves his high screaming register for the end of the chorus (2:11), with the background vocal on the higher notes reaching as high as "Trashed" and "Disturbing the Priest." His agile vocal facility is probably best demonstrated in the bridge (3:50–4:44): notice how he goes in and out of his high screaming register with ease (e.g., 3:53–3:59) and how he uses three distinct registers of his voice. Also, the soul-like inflections give the vocal line an interesting character. For instance, the first two chords of the bridge (3:50–3:59, 4:08–4:17, and 4:26–4:35) are like the first two in Ray Charles's "Georgia," affecting the notes Ian sings. Geezer plays rather simply, always tasty, and with a bright tone. He said he used an eight-string bass on "Born Again," but he did not specify if it was the song or the album. The type of eight-string he had pairs each of the four strings with a string an octave higher (like how a twelve-string guitar is strung), giving it a bright tone. This bass is visible on the 1975 Don Kirshner's Rock Concert. Bill plays in his characteristic style, in particular by placing the snare drum in unexpected places. There is some nice percussion work later in the song (4:47), including a gentle use of the wind chimes for additional color (4:45, 4:53, and 5:02—although only the second one is easy to hear).

The Mystery of Tony's Flute

Tony is credited with playing flute on the album, yet its appearance on the album has never been made clear. Even when asked, he could not remember. Geoff's custom Mellotron tapes reveal one place where the flute was played: at the start of the first verse of "Born Again" (0:52). The vocal track can be heard in the background of the flute sample (likely Tony recording with studio monitors playing instead of using headphones). The lyrics are clearly "through my window." In the sample, Tony plays a quick five-note flurry twice as "pickups" into the first and second beats of the verse (0:52 and 0:53). The first flurry is barely audible in the final mix, and the second one is buried by the vocal. The same pair of brief flurries were probably played every eight seconds each time the two-chord progression repeats. They can be heard on the album at 1:01, 1:10, 1:18, 1:19, 1:27, 1:28, 1:45, and 1:46, and also in the second verse. A synthesizer may have doubled this flute part, as the timbre sounds warmer than Tony's flute tone. At 5:01, just before the start of the guitar solo, there is a melodic part in the right channel that might be a flute, but it sounds more like a synthesizer. It lasts through the end of the song.

"Hot Line" is a straightforward rock number along the lines of "Lady Evil," with similarities in feel, blues-based riffs, bass line, and tempo ("Hot Line" is only slightly faster). The drumming is much more straightforward here than on "Lady Evil" and many other songs, so I would have guessed it was Vinny or Malcolm if Bill wasn't credited. Ian shows off his vocal range by starting in his medium-high register and descending into his low register but also utilizing his high, screaming technique. In 0:38–0:44, for instance, he uses all three registers. Ian also effortlessly navigates into high screaming, even midword (e.g.,

STONEHENGE AND THE REVOLVING DOOR OF MUSICIANS 123

"line" at 0:55–0:59). After "take me to the river," Ian sings, "Lead me to religion, take me up them stairs." The church next to the manor house is on higher ground above the river/canal, so it's as if this location inspired the metaphor and the imagery. Ian spent some time on the river and for a while had a boat moored there (until Bill sunk it in retaliation for crashing his car!).

Setting up a much different character, "Keep It Warm" is the only song on the album in which Ian does not start the verse in his medium-high register. Instead, he begins in his medium-low register, but he ascends to his usual medium-high register for the second half of the verse (0:29). The song has a blues-like character, especially in the vocal melody and guitar riffs. Tony said the riff dates back to the days of *Mob Rules*. Bill said the song "reminds [him] of a blues standard," comparing it to "Lonely is the Word," which he said "also [has] a blues feel."[13] The chorus uses more pop-like chords and melodies, contrasting the blues-influenced verse sections. The openness of the chorus allows Geezer the room to play busier (e.g., the triplet figures, especially at 4:05, 4:31, and 4:47). The bass and drums open up with increased activity in the repeated choruses at the end (e.g., the double bass drum work at 4:54 and 5:08). The solo section recalls the solo section from "Dirty Women" in that both go into a double-time feel in the middle of it (2:44).

Some releases say "Hot Line" and "Keep It Warm" were written by Geezer, Ian, and Tony, and the other songs by Bill, Geezer, Ian, and Tony (Geoff was not given songwriting credit). Other releases list all songs written by Black Sabbath. Curiously, Bill was omitted from credits from those songs, but he is listed with the American Society of Composers, Authors and Publishers (ASCAP) as a coauthor. Perhaps the band felt the songs were fully formed with Malcolm's temporary drum parts, thus he didn't change them enough to warrant songwriting credit. Or perhaps it was contractual and Bill was to receive less than 25 percent writing credit, so someone arbitrarily chose those two.

BORN AGAIN TOUR AND THE REVOLVING DOOR OF MUSICIANS

Bill fell back into alcoholism while still at the manor, so Electric Light Orchestra drummer Bev Bevan, also a Birmingham native, was hired for the tour. This tour is infamous for having too-large replications of Stonehenge as part of the stage set. Ian said Geezer came up with the idea when they returned to Light and Sound Design studios for tour rehearsals—this would have been the second week of August 1983. Geezer said it was Don Arden's idea. It has been commonly reported that the "Stonehenge" idea for the movie *This Is Spinal Tap* (1984) came from Sabbath's 1983–1984 tour. It should be clarified that the "Stonehenge" scene appears in the twenty-minute short *Spinal Tap: The Final Tour*, which went into production in 1981/1982, thus predating Sabbath's "Stonehenge" by two or three years. Unless the band—or someone close to the band—had known about this short, this was one of rock's great coincidences.

Ian left the band after the tour, Bill came back briefly, and they worked with another singer, David Donato, for a while. They recorded a demo for a song called "No Way Out," which became "The Shining" on Sabbath's 1987 album *The Eternal Idol*. Bill and Geezer left the band, and Tony started to work on new material without David. Tony hired Gordon Copley (bass) and Eric Singer (drums) of Lita Ford's band. With Geoff, the four worked on new material with singer Jeff Fenholt, songs that would later be recorded for the album *Seventh Star* (1986). Listen to the recordings of the sessions with Jeff to hear earlier versions of the songs, such as "Star of India," which became "Seventh Star." These demos can offer much insight into the development of the songs. For instance, an early version of "Danger Zone" has a chorus section with an interesting chord progression that never made its way to the album version.

In June 1985, Tony asked singer Glenn Hughes of Deep Purple fame to record a solo album using much of the existing material. Geoff claims to have written 75 percent of the lyrics and melodies on *Seventh Star* because they couldn't legally use Jeff's contributions. Glenn claims to have written 90 percent of the lyrics. The album's liner notes state that music and lyrics were written by Tony and that "additional" lyrics were written by Geoff, Glenn, and the producer, Jeff Glixman. However, legally with ASCAP, writing credit was only given to Tony. Gordon went to Hawaii to work with Lita Ford, so bassist Dave Spitz was brought in to replace his recorded bass tracks. Because of difficulty matching the pitch of Dave's bass to the other parts on "No Stranger to Love," they decided to keep Gordon's parts for the one track. The entire album is slightly below standard pitch (i.e., not just guitars tuned down but keyboards pitched low too), so the pitch issues on the album may have to do with tape speed. The tempos of the songs are about 96 percent of what they are on the demos and isolated rhythm tracks, so perhaps it was recorded or mastered at the wrong tape speed, thus affecting the pitch and tempo.

After completing most of the tracks at Cherokee Studios in LA in July, they went to Cheshire Sound Studios in Atlanta in late August to record "Angry Heart" and "In Memory. . ." Glenn played bass on those two tracks. When it came time to release *Seventh Star*, Don Arden and Warner Bros. decided against releasing it as a Tony Iommi album but billed it instead as "Black Sabbath featuring Tony Iommi." Note that this was the first Black Sabbath release with only one original member. Because it was released as a Black Sabbath album, *Seventh Star* is included in this book. Moreover, it plays an important role in Sabbath's history and development as a band and deserves a closer listen.

SEVENTH STAR

"In for the Kill" starts with Eric's twenty-four fast snare drum hits and proceeds to the main riff in an unusual meter: fifteen beats long at 160 bpm (0:03–0:09). Eric plays a standard rock feel in four, and because of the odd-number of beats in the riff, the beat gets turned around each time it's played (0:03, 0:09, 0:15, etc.). The unusual meter makes for some interesting vocal phrasing. The riff evens out at 0:26 for a pre-chorus phrase that sets up a more stable chorus (0:29). To contrast the darker sound of the verse, the chorus uses major chord harmony and includes harmonized vocals. Here, Dave plays some nice bass fills (0:40 and 0:46) and is even busier on the second chorus (e.g., 1:22–1:25). The harmony takes a darker turn at 1:55 for the guitar solo, which is like a duet because there are two guitars playing almost the same thing. Eric's drumming on this track is very solid; his double bass drums really come through, afforded by the space between the chord hits in the transitional riff (1:49). His style is far closer to Vinny's than to Bill's, as he favors straight-ahead drumbeats over an improvisatory/reactionary style. As on most of Sabbath's songs, Geoff's performances are minimal but tasteful and effective; listen for him on the choruses.

"No Stranger to Love" could be described as a "power ballad" for its vocal style, keyboards, slow tempo, and hard-hitting drums but without having a doomy, heavy guitar riff. Unlike earlier ballads such as "Changes," this has a hard-hitting eighties pop/hard-rock style about it. Geoff lays claim to writing the song and said the earliest version of it was modeled after Foreigner's "I Want to Know What Love Is" (1984), a very keyboard-driven song. Glenn said that most of the album was written by Geoff and Tony before he entered the project, but this song was one of three to which he contributed writing. The song structure is very simple, consisting of only verse and chorus sections. As heard on a demo recording with Jeff Fenholt, a bridge with a clever chord progression that changes key was omitted for the album version. Perhaps they opted to simplify the song to be more radio friendly. There is some nice interaction between Tony and Eric during the guitar solo (3:14–3:20), especially when Eric picks up on Tony's triplet rhythmic idea (3:17).

Starting at 242 bpm and reaching 248 by the solo, "Turn to Stone" was Sabbath's fastest song to date. If the tape speed was indeed too slow, then it was actually recorded at 252–258 bpm and thus even faster than the middle section of "Into the Void." The demos and isolated rhythm tracks for this song are also in the 250s range, so it is quite plausible. Tony's guitar solo is much different than his usual style. Listen for the Nashville-style picking and contour, far different from the bends, slides, and hammer-ons/pull-offs he often uses for solos. Eric's double bass drum work is punchy and solid; in addition to the beginning, there are moments where he brings it to the fore (e.g., at the end of each verse riff: 0:14, 0:22, etc.). He and Dave cleverly delay the hits after the guitar solo (2:20 and 2:22) rather than playing a predictable downbeat; if not paying attention, they make it sound as if the hit at 2:23 comes in early. It is a short song due to the fast tempo and because the bridge, as can be found in an earlier version of the song, was removed.

"Sphinx (The Guardian)" is essentially an introduction to "Seventh Star," scored for synthesizers alone. The timbre of Geoff's keyboards is smooth and unassuming, creating an ominous mood. The notes navigate gently, and at 0:27 the harmony changes, hinting at something new, but it returns to its static state at 0:31. A higher synth begins to fade in at 0:39, and it remains on the same pitch for a while, creating suspense. The chord changes at 0:50 as it did at 0:27, but this time the activity continues as the high synth remains motionless. The chords cease activity, so 1:04 sounds like a point of arrival. However, at 1:07, the high synth ascends in an almost Pink Floydian way (e.g., "Shine on You Crazy Diamond Part One"), jumpstarting the energy to set up "Seventh Star."

Eric's drumbeat and the three-against-four rhythm in Tony's guitar riff at the start of "Seventh Star" recall Led Zeppelin's "Kashmir" (1975). Another connection to "Kashmir" is the change in harmony at 2:54, which has the same relationship found in the middle sections of "Kashmir" (e.g., the "ooohh yeah" part at 7:35). Both songs use similar exotic-sounding scales, an element that likely had to do with Jeff Fenholt's "Star of India" title for the earlier version, as Geoff said they thought it had an "Indian feel."[14] Ironically, the lyrics for "Kashmir" were not inspired by Kashmir, India, but by the Sahara Desert in Morocco. The first line of "Seventh Star," "there's a vision in the sands," conjures similar imagery. Geoff's lyrics were inspired by his interest in ancient mythology, theology, biblical prophecies, and Egyptology. This song, he explains, came from "an idea from ancient times about the coming of Armageddon when seven stars lined up."[15]

Tony's riff continues for the verse, over which Glenn sings in a blues-inflected rock style. The harmony changes at 0:36 for the chorus, but the main riff returns for the latter two-thirds of the chorus (0:42–0:54). Here, the harmonized vocals interrupt Glenn's "ages" with "the call." Without an interlude, the chorus moves directly into the second verse (0:54). The second chorus is performed twice (1:18 and 1:36). Notice on the second time that Dave and Tony don't return to the main riff but instead play a new riff (1:43). Here, Geoff's Mellotron choirs create a dramatic background, perhaps in response to the "hear a thousand chanting souls" and "hear the sound of fallen angels" lyrics.

Set over a chord progression recalling "Dirty Women," Tony solos in his classic, melodic style. The solo is succinct and effective, as in "Snowblind." The music takes a significant turn at 2:18 when Geoff's synthesized strings introduce a new scale, one that was certainly used to sound "exotic." The use of strings is another connection to "Kashmir." Tony picks up on Geoff's exoticism at 2:42 by using the same type of scale for his melodic line. At 2:54, the harmony changes again, the aforementioned "Kashmir" part (sing Plant's "oooh yeah" melody, and you'll see what I mean). That leads the music back into the main riff at 3:00 to close this prog-like middle section. Perhaps the producer Jeff Glixman, who produced four albums by the prog-rock band Kansas in the mid-seventies, had some influence here. Geoff said that for the next album, *The Eternal Idol*, Jeff "kept trying to push me to put in all these Kansas-type keyboard flurries,"[16] so it wouldn't be surprising if that were the case for moments on *Seventh Star* as well. "Kashmir" and the rest of *Physical Graffiti* isn't full-on prog, but the elements are present, as is the case here. The simplicity of the bass and drums in "Seventh Star" is certainly not prog, but their performance at times channels John Paul Jones and John Bonham. That aside, notice Eric's offbeat cymbal hits, first on the bell of the ride cymbal (2:19–2:40) and then alternating between the bell and a crash cymbal (2:42–2:52)—a detail in his drum part that is small but largely effective.

After a third verse, they do another extended chorus, this one even longer than the second one. At 3:57, Glenn goes into his higher register, emphasizing "fallen angels" unlike before. At 3:59, the new riff from the second verse and Geoff's Mellotron choir return. Instead of going into another solo at 4:11, the refrain from the chorus is repeated twice more. The riff here is especially heavy, thanks to Dave playing power chords on the bass (4:11–4:16). The riff repeats until the end without vocals, but an uncredited flute solo (likely Tony) is only somewhat audible in the thick texture. It is easier to hear when he goes higher (4:47–4:50 and 5:05–5:06). He plays some nice blues licks and utilizes the same Dorian scale that he uses on the guitar when evoking a jazz style. It is possible that it is a keyboard, but the timbre sounds closer to an acoustic flute than an electronic keyboard, especially 5:05–5:11.

"Danger Zone," like the intro to "Air Dance," begins with a harmonized riff played by two guitars. The riff continues for the verse, and then a postverse (0:55) ends with the "Danger Zone" refrain. Instead of going into a chorus after the second verse as it does in the demo, the postverse returns at 1:43. The third verse is half the length of the first two, letting the song's inertia lead us into a guitar solo over the postverse and a new progression (the demo had a return of the chorus section here). Listen for the tightness in the bass, drums, and palm-muted guitar in the breakdown section after the solo (2:42–2:55). Glenn returns for the bridge section (where the guitar solo used to be). The main riff returns at 3:19 for the remainder of the song. Instead of giving us a fourth verse, Glenn recalls earlier material, including the refrain.

STONEHENGE AND THE REVOLVING DOOR OF MUSICIANS

Note that the song lacks a true chorus, but a simple refrain acts as a recurring hook instead. To avoid confusion by those unfamiliar with the song, it should be noted that it slightly predates the popular "Danger Zone" song from the movie *Top Gun*, also released in 1986.

"Heart Like a Wheel" has the most direct connection to the blues on the album. Dave and Eric lay down a slow blues shuffle, Tony provides some blues chords (e.g., 0:45), and Glenn's melodies are blues in-flected. Remember that the band was approaching the album as a Tony Iommi solo project, not a Black Sabbath album, as stated by Eric, Geoff, Glenn, and Tony. It's still a rock blues: Glenn's voice at times, 2:07–2:10, for instance, has a Steve Perry–like timbre and style about it. Compare those few seconds with Journey's "Lovin', Touchin', Squee-zin'," which has the same slow blues shuffle feel, or with "Lights," which has the same meter and similar groove. Dave and Eric begin to stray from simply laying down the groove late in the song. For instance, notice Eric's syncopated bass drum hits at 5:55, and Dave abandons the heartbeat-like rhythm in favor of a smooth, descending bass line at 6:00. Regarding Geoff's lyrics, the wheel imagery was inspired by a movie about a female racecar driver's struggle for equality in her sport.

Notice the similarity in pulse between "Heart Like a Wheel" and "Angry Heart" that momentarily tricks the ear. Within the slow 64 bpm blues at the end of the previous track is an underlying pulse of 192 bpm. Eric's opening drum fill (snare–bass–bass–snare–bass–bass–snare) makes it sound as if he's continuing the same feel/groove. However, the band enters at 0:02 with a medium rock groove (102 bpm), the underly-ing pulse only slightly faster (204 over 192). It may seem like a coinci-dence, but the tempo relationship and Eric's fill seem quite intentional. The 1986 Cleveland performance places "Angry Heart" *before* "Heart Like a Wheel" without a break, cleverly exploiting this relationship, so certainly the band was aware of the similarity. "Angry Heart" is a straightforward rock song with some rock organ from Geoff, as if nod-ding to Glenn's background with Deep Purple. The backward piano throughout the song is a nice effect (0:08–0:11, 0:22–0:25, etc.).

The last chord of "Angry Heart" sustains, and "In Memory. . ." be-gins without a break, marked by a hit by Glenn and Eric. Tony's acous-tic guitar retains the same pulse as before (202 bpm), but Eric's drums set up a slow rock groove (50.5 bpm). Tony starts his pattern with only three notes instead of four, so it tricks the listener by making the high notes of his guitar part sound like "upbeats" instead of being on the beat. As a result, he only plays fifteen of the sixteen notes of his pattern before the band comes in, so it sounds like Eric and Glenn come in early. With the same basic pulse and same key, it sounds like "In Memory. . ." is a continuation of, or coda to, "Angry Heart." At 0:55, the listener might expect a second verse, but the "haunts me" refrain functions like a chorus. The listener might expect a second verse at 1:35 or 1:45, but instead Glenn sings the refrain. Without a contrasting section or chord progression, it feels like not a stand-alone song but more of an extended coda to "Angry Heart" in the way that "Stonehenge" feels like an extended introduction to "Disturbing the Priest." Lyrically, however, it does stand alone, as Geoff wrote it about the loss of his mother.

SEVENTH STAR TOUR AND LINEUP CHANGES

Glenn was unhappy with *Seventh Star* being released as a Sabbath album, especially because he was expected to tour with the album and sing songs from their existing repertoire. They rehearsed from mid-January to late February at the Alley Music Studios in North Hollywood, preparing the set. Meanwhile, *Seventh Star* was released. The press was invited to the final rehearsal, at Desilu Studios (Culver City Studios), and a bootleg of this private performance exists. Around the time of that final mid-March rehearsal, Glenn got in a fight that left blood residue negatively affecting his ability to sing. As you can hear from the Culver City, Cleveland, and Detroit recordings, he had difficulty singing in the upper part of his range. He would avoid high notes by taking them lower, sing them falsetto, or miss them outright. From all reports, things did not improve after those first few concerts. He was only on the tour for a week before he was fired and immediately replaced by the relatively unknown singer Ray Gillen.

According to the Associated Press, about fifty people gathered at the Glens Falls Civic Center on Wednesday, March 26, protesting against the concert, which was scheduled for Good Friday. One of the protesters, Reverend Charles Semple, said that Sabbath's music and stage antics had a "Satanic overtone."[17] The story made national attention, including CNN's *Showbiz Today*. On the day of the show, the *Schenectady Gazette* wrote that the show in Glens Falls would be a "theatrical, drama-drenched metal extravaganza, reportedly involving lasers and simulated human sacrifice."[18] Perhaps they, like many others, had confused Black Sabbath with Black Widow, which had staged human sacrifices sixteen years prior. The AP announced on the day of the show that it would be canceled, affording Sabbath another day to rehearse with Ray.

Ray's voice was very agile, and he had no trouble stepping in last minute, hitting high notes, and comfortably executing his predecessors' vocal lines. Check out the songs from the June 2, 1986, concert released on the deluxe edition of *Seventh Star* to hear a Ray-fronted Sabbath. There are also several bootlegs of other concerts from this short tour worth a listen.

With Ray as the new lead singer, Sabbath spent some time in Henley-in-Arden, about a half hour south of Birmingham, working up material for a new album. According to Eric, they then took a six-week break and resumed work in Monmouth, Wales. Tony said they spent six weeks in London writing songs, and although the timeline in his book implies it was in the summer, it was probably around November. In September, they went to AIR Studios on the Caribbean island of Montserrat to record. Dave left the project at the end of September for personal reasons. They immediately brought in bassist Bob Daisley (Ozzy, Rainbow, and Uriah Heep), and he recorded his parts in early October. He said that when he arrived, the bass, drums, rhythm guitar, and guide vocal melodies had been recorded. Just as Geezer asked not to hear Craig Gruber's bass parts on *Heaven and Hell*, Bob asked Jeff not to show him Dave's work to avoid having his "ideas swayed in any way."[19]

Sabbath left Montserrat sometime in October and continued work at the AIR Studios in London with a different producer, Vic Coppersmith, who had worked as an engineer on Sabbath's *Vol. 4* album. Bob once said much of the lyric writing had been done when he was in Montserrat and that he wrote additional lyrics once the band relocated to London. Later, he recounted that he did not start writing lyrics until after he returned to England. He said they kept some of Geoff and Ray's lyrics, although by his reports there wasn't much beyond song titles and a few lines when he arrived. According to Bob, Dave, and Geoff, Ray struggled with recording the vocal parts. Ray left the band because management wasn't paying him. The eight-song album as it stood when he left has been released as disc two of the deluxe expanded edition of

The Eternal Idol and on several unofficial releases. It is an interesting relic and insight into what the Ray-fronted Sabbath sounded like in a studio setting. After his time with Sabbath, Ray had a brief career with Badlands and a few other projects. He died of AIDS-related illnesses in 1993.

7

A TONY MARTIN TRIPTYCH

After leaving AIR Studios in Montserrat in October 1986 and relocating to AIR Studios in London, Black Sabbath switched studios again, moving to Battery Studios to work with Chris Tsangarides to finish what would become *The Eternal Idol.*[1] With Ray Gillen gone, Sabbath needed a singer. Instead of releasing the album with Ray's work while someone else fronted the band on tour, they hired Birmingham native Tony Martin to rerecord all of Ray's vocal parts. Like Ray, he was relatively unknown at the time he joined Sabbath. He said he was instructed to copy Ray's parts exactly. According to Bob Daisley, it was "all [Ray's] phrasing and vocal ideas,"[2] which probably means that Ray came up with the vocal melodies. Tony said, "They wouldn't let me change anything, not the slightest thing."[3] This can be mostly confirmed by playing both versions of the eight songs simultaneously. His version is remarkably close to Ray's; most of the pitches and rhythms are identical. Listening to the differences may offer insight into Tony's contribution to the album and into his personal style.

The primary differences between Tony's and Ray's vocal parts are high notes and endings of songs. The high notes Tony avoided are present in other songs, so it's not as if he wasn't capable of hitting them. I suspect it would have been an artistic decision to change them, saving high notes for fewer moments in the song. For instance, he avoids Ray's high note in the second chorus of "Nightmare," saving it for a single climax near the end of the song (4:24). Ray changes the melody for the third verse of "Ancient Warrior," but Martin uses the melody from the first two verses; perhaps they decided to keep the verse melodies consistent with one another. At the ends of songs—especially ones with a repeated chorus, refrain, or riff—the vocal parts sound improvisatory. Tony uses many of Ray's parts in these outro sections but sometimes sings them in different places. Maybe they allowed him the opportunity to put a personal stamp on the sections Ray sang less strictly. Tony also sings new lyrics, such as at the outros of "The Shining" and "Lost Forever."

Other differences between the two versions include a Ronnie James Dio–like vocal ornamentation added to several of Ray's parts. There are some other minor vocal additions such as "ooh yeah" and "mmmm" not present in Ray's version. Due to these differences, Ray's parts were copied not exactly but mostly. However, it's possible that the changes to the vocal melodies were made with Ray still in the band. If that is the case, then either the changes never made it to tape or the available recording with Ray isn't the final version before he left. Thus, the comparison of the two versions cannot confirm or disprove Tony's statement about not being able to change the "slightest thing." In any case, the two versions are very similar, showing that he did a fine job replicating Ray's parts.

THE ETERNAL IDOL

The album opener, "The Shining," is like early Sabbath in that it has at least six different riffs, but the sound is clearly more eighties mostly because of the vocals, keyboards, drums, and overall production. Bob plays very melodically on this track (e.g., 0:15–0:36). The tone and the smoothness in that intro bass part makes it sound like a fretless bass, an instrument less common in rock, especially metal. Although he has recorded with fretless, he implied that he only brought one bass with him to Montserrat. Thus, it's probably the effect that gives it that sound. He also plays a high melodic line through much of the slow section (3:02–3:47) and has some nice fills in various parts of the song. Geoff Nicholls can be clearly heard in the verses as Iommi lays out in these parts.

"No Way Out," the 1984 version of "The Shining" with Bill Ward, David Donato, Geezer Butler, and Geoff, has the same riffs, chords, and song structure. The recording fades out during the solo, so it is unknown if the postsolo riff existed and whether the chorus returned. Although these riffs are more than likely Iommi's, I wonder how much input Bill and Geezer had on the song before leaving the band. The groove in the verses had very much a "Heaven and Hell" vibe, but that connection was somewhat diminished with Bob's and Geoff's parts. Iommi concurs, describing it as "like a faster 'Heaven and Hell'; it had a similar sort of tempo."[4] His description is accurate as "The Shining" was recorded at 99 beats per minute (bpm) and "Heaven and Hell" at 88. One could use the two versions to compare Bill's drumming to Eric Singer's, but Bill doesn't play too distinctively on this demo other than his liberal use of crash cymbals. Bob plays more melodically on this song than does Geezer, which is notable because Geezer so often plays quite busily.

"Ancient Warrior," as Bob describes it, is about the "futility" and "stupidity" of war, and how society has the insight to stop the greed.[5] He says the ancient warrior is a "prophet who tells us that we all potentially have the gem of wisdom within us."[6] Instead of singing the line "some say I'll be put away" as did Ray, Tony delivers the line with aggressive speak-singing (*sprechstimme*). The phrasing of the riffs in this song is unusual, giving the music a sense of uncertainty. To clarify, instead of the usual four-, eight-, or sixteen-bar lengths, the verses have fifteen, the first and third choruses have nine, and the postchorus riff is four and a half bars long. Iommi incorporates some "exotic" notes into his main riff, similar to the scale used in "Seventh Star" (0:32–0:34, 0:36–0:38, etc.). He also uses that scale to start and end his solo (2:57–3:05 and 3:33–3:35), bits that were not present in the version with Ray. From 2:57 to 3:42 during the guitar solo, Geoff's thick layers of keyboards paired with Bob's pedal bass give it a Genesis-like sound. Given its place in history, this section is like a heavy metal version of neoprogressive rock (neoprog; e.g., Marillion). With the unusual phrase lengths, neoprog middle section, and some exotic notes, the song has a certain progginess about it.

Bob says that "Hard Life to Love" was likely his second warning to Ozzy Osbourne and his crazy lifestyle, the first being "Suicide Solution" from *Blizzard of Ozz* (1981). Tony adds a Ronnie-like inflection to Ray's vocal melody on the words "insane" (1:22) and "die" (2:27). The song alternates a fast tempo (148 bpm) with a half-time moderate tempo (74 bpm), but it never loses energy. Listen to Bob's melodic bass lines during the half-time parts of the verses (e.g., 1:12–1:15).

The opening of "Glory Ride" may remind you of the opening of "Shock Wave." Both use double-tracked guitars, have a similar contour, and are in the same tempo. With Bob's pedal bass and Geoff's chords, the verses are like Journey's "Separate Ways (Worlds Apart)." Even Tony's palm-muted guitar part is similar, but he uses the heavy metal gallop rhythm instead. These elements plus Eric's big "two and four" drum hits at 3:35–3:40 (which used to be in the intro as well) give it an eighties pop metal sound. There is some seventies-style rock as well: listen for Bob and Eric's "Immigrant Song"–like groove in the guitar solo (2:31–3:14) and for the "Pinball Wizard"–like breakdown (3:18–3:34). The song seems to open up at 1:44 with the half-time feel: there is space for Bob to play melodically and for the acoustic guitar to cut through. Regarding lyrics, the song is about World War II fighter pilots: the Royal Air Force and the German *Luftwaffe* in the Battle of Britain and the Japanese *Kamikaze*.

The main riff for "Born to Lose" uses the "Cat Scratch Fever"–like inverted power chord, giving it a classic rock 'n' roll sound but with an up-tempo eighties rock feel. Tony adds a Ronnie-like hum to Ray's vocal parts at 0:51 and a nice ascending background vocal line during the choruses (right channel only at 0:37, 1:21, and 3:05). He also changes Ray's melody in the bridge to use the same scale found in "Ancient Warrior" and "Seventh Star" (1:43–1:45 and 3:14–3:16). It may not have same exoticism, but it matches nicely with the guitar riff. The guitar solo is very melodic, and the lick at 2:30 is pure Tony.

Iommi said that the band was asked to write music for the movie *A Nightmare on Elm Street*. Given the timeline, it was likely the third in the franchise, *Dream Warriors* (1987). Contract negotiations failed, but they had already written the song: "Nightmare." Bob says the lyrics are a "warning not to be sucked in by negativity."[7] After a creepy introduction from Geoff, Eric's drum fill introduces the main riff. Similar to the live-only unfinished song known as "Sometimes I'm Happy," the main riff's funky, swinging rhythm recalls the seventies Sabbath style. Bob's Geezer-like bass fills and the move into double time also recall an earlier Sabbath style, but much of the song is indicative of the eighties. Also note that the laughing (2:48–3:00) is actually Ray, not Tony.

"Scarlet Pimpernel" is a brief instrumental piece for guitars, synthesizers, and percussion, the latter credited to Bev Bevan. It is a simply structured piece with only two alternating sections. After a brief intro, the main theme is played twice by the guitar (0:09 and 0:18). Bev's rolling cymbal builds into the B section, where Geoff enters (0:27). Although the beat remains consistent, the meter is obscured with washes of synthesizers, giving it a freer, looser feel. When the A section returns at 0:47, the theme is played three times and with more intensity. With Geoff in the texture this time, the sound is much fuller. There may be some faint drums in the background in this section. The B section returns once more (1:13), and the piece closes with the A section (1:33–end). As the theme is repeated four times, another guitar and a synth provide additional melodic motion. After 1:40, toms are faintly heard beneath the cymbal rolls (clearest at 1:52–1:56). This piece was a late addition to the album, done around the time of mixing, thus after Eric had left the band.

In stark contrast to the instrumental number, "Lost Forever" begins with a fast palm-muted guitar riff on a repeated note. Although it uses inverted power chords as in "Born to Lose," its conjunction with the heavy metal palm-muted riffing loses any classic rock connotation (e.g., "Cat Scratch Fever" or "Smoke on the Water"). The lyrics are dark, about someone facing the death penalty. It is very dramatic when Ray hits the highest note of the song on the last syllable of "forever," a climactic moment of the song (1:47). However, Tony sings it lower, lacking the same impact. He saves the high note for the "lost forever" refrain during the outro of the song, which is effective in a different way. The music takes a sudden turn at 1:50 when the key abruptly changes, and another very melodic guitar solo is heard over a chord progression that sounds like something Geoff would have come up with (cf. "Neon Knights"). It's a wonderfully constructed solo, especially when Tony recalls the 2:01–2:04 lick at 2:12–2:16.

"Eternal Idol" may remind the listener of "Black Sabbath" and "Megalomania" for a variety of reasons. For one, all three songs have soft verses that lead into a contrasting heavier section, creating dramatic effect. The guitar riffs for "Megalomania" and "Eternal Idol" begin the same way, albeit in different keys (0:00–0:03 in both songs). The same type of "dark" chord found in the heavy parts of the "Megalomania" verses (e.g., 0:49, 0:52, etc.) is incorporated into riff 2 of "Eternal Idol"

(0:34, 0:56, etc.). The same "reverse reverb" effect was used on the vocals on "Megalomania" and "Eternal Idol," although analog on *Sabotage* and likely digital on *The Eternal Idol*. The lyrics for "Eternal Idol" evoke Geezer's religious themes on "Black Sabbath" and other songs. The outro verse takes a political turn, a topic that Geezer has also tackled. Bob and Ray worked on the lyrics together, with mostly Ray's being used.

Eric approaches the verses of "Eternal Idol" comparably to the verses of "Black Sabbath." In the verses of "Black Sabbath," Bill plays toms throughout, adding accents in different places. Starting in the midseventies Bill played it more sparsely, saving the tom hits for the second half of the riff or for the very end of it. Bev Bevan and Vinny Appice took the latter approach. When Eric plays the "Black Sabbath" verses, he uses cymbals in the first half of the riff and toms throughout the second half, thus not as sparsely as Bev, Vinny, and post-1974 Bill. Whereas Eric plays consistent rhythms in "Black Sabbath," he takes a more improvisational and reactionary approach in "Eternal Idol." Instead of playing a rock beat throughout the soft verses, he approaches the drum set like a percussionist (tom and cymbal rolls, tom hits, light cymbal hits, etc.). I find this to be Eric's finest and most creative playing on *Seventh Star* and *The Eternal Idol*. According to Bob, this track was recorded with the entire band playing together, and perhaps that's why Eric plays differently here. He plays the first verse (1:15–1:45) especially sparsely, only playing the toms about 25 percent of the time. He is more active the second time around (2:16–2:46), playing the toms about two-thirds of the time and with longer phrases (e.g., 2:36–2:39). He splits the difference on the third time (4:12–4:43) by playing the toms about half of the time. In all three cases, though, it's much sparser than a rock beat charging through.

Martin begins in his lower register. The only other time he sings in this register on the album is on the tag of "Born to Lose" (3:28–3:32) and the first two notes of "Nightmare" (0:52). Generally, he sings in Ronnie's usual register on this album. Remember, though, these parts were written for Ray's voice. Moving into the heavier section is made especially dramatic by Tony singing in three distinct registers: low ("now," 1:41), medium ("see," 1:45), and high ("sinners," 1:47). The guitar and bass hit a tritone at 1:47, making the vocal climax sound scarier. It also supports "your judgment day," so the lyrics supported by a dramatic tritone recall "Black Sabbath." By switching vocal registers, Tony brings out the drama of the lyrics. For instance, he sings the lowest note on the album at 4:17 ("our souls") and then leaps way up to "he's not" (4:21); this leap is even larger than Ian Gillan's in the first verse of "Born Again." He then leaps down to his middle register to complete the line ("one thing," at 4:23); again, there are three distinct registers. At 3:13, Tony pops out the highest note on the album as part of his vocal ornament on "why," a very dramatic moment in this song.

The simple distortion-less guitar part, sustained bass notes, and sparse percussion leave room for other textural sounds beneath Tony's vocal parts. For instance, fading in at 1:00 is what sounds like guitar played with an e-bow. It sustains a note, changes at 1:07 for two more notes, and fades out by 1:21. It returns at 1:25, changes pitch at 1:30, and fades out by 1:36. A similar sound—maybe Geoff this time—comes in at 2:02 for the second soft verse. Here it has a brief melody (2:13–2:16) and fades out by 2:23 and returns from 2:29–2:38. It is most prominent when it returns at 3:50. It has synth-like qualities, but the slide down at 4:12 sounds like guitar. Tony could have played with an e-bow highly processed through effects. These sounds are mostly in the right channel, so they are easier to hear if the left channel is muted. There is some light synth work throughout the verses (e.g., 1:04–1:45), and the synth washes and cymbal rolls blend nicely with the effect on Tony's voice.

Bob plays very dramatically in the loud verses, enhancing the lyrics. For instance, there is a short bass slide at 1:54 and then a lower slide at 1:56. He plays very sparsely in the first verse to provide a place from which to build intensity. He adds notes on the second time around (e.g., 2:06) to complement the guitar, but he keeps it simple to leave space.

For a song over six minutes long, the structure is surprisingly simple. It is comprised of only three different riffs and has no guitar solo (not including the few seconds of a faint solo in the fade-out). Riff 1, the soft one, is used for much of the song. Riff 2 comes in at 0:30, but it doesn't return until 3:19 in order to continue the heaviness of riff 3. When riff 3 is introduced, it has a feeling of a chorus because it's louder and climactic. Its first appearance is brief, only fifteen seconds, and the energy dissipates for another verse (1:46–2:01). When it returns at 2:47, it's twice as long and has greater dramatic impact. After riff 2 comes back (3:19), there is another soft/loud pair of verses. Riff 2 returns at 5:16

and is repeated for over a minute as the song fades. An outro verse begins at 5:31, which comes as a surprise because there hadn't been vocals over this riff before. This is the political verse that gives a different slant to the previous lyrics. At 5:53 on the word "know," Martin introduces a new melody in beautiful counterpoint to riff 2. Originally, it came later in the fade-out on the syllable "whoah," but they cut a few of Bob's lines of lyrics in order to start it sooner, allowing Martin to repeat it several times before the band stops.

Two additional songs come from this time: "Black Moon" and "Some Kind of Woman." The former was released as a B side to "The Shining" on a seven-inch single, and both were on the B side to the twelve-inch single and on the deluxe expanded edition of *The Eternal Idol*. Bob said they began working on ideas for those two songs in Montserrat. Geoff said that "Black Moon" was rerecorded in London (i.e., after Bob had recorded his bass parts), so he played bass instead, uncredited. Geoff also lays claim to writing the lyrics for it. The song was slightly revised and rerecorded for their next album, *Headless Cross* (1989). The earlier version is more keyboard heavy, is less drum heavy, and lacks the repeated chorus found at the end of the later version. Geoff said that the rhythm tracks for "Some Kind of Woman" were done in Montserrat with Dave Spitz, so perhaps Dave makes an appearance on the album after all. Bob said he recorded both of these B-side tracks in Montserrat. Geoff also said it was rerecorded at Battery Studios in London, making the bass credit dubious. The Van Halen style is evident with the heavy metal boogie guitar riff, David Lee Roth–like vocal inflections, and Eric's "Hot for Teacher"–like drum groove.

THE ETERNAL IDOL TOUR AND MORE LINEUP CHANGES

With the album complete, Iommi hired Bev and Geezer to rejoin the band. After a few days of rehearsal in mid-July 1987, Geezer left and was quickly replaced by Dave in time for their July 21 concert in Greece. Refusing to play in South Africa due to apartheid laws at the time, Bev left and was replaced by Terry Chimes (the Clash, Hanoi Rocks, and the Cherry Bombz). Dave left after the South Africa dates and was replaced by Jo Burt (Virginia Wolf) for a three-week European tour.

The Eternal Idol was released that autumn. Dave was incorrectly credited as bassist along with Bob even though his tracks had been replaced. As of late July/early August, Dave was going to be the touring bassist, so perhaps they wanted to give the appearance of continuity and stability. Another reason for Dave's inclusion in the credits could have been the possibility of including "Some Kind of Woman" as an album track, if he did indeed play on it. Bev was credited for "percussion" for the cymbal rolls—and probably for the toms as well—on "Scarlet Pimpernel." Bob, Geoff, and Ray were not credited with the lyric writing, Geoff was not credited for contributing to the songwriting, and Ray was not credited for writing the vocal melodies. Only Iommi got writing credits for the album.

Iommi teamed up with veteran drummer Cozy Powell (Rainbow and ELP) for plans for another album. Cozy said Sabbath needed to show "strength and stability" so they kept Martin because he had "proven himself brilliantly" and Geoff because he was "responsible for a lot more than people think."[8] They hired bassist Laurence Cottle to record the bass tracks. At the time of recording, at only twenty-six years old, Laurence already had album credits with Don Airey, Eric Clapton, Alan Parsons, and many others. Sabbath once again had an all-British lineup, and the band remained in England to write and record the album. Preproduction took place at Rich Bitch Studios (Birmingham), and the album was recorded from August to November 1988 at Amazon Studios (Liverpool) and Soundmill Studios (Slough, Berkshire), but primarily at Woodcray Studios (Wokingham, Berkshire).

Iommi said that Cozy was involved in the songwriting process, calling it a "joint effort." Cozy said "it's nice for me to get involved from the start of the project" instead of other recording projects where he comes in late into the process and merely lays down drum tracks. "This time I've actually had the chance to write with Tony [Iommi]," he continued.[9] Iommi said that Martin wrote all the lyrics, but Geoff claimed lyric-writing for "Black Moon" as mentioned before. "Satan," "devil," or "Lucifer" is mentioned in most songs, giving the lyrics on *Headless Cross* a much darker character than previous albums. The liner notes for the album states the songs were written by "Black Sabbath" instead of solely Iommi. The American Society of Composers, Authors and Publishers (ASCAP) lists Geoff as a cowriter for seven of the songs, so it was the first time he was officially credited for his songwriting contributions after nearly a decade with the band. Regarding the songwriting Cozy said, "I think it really makes a lot of difference if everybody can get involved and really put their little 'stamp' on it."[10] If there were one "stamp" Laurence put on *Headless Cross*, it would be his intro to "When Death Calls."

HEADLESS CROSS

"The Gates of Hell," the introduction to "Headless Cross," is scored for synthesizers and sound effects. It was also used in live performances. A synth choir on "ahh" sounds several times with its pitch bent down slightly. At 0:44 the synth choir is louder, lower, and more dramatic. A final low "ahh" bends down softly at 0:49.

"Headless Cross" begins with a simple drumbeat through an eighties-sounding gated reverb effect. The gated reverb sound on drums, made popular by Phil Collins in the early eighties, was widely used throughout the decade. Cozy and Iommi were credited as producers on the album. Cozy said, "If you listen to *Headless Cross*, the drums on there—that's my production."[11] The drums on the album sound huge and are loud in the mix. Compare the two versions of "Black Moon" to hear the difference.

The tempo (88 bpm) is the same here as it is on "Heaven and Hell," and Laurence plays a "Heaven and Hell"–like bass part underneath Iommi's intro riff (0:12). The relationship of the guitar to the bass is like Van Halen's "Runnin' with the Devil," but the riffs are not the same. The music changes key at 0:33 for the start of the main riff. Interestingly, it stays in the new key for nearly three minutes. By then, the original key area has nearly been forgotten, making its return for Tony's guitar solo sound surprising (4:21). Laurence maintains the same bass rhythm, the so-called heavy metal gallop, which, by 1988, had become a heavy metal trope.

At the start of the verse (0:55), Tony's guitar chord fades out and Geoff takes over his role of providing the harmony. Cozy and Laurence continue in a subdued fashion, leaving plenty of room for the vocals. They play very tightly together, even hitting an unexpected syncopated accent together at 1:27. Laurence plays a nice bass fill marking the halfway point of the verse (1:15–1:16; also at 2:20–2:21 and 3:36–3:37).

Tony hits a vocal climax at 1:36, triggering Cozy's snare fill, Laurence's upward slide, and Iommi's lead-in to the chorus. To close the chorus, Cozy plays a huge drum fill and Tony sings the song's refrain, "at the headless cross," in his upper register. "Head" is the same high note at 1:36 and on several places on *The Eternal Idol*. The background vocals, which are more audible later in the song, include even higher notes. The main riff returns, Tony repeats the refrain but in his middle register, and the volume comes down for another verse.

After the second verse and chorus, a dark and unusual riff played by guitar, bass, and synth choir comes in. It is brief (3:05–3:16), but it adds enough variety before the third verse and chorus. A big synth choir chord fades as the main riff returns to close the instrumental interlude (3:16). Notice Cozy and Laurence's coordinated fill at 3:26 to bring in the third verse. Another huge fill from Cozy (4:08–4:10) closes the chorus and sets up the vocal refrain. Here, and at the end of the second chorus, it is easier to hear the background vocals (2:53–2:57 and 4:09–4:13). Above Martin's melody are two additional parts, the highest of which is even higher than Ian's screams on *Born Again*.

The song abruptly changes key at 4:21 for the start of the guitar solo, giving the music a new dimension. Sabbath has used this technique for years to provide contrast and variety. Halfway through the solo (4:43) it changes key again, returning to the main key of the song. What's revealed is that they used the key relationship from the intro (0:12–0:54) for the solo (4:21–5:04), a clever reworking of earlier material with some minor adjustments (pun intended). There is a wonderful moment in Tony's guitar solo when Laurence answers a guitar lick (4:46 and 4:47), giving the impression that they are in the same room musically interacting. This type of call-and-response is commonplace in jazz, and Laurence's background as a jazz bassist shows here. He agrees, calling this moment "jazz sensibility."[12]

The final verse follows the solo, and Cozy plays another big fill to take it to the chorus (5:24). This fill, twelve fast snare hits followed by twelve more on the double bass drums, is indicative of his drumming style, although many other drummers have used it. With Tony altering his vocal melody, the background vocals are most audible this time around (5:47 and 5:58). The main riff is repeated for the outro and fade-out, during which Tony borrows Ozzy's vocal melody for "where can you run to" from "Sabbath, Bloody Sabbath" for the line "where will you run to" (6:10). With the similarity in both melody and lyrics, it could have been a hat tip to seventies Sabbath.

"Devil and Daughter" is a midtempo rock shuffle made especially heavy by Cozy's bass drum part. Geoff and Iommi take the melody in the intro and then harmonize each other at 0:28. Like many other songs on *Headless Cross*, keyboards play a prominent role in the texture. The rhythm of the verse riff (0:45–0:49) is the same as "Children of the Grave": notice the shuffling gallop and the two long hits at the end of it. Martin recalls this song for having a really high note, calling it a "stupid note" and asking himself, "Why am I singing such a note?"[13] He may be referring to the high note 1:48 and 3:46, or he confused it with his background vocals on "Headless Cross" that are even higher (which has a note that he specified as "A-sharp"). The guitar solo (2:17–3:20) is a bit stylistically different for Tony. For instance, the middle part of the solo (2:56–2:59) has two guitars, one in each channel, playing fast trills. Because the two guitars play different notes, their composite sound gives the aural effect of blazing-fast tapping, a technique normally not associated with Tony.

"When Death Calls" begins with a gorgeous bass solo in which Laurence plays chords, something bassists rarely do. He plays the top two notes of each chord with artificial harmonics, a difficult technique that produces higher pitches. It is an uncommon technique for bass, especially in rock, and perhaps it is a Jaco Pastorius influence. Laurence said that Neil Murray jokingly scolded him for writing that bass part, as Neil would have to reproduce that in live performance. Laurence alternates between two chords that recall "Born Again," and Cozy and Geoff fill out the texture with cymbal rolls and synthesizers. The dark melody note and chord at the end of the verses (1:20 and 2:57) sets up a mood change for the chorus, which has very much an eighties sound and style, especially with the background vocals on "when death calls." At 3:35, that dark chord also sets up a second significant change, when they go into double time, taking the music in yet another direction. Another highlight of the song is the guitar solo from Brian May (Queen) at 4:28–5:04, the lick at 4:38–4:41 especially.

Although the verses of "Kill in the Spirit World" are pretty straightforward, the choruses have a much different flavor than other songs on the album. Here (0:42, 1:59, and 3:53), Tony has an effect on his voice, Cozy plays toms instead of a rock beat, and Laurence and Tony play a chromatic riff that is reminiscent of the "Monsters!" section from Rush's "La Villa Strangiato" (1978). The seemingly unrelated five-second intro riff returns at 1:38 to set up the middle section. After another chorus, it goes into half time for a guitar solo in his classic style: fast licks over a slow-moving descending chord progression.

"Call of the Wild" begins as another straightforward rock number, but the band gives an "exotic" flavor to the postverse refrains (1:03, 1:54, and 4:03); even Cozy changes his parts up a bit here. The choruses (2:11 and 4:20) have the eighties-style background vocals, a mainstream sound to balance the strangeness of the refrains. Cozy references his altered groove from the refrains in the bridge (2:29–2:45), but the music is very different. Here, Iommi plays a palm-muted part that sounds like a string orchestra playing staccato, a nice musical gesture to complement the others. The refrains already hinted at another key, but it changed yet again for the middle section (2:29–3:28). This key change at 2:29 is done rather smoothly, but the change back for the third verse is very abrupt as if to pull the listener back in (3:28).

"Black Moon" is a classic blues shuffle but with a metal approach and eighties sound. Its working title, "The Boogie Song," describes the groove. The blues-based riff may remind the listener of "Evil Woman" from Sabbath's first album. There is plenty of space within the riff, filled in with drums, vocals, and organ. Notice Cozy's huge bass drum sound, especially at 0:57, 1:43, and in the choruses (0:44, 1:26, 2:09, etc.). Comparing it to the 1987 B-side version, not too much was changed. To fill in some awkward emptiness in the earlier version, they put reverse reverb on the snare drum at 2:23 and added a guitar lick at 2:39. The main differences come at the end of the song. After the third verse, this version skips a seven-second instrumental riff and goes directly into the chorus (2:49). Instead of immediately going back to the main riff as in the 1987 version, the chorus is extended (2:56–3:11). The main riff comes back, but instead of repeating it for the fade-out, they do the chorus some more. Clearly, the *Headless Cross* version is more chorus focused.

Acoustic guitars fade in through what sounds like a cloud of granular synthesis for the album's closer, "Nightwing." From 0:27–0:42, Laurence plays a beautiful solo on the fretless bass. Listen for how he takes advantage of the instrument's unique construction by sliding and achieving a warm tone. Tony's slow vocal trill on the words "night" and "wind" (0:54, 2:04, and 4:44) evokes Ronnie's performance on "Children of the Sea," insomuch as I almost expect Bill Ward to come in with the big drum fill at 0:56. Iommi tricks us with expectation at 3:26 when we expect heaviness, and perhaps another blazing guitar solo. Instead, he plays a solo on an acoustic guitar, but it is mixed loudly enough to be in the foreground.

"Cloak and Dagger" was an additional song that was recorded in these sessions and was released as a B side to the "Headless Cross" single. It has a slow blues shuffle feel along the lines of "Heart Like a Wheel." It may be Cozy's most intricate playing on these sessions and is well worth a listen.

HEADLESS CROSS TOUR AND ENTER NEIL MURRAY

Laurence was only hired to play on the album, so they hired veteran bassist Neil Murray for the tour. Neil had played with Don Airey in Colosseum II, with the Canterbury/jazz/prog-rock band National Health, and with Bill Bruford (Yes and King Crimson). In short, he had experience playing complicated music. He also had worked with metal bands, having spent a decade with Whitesnake and Vow Wow. Check out the video footage from the tour, if only to see Neil execute Laurence's "When Death Calls" intro. Nearly all of the U.S. tour was canceled, but they toured Europe and Japan for several weeks, and then to the U.S.S.R. for three weeks. The latter is very surprising considering they were on the U.S.S.R.'s 1985 "approximate list of foreign music groups and artists whose repertoires contain ideologically harmful compositions." Sabbath's "type of propaganda" was "violence and religious obscurantism."[14]

After the tour, Sabbath returned to Rich Bitch Studios for preproduction for a new album. Martin described the songwriting process as starting with Iommi's riff, and then Geoff at times would come up with melodies and chord progressions. For the times Iommi was absent, Martin played a temporary guitar track allowing Cozy, Geoff, and Neil to come up with ideas. He would come up with three different versions of his vocal parts and let the band choose which to develop. With his lyrics on a variety of topics including Norse mythology, the Ten Commandments, and love, Martin said they were "consciously getting away from the whole Devil thing" that was so prevalent on *Headless Cross*.[15] Songwriting credits were given to all five members of the band with the exception of the instrumental "The Battle of Tyr," which omitted Martin from the credits.

Leaving Birmingham for Wales in February 1990, they started recording at Rockfield Studios, the rural residential studio where Sabbath wrote some of *Paranoid* and *Vol. 4*. Later that month, Sabbath returned to Woodcray Studios and finished recording by June. The album's title came late into the process, likely well after it had been recorded, on the suggestion from the band's management. Thus, *Tyr* was not recorded as a concept album as some have assumed, but the title does relate to the tracks "The Battle of Tyr," "Odin's Court," and "Valhalla."

TYR

Tony starts the album with a gentle guitar pattern that, for a few reasons, will remind listeners of the opening of "Children of the Sea," especially just before halfway through his phrase (0:05–0:07). Moreover, vocals enter at roughly fourteen seconds in both songs. Providing another association, the melody note on the background vocal's "sanctus" is the same for Ronnie's "in the mist" (0:14).

Although not printed in the album's lyrics sheet, the lyrics here are "spiritus sanctus, anno, anno mundi." *Spiritus sanctus* translates as "Holy Spirit," and *anno mundi* as "year of the world." The repetition of *"anno"* was certainly a rhythmic phrasing decision. Perhaps the idea to include Latin lyrics came from their *Headless Cross* tour, as they opened their concerts with a recording of Jerry Goldsmith's *Ave Satani* from the movie *The Omen* (1976). Martin thought that 1990 was the year everyone was going mad trying to save the world, so the song became "Anno Mundi." The subtitle "The Vision" appears on the album sleeve but not on the back of the album cover.

The first verse has Tony singing in his comfortable middle register, only leaping up a couple of times. The vocal phrases run into one another, and at 0:49, the fourth phrase actually interrupts the third. A brief extension at 0:55 closes this part of the song. The music suddenly changes at 0:57 when the heavy guitar riff comes in, with Neil following Iommi. Listen to Cozy's bass drum part in this section; it's not terribly interesting, but it's not your standard fare either. Although the key has changed for the new riff, Martin remains in the same middle register. As before, he goes higher only a couple times, as in the bluesy line at 1:48. Iommi adds some variety at 1:52 with an additional guitar playing some nonobtrusive licks in the left channel. Some nice background harmonized vocals spill into the chorus (2:02–2:10). It's a powerful chorus, an aspect of songwriting this lineup has refined since *Headless Cross*. The postchorus riff (2:31) sets up the refrain, "anno mundi," followed by a break at 2:37 to show off the high background vocals.

The second verse begins immediately after the break, riding the momentum of the chorus. Iommi plays an additional guitar in the left channel throughout the verse to enhance the texture, and yet another guitar enters at 2:50. Tony's slow vocal trill on "alone" (3:03–3:08), the same ornament he did in "Nightwing" and Ronnie did on "Children of the Sea," takes it to the chorus. Cozy is especially aggressive here; listen for the big fill at 3:15, for instance.

Suddenly the song changes key to start the instrumental middle section (3:32). The background vocals soar above the first two chords while Iommi plays a melody line. The chords in this part are similar to the middle sections of "Seventh Star" (2:48–2:58) and Led Zeppelin's "Kashmir" (7:28–8:39). He repeats the line, taking it to a surprise chord at 3:45, and the music quickly dissolves. With his left foot keeping time on the hi-hat, Cozy plays some light cymbal hits. Geoff soon enters in the left channel with the Korg M1's choir sound.

At 3:52–4:05, it recalls the "Spiritus" vocal choir part, but Geoff's organ sound in the right channel temporarily supplants Tony's intro guitar part. The counterpoint between the synthesized choir in the left, the organ in the right, and the Latin choir in the middle are fascinating and worth a few listens. Iommi sneaks in at 4:05, but his presence is known by 4:11 with the "Children of the Sea" motif. Tony sings a little blues lick in his low register for the first half of the verse. In the second half of the verse, Cozy and Neil play the eighties-style "two and four" bass and drum hits (as Eric did at 3:26 in "Glory Ride," and so many rhythm sections of the time did).

As it did at 0:57, the song changes key for the heavy verse (4:40). Tony does the "Nightwing"/"Children of the Sea" vocal trill again at 5:04, and the chorus returns at 5:06. Cozy's aggressive playing style is again heard throughout the chorus, especially the four-second fill at

5:36. He and Neil coordinate a striking moment at 5:29, and although Neil is pretty low in the mix on the album, the tightness between his bass and Cozy's snare drum is evident.

The several allusions to "Children of the Sea" may have been unintentional, but they are there. The listener may have noticed that "Anno Mundi" develops in a very similar way to how "Children of the Sea" develops. That is because the two songs have nearly the same structure. They both have a guitar intro followed by a soft verse. The songs then change key and go into a heavy riff, followed by a second verse over that new riff. Both songs then go into a chorus, a second heavy verse, and another chorus before changing key again for an instrumental section. Then, both songs change key and go back to the intro, have another soft verse, and then change key for the heavy parts—astonishingly similar. The only difference is at the end when "Children of the Sea" goes into the chorus and then another heavy verse, but "Anno Mundi" reverses that order. For those familiar with the music of Ronnie-era Sabbath, the effect is that "Anno Mundi" develops with expectation and fulfillment, and thus seems natural and logical.

"The Law Maker" stands in contrast to the slow and medium-tempo songs of *Headless Cross*. At about 256 bpm, it is Sabbath's fastest song and comparable to "Turn to Stone" and "Some Kind of Woman." It has a slight swing feel to it: not as straight as "Turn to Stone" but not nearly as swung as "Some Kind of Woman." Notice the nice background vocal part in the second verse (1:04–1:18). Also notice how Geoff's fast arpeggiating keyboard part and the chords Iommi, Neil, and he play give the bridge (1:51–2:06) a prog-like sound and style. What's hard not to notice is the volume of Cozy's bass drums throughout the guitar solo. Although Leif Mases mixed the album, Cozy and Iommi coproduced again, and this is one example of Cozy's preference for a drum-heavy mix.

The introduction of "Jerusalem" exemplifies two sides of Sabbath. Compare the metal riff (rhythm guitar, bass, and double bass drums all in unison) underneath a classic tritone-focused single-line guitar melody at 0:12–0:19 to the commercial-oriented, big-vocal sound immediately following (0:19–0:24). It has a typical eighties-style chorus refrain (e.g., 0:58–1:04), and the song even ends with those multitracked vocals (3:53). Neil describes *Tyr* as having a "good mix of material from the very heavy, to the epic, to the commercial."[16] The lyrics were inspired by reports of an American TV evangelist taking people's money and living lavishly. Lines such as "and an angel cries 'beware your lies,'" "better watch your lies," and "where will you go when it all goes wrong?" are directed at lying evangelists.

The opening riff to "The Sabbath Stones" is essentially the "The Wizard" verse riff played slower and lower. The slow tempo (61 bpm), the dark chord (e.g., 0:04), Tony singing in his low register (0:18), and the reverse reverb vocal effect provide a particular mood. Neil is fairly low in the mix for much of the album, but he is very prominent in the softer sections (1:36–2:24 and 3:45–4:32). Moreover, Cozy plays lighter and Tony's guitar is softer with no distortion clearing some sonic space. Check out Neil's bass solo from 3:45 to 4:00. Underneath the synth strings during the bass solo is the sound of an acoustic violin, but it is faint. The solo violin line at 1:36–1:56 is more audible. I suspected it might have been Martin, as he played violin on some of his solo work, but he recalled it being a Mellotron. In that case it would've been the rare M300 solo violin tapes (i.e., ca. 1968 samples of an acoustic violin), as the far more common M400 used multiple violins, not solo. However, the timbre is brighter and fidelity is clearer on the album than on the samples on those tapes, so if Sabbath didn't hire a live violinist, there was some studio trickery to make the Mellotron sound as if it was. It's not a synthesizer because Geoff had switched to using Korg's digital keyboards by 1990, and the M1 did not have solo violin and the T-series sound is different from what is on this song. At 5:04, after Tony sings "the Sabbath stones," the band suddenly changes tempo from 61 bpm to 137 (significantly faster), and at 5:08, Cozy pushes it even further to 142 bpm. This transition section is like the transition into the fast part of "Heaven and Hell" (4:26–4:44) for its similar pedal bass part and chord progression. Excluding the acoustic outro of "Heaven and Hell," both songs go into a fast feel for the latter quarter of the song. Sabbath also did this on "Black Sabbath." Regarding the lyrics, the "Sabbath stones" refer to the Ten Commandments.

"The Battle of Tyr" is a brief instrumental piece for synthesizers alone. A faint horn call comes out of the sound effect at 0:04 and is repeated higher at 0:10, as if to represent a distant Viking horn call. The horn calls return at 0:51 and 0:58, but louder, implying the Vikings are nearer. A loud synthesized orchestra enters with three descending chords, each one minor—without regard to a key—to give it that dark,

ominous sound. Geoff builds it back up with a melody sequencing upward through different keys (0:22–0:33) and reaches its climax with four
descending chords (0:33). The way the harmonies relate to one another
may remind the listener of late nineteenth-century classical music or
film music for a reason beyond the scope of this book. Geoff uses the
Korg M1's "WindBells" to close the piece, and it spills over into the next
part of the Norse-themed trilogy.

Although the sounds date it to 1990, "Odin's Court" has very much a
seventies style about it (Tony's use of the clean guitar, background
keyboard melodies, etc.). Even the little guitar fill at 0:52 has a David
Gilmour/Pink Floyd–like essence, and perhaps the solo does too
(1:11–1:38). Tony's strumming pattern at 1:06 is like a slightly slower
and lighter "Air Dance" chorus with echoes of the "Tide Pools" section
of Rush's "Natural Science" from *Permanent Waves* (1980). This section returns at 2:22 as a transition to part three of the trilogy. The music
belongs to "Odin's Court," but the lyrics belong to "Valhalla" according
to the lyric sheet. The timing printed on the LP honors the music, and
at 2:43, it segues into the next track.

"Valhalla" begins when Tony sings the word "Valhalla" and the full
band comes in heavy. The style changes abruptly into modern-for-its-
time mainstream metal, complete with an eighties-style big vocal chorus refrain (0:58) as in "Jerusalem." Neil's bass is turned up on this track,
so it makes it easier to hear his fine bass work (0:41, 0:56, 1:45, the
bridge 1:48–2:07, 2:59–3:04 behind the guitar solo, etc.). The highlight
of the song is its prog-lite bridge section (1:48–2:08), which has some
nice harmonies provided by background vocals and rock organ, giving it
a Boston-like character.

Following the prog-leaning, eight-and-a-half-minute, Norse-themed
trilogy is "Feels Good to Me," which Martin describes as a "commercial
radio track"[17] and classifies it as a "love song."[18] Those introduced to
this song through the music video or the single/radio edit are treated to
a fine thirty-second intro solo from Iommi on the album version. His
use of bends is very tasty (the "sighing" bend at 0:02, the "blues" bend
at 0:14, etc.). Martin turns on what he calls his "Journey"-like experience from his pre-Sabbath days in this song (compare "forever yearn-
ing" at 1:48 and 3:00 to Journey's "Forever Yours," for instance).

The album's closer "Heaven in Black" starts with a drum fill from
Cozy, eighty-five hits in only six seconds, that may remind listeners of

the fast part of his opening fill to Rainbow's "Stargazer" from *Rising* (1976). When he does a similar fill at 2:47, Tony plays a fast flurry with him to end his guitar solo. Some might recognize the opening fill from "Sick and Tired" from Sabbath's 1995 album *Forbidden* and expect a slow (69 bpm) blues shuffle to follow. Cozy instead sets up a tempo and groove similar to "Devil and Daughter." The songs are alike, but "Heaven in Black" is much less keyboard driven. There is some rock organ, but it is pretty buried in the mix. Having recently been in Moscow for several performances, inspiration for the lyrics came from the Russian legend that the czar Ivan the Terrible ordered the architect of St. Basil's Cathedral in Moscow to be blinded and then killed in order not to reproduce the building elsewhere.

Tyr Tour

The record sleeve optimistically said, "See you on the Black Sabbath World Tour '90–'91," but they never went further than Europe, nor did they make it to 1991, for the tour ended in November. With no dates in the United States for the *Tyr* and *Eternal Idol* tours, and only about twenty-five dates in the United States for both the *Seventh Star* and *Headless Cross* tours combined, the future looked bleak. Even some dates in the UK were canceled due to poor ticket sales. There are some bootlegs of this tour, including one with Geezer and Brian May as guests. Check out Cozy's drum solos, as they incorporate the "Mars" movement from Holst's *Planets*, the piece that inspired the "Black Sabbath" riff. Although the *Tyr* lineup mostly dissolved after the tour, they would work together again soon.

8

RONNIE RETURNS

Summer 1990: It had been eight years since Ronnie James Dio and Vinny Appice left Sabbath. Although Vinny had been playing in Ronnie's band "Dio" for several years, he had left the band by then. On August 28, Geezer Butler "sat in" with Dio for a performance of "Neon Knights." Eleven days later, Geezer "sat in" with Sabbath during the *Tyr* tour. These events set off conversations between Geezer, Ronnie, and Tony Iommi of doing another album together. By December, after the *Tyr* tour had finished, Geezer was back working with Sabbath. With Cozy Powell and Geoff Nicholls remaining, Sabbath worked up new material, and Ronnie entered the project in 1991. As heard on demos, much of this material ended up on their next album *Dehumanizer* (1992), but some of it was saved for later albums such as *Cross Purposes* (1994), *Forbidden* (1995), and Iommi's solo album *The 1996 DEP Sessions*. Due to personality clashes, Tony Martin briefly replaced Ronnie for this project. One song from these writing sessions was eventually released as "Raising Hell" on Tony Martin's solo album *Scream* (2005), with writing credits to him and Geoff, but not to Cozy, Geezer, or Tony Iommi.

Due to what Geoff and Neil Murray called a "huge"[1] monetary package from the record company, Ronnie was brought back into the project. There was animosity between Cozy and Ronnie that likely dated back to the 1970s when they worked together in Rainbow. Moreover, Ronnie thought that Cozy was musically not "the right player for Sabbath." He continued, "It would be like me not being the right singer for

Yes."² Cozy had a hip injury later that year, and Vinny was invited back, effectively reuniting the *Mob Rules* lineup.

Vinny said that with some songs already written by the time he joined, they only spent two weeks writing material before spending six weeks rehearsing and recording demos at Monnow Valley Studios. The studio is located in southeast Wales only a mile north of Rockfield Studios, where Geoff and Tony had just done some work on *Tyr*. Instead of writing material in LA as they had for *Mob Rules*, they rehearsed in Henley-in-Arden, the same town in which Sabbath started writing songs for *The Eternal Idol*.

Sabbath recorded "Time Machine" for the movie *Wayne's World*, and although production credits on the soundtrack went to the band, Vinny said they worked with producer Max Norman (who had done Ozzy Osbourne's early eighties albums). He said the studio was on a farm near an airport, so my guess is that it was Ridge Farm Studios, which was only five miles from London's Gatwick Airport and where Max was the resident engineer. As they did with "The Mob Rules," Sabbath rerecorded the song for the album. The band returned to Wales to record *Dehumanizer* but this time at Rockfield. There, they worked with producer Reinhold Mack, best known for his work with ELO and Queen.

DEHUMANIZER

Tony said in 1992 about *Dehumanizer*, "Geezer's come up with more riffs and ideas than he's ever had on this album."³ Geezer follows up: "Everybody's had a lot more input than the other albums; it's like more of a team effort."⁴ Although Geoff also contributed to the songwriting process, only Geezer, Ronnie, and Tony were given songwriting credits. "Master of Insanity" was a song from Geezer's solo project, the Geezer Butler Band (GBB). According to GBB's guitarist Jimi Bell, it was written in 1987 and he wrote the music, Geezer wrote the lyrics, and the singer Carl Sentance wrote the vocal melodies. A recording of that band reveals that the guitar parts, lyrics, and vocal melodies are nearly identical to the *Dehumanizer* version, yet Carl and Jimi were not credited.

Sabbath "didn't want another *Heaven and Hell* and *Mob Rules*," said Tony. "We wanted to be in the nineties. We were conscious about it in making a heavier album, more involved, more riffs."[5] Geezer said whilst grinning, "We set out to make it as heavy as we can; That's what everyone wanted."[6] So that the *Dehumanizer* tour could include the new songs in the set list, Geezer said that instead of using "loads of overdubs and effects . . . the whole thing's been written so [we] can produce everything live."[7] Tony said in order to "retain a live feel" on the album, the band only did one, two, or three attempts ("takes") per song.[8]

As with his hi-hat splashes that open *Mob Rules*, Vinny is the first to be heard on *Dehumanizer*. After fifteen seconds of sound effects to start "Computer God," his drums enter in a most powerful fashion. The snare and bass drums sound very punchy, as do the toms once they are used later in the song (e.g., 1:31–1:33). In this intro, he doesn't play as straightforward as he did on *Mob Rules* or as Cozy did on the demo for this song. For instance, instead of playing a simple bass–snare–bass–snare pattern, he adds some nice rhythms at 0:18–0:20 and delays the snare at 0:22 in the way Bill Ward might.

Geezer and Tony enter at 0:26 with an aggressive, punchy riff that is especially dark due to the scale they use. It's the second chord of the riff (0:27 and 0:32) that gives it its distinctive character. The riff has an unusual meter of seven beats, giving it a slightly off-kilter feeling (three beats: 0:26–0:28, two beats: 0:28–0:29, and two beats: 0:29–0:31). It is played twice, with the third part changed on the second time (0:34–0:35, when Geezer goes low). Instead of playing in the "seven" feel, Vinny plays the simple bass–snare alteration pattern as if it's a usual "four" feel. Because the riff is played twice, the total length is an even fourteen beats so the simple bass/snare alteration works without notice. However, he hits a crash cymbal at 0:31 to acknowledge the riff repeating after seven beats. From the guitars' perspective, it turns around the beat into a snare/bass alteration at 0:31. Eric Singer took the same approach to the fifteen-beat riff in "In for the Kill," as discussed in chapter 6.

Once the verse begins at 0:36, the feel is evened out to eight beats long, thus more stable. The verse riff consists of the first four beats of the intro riff followed by silence for Ronnie and Vinny. Notice that the lyrical content of this song (and the rest of the album for that matter) is different than *Heaven and Hell*, *Mob Rules*, and albums from other bands that Ronnie is on (Elf, Rainbow, and Dio). They decided that the imagery used in past lyrics such as rainbows, dragons, and so forth, would no longer work for the band. Borrowing its title from a Geezer Butler Band song, "Computer God" took on a futuristic sci-fi theme. Ronnie said it "was probably the song that started us off into the direction we ended up with."[9] Like "Voodoo" and other songs, the first verse has a brief extension (0:57–1:00) before going back into the verse riff. There is no extension at the end of the second verse, and it heads directly into the prechorus (1:22). Because the listener expects the extension to return, the effect is that the prechorus comes early, thus pushing the song forward. The third verse heads into the prechorus (2:15) with no extension as well. Geezer and Tony play some nice fills in the second and third verses, respectively. The bass fill at 1:10 (after "engergize") is loud, and the tone is amazingly piercing. The guitar fill at 2:03 (after "reality") is played in the corresponding location in the third verse.

The key changes for the prechorus and chorus, giving it a much different character. Ronnie ditches the blues-based melody of the verses for a more scalar approach (e.g., "take a look at the toys around you" descends down a scale). Tony plays the prechorus riff with many pinch harmonics (the squeal-like sounds), giving it a brighter timbre. Geoff's keyboards can be heard at 2:21, whereas they are absent in the verses. Also in these sections, Vinny's toms sound punchy and huge (under "it turns to steel" at 1:31 and "the toys are real" at 2:25). Notice how the music skips a beat (less than one second) at the end of the first chorus (1:54). The start of the third verse is especially dramatic because it comes in early and the key abruptly changes. At 2:45, the listener expects the end of the second chorus to do the same, but instead it continues to a postchorus riff that links to the next part (3:04–4:03).

Tony's chord pattern starts off the soft middle part, Geoff enters at 3:15, and then Geezer enters with four fast pickup notes into the middle verse. His tone is different here, this time big and fat and not cutting like before. He plays the four-note lick again at 3:36 but much lower. Notice his low note at 3:37, only playable on bass detuned down three half steps as he did on some earlier albums. Instead, he plays this on his Vigier Passion five-string bass, thus not requiring detuning. Even with the fifth string at his disposal, he rarely uses it and saves the very low register for special moments such as this one and the slide in the fourth verse (4:05). Ronnie's timbre for the middle verse (3:26) is also different, using his growl-less pure/straight tone as in "The Sign of the

Southern Cross." As he did in that song, he sings in his lower register and reaches the same low note ("soul" at 3:33). It is evident that he prefers his lower register for softer sections in order to be more expressive and for when he does not have to project over bass, drums, and distorted guitars. Ronnie's third phrase (3:47) is extended to close the middle part, and Vinny brings it back to the heavy verse riff.

The fourth verse is shortened to only two vocal phrases. Thus, it acts more like a transition to the fast part. The riff that leads into the extension from the end of the first verse (0:56) comes back at 4:12. This extension is twice as long (4:14–4:19) and is propelled by five syncopated chords all set up by Vinny. His drum fill at 4:17 sets up a double-time feel for the next part.

In true Sabbath fashion, the key changes to correspond with the tempo change as the guitar solo starts (4:19). After ten seconds of soloing, the backing riff changes to a chord pattern not unlike the "Neon Knights" solo and sounds like something Geoff would have come up with (4:29–4:40). Two more chords (4:40–4:45) take it back to the first key with a new backing riff to end the solo. This whole section (4:19–4:45) is repeated, but Ronnie sings instead of Tony soloing. Because of the repeat, the key changes again (4:55), so we hear it is a bridge. Thus, retrospectively, Tony was soloing over the bridge, but we wouldn't necessarily have known that at the time. It is a clever way of presenting material twice but in a different light. The main bridge riff (4:55, "deliver us to evil") leads to the bridge chord progression (5:05, "virtual existence") that is extended with two chords (5:16, "termination of our youth"). The postbridge riff (5:21) is continued beyond its original length of ten seconds for a second guitar solo. At 5:42, Tony picks up on a rhythmic idea from Vinny's drumming and incorporates into his solo. Vinny plays an impressive fill using the snare drum and double bass drums at 5:39, and Tony reacts to it. The drums were completed six weeks before the album was done, and they did the bass, guitars, keyboards, and vocals later. Tony, overdubbing his guitar solos, would have played off of what Vinny had recorded first. The end result, however, is what sounds like a band jamming and reacting to one another.

"After All (The Dead)" is Sabbath's slowest song but only by a small margin to "Black Sabbath" and "Season of the Dead." Vinny calls the song "a very slow, pumping song, and there's a lot of things I can do in there because it's so open."[10] Although the intro and verse may be felt at about 63–64 beats per minute (bpm), a half-time feel is implied when Vinny plays the backbeat during the postverse riff, thus the tempo here is 32 bpm. Imagine a crowd trying to clap a backbeat every four seconds; that's how slow this is. Tony's trill on Vinny's first and third backbeats (1:04 and 1:12) is reminiscent of the "Black Sabbath" trill, but for some reason this one sounds more evil. The reverse reverb on the guitar on the intro recalls the verses on the first part of "Megalomania." Tony's riff at 1:48 picks up the tempo to 69 bpm, but it is still moderately slow. Geoff's synths accentuate that riff with three descending notes each time, and Vinny picks up on that and turns it into a drum fill (1:58). There are too many interesting moments in the song to mention here, but take notice of Tony's picking pattern on the higher guitar at 2:43, the "surprise" hits in the middle of the verse (3:33), and Vinny changing up the rhythm at 5:09. Note that Geezer uses the five-string on this song and plays even lower than ever before (2:23 and even lower at 5:16).

At 216 bpm, "TV Crimes" is one of Sabbath's fastest songs, thus it is in stark contrast to "After All." The song is about the greed of TV evangelism, but its original title was "Nursery Crimes," explaining lines such as "Jack is nimble, Jack is quick." Ronnie said they changed it because another band had used the title. That must have been Genesis's *Nursery Cryme* (1971). Vinny said there are "a couple of parts . . . where I'm not just playing a beat. I'm playing more of a melodic part that I created."[11] He was probably referring to the soloistic parts at 1:54–2:03 and 3:51–3:54, but he also plays melodically in the second part of the verses (0:48, 1:15, and 3:00). By approaching the drum set melodically instead of a playing a straightforward rock beat, Vinny plays in these parts some of the most creative and interesting drumming that he ever did with Sabbath. Geezer said he "couldn't think of a bass [part] to come up with" and that it ended up being the last song he recorded for *Dehumanizer*, only a day before recording the vocals.[12] Knowing the bass part was recorded long after Vinny had recorded his parts and left, we can conclude that Geezer left space for Vinny's first solo (1:54) and played a melodic line to complement his second (3:51). Geezer's moving line in the verses also complement Vinny's melodic parts (0:49, 0:53, etc.). Geezer's performance on this song is stellar, especially at 1:29–1:31, 3:09–3:11, and throughout Tony's solo (2:12–2:42). Notice the drums, bass, and rhythm guitar end the solo section in the same way that they close the solo from "Turn Up the Night": compare 2:37–2:42 in "TV Crimes" to 2:07–2:11 in the other. Another point of comparison to make is Vinny's "train" snare part in the verses to Bill's "train" snare part in the fast part of "Heaven and Hell."

"Letters from Earth" is a slow (60 bpm), heavy song generated from its intro riff. The first three power chords of that riff become the first part of the main riff (0:25) and of Ronnie's vocal melody for the song's title (0:56). In the fade-out, it is sung at the bottom of Ronnie's range (3:50, 3:58, and 4:06), so low that it doesn't sound like him. The ringing-out/arpeggiated chord in the intro riff (0:04, 0:12, and 0:20) comes back in the bridge (1:49 and 1:57), connecting the two sections. The bridge sets up a double-time feel for the guitar solo. Leading up to the solo is a guitar riff with liberal use of pinch harmonics, giving it an eighties and early nineties sound. The first part of the solo is blues-based, but the last part of the guitar solo (2:28–3:36) has slides and whammy-bar use that is similar in style to Eddie Van Halen.

"Master of Insanity" starts with a riff in the unusual meter of "fourteen," giving it a prog-metal feel. The first part of it is played in groups of three, as if to imply a slow groove at 63 bpm. But the three-grouping is abandoned partway through, so the underlying pulse is 189 bpm. The riff comes back in the middle of the song and again at the end, but 6–8 percent slower, giving it a doomier sound later on. Although it is first heard in the bass, it could have been Jimi Bell's riff (especially considering its unusual meter that Sabbath doesn't use in other songs). The chorus riff (0:37) is very unlike Tony's style (e.g., the rhythm, the Van Halen "Panama"-like bit at 0:41, etc.). The verse riff (1:00) is much more like his style and, not coincidentally, slightly different from the earlier, Geezer Butler Band version. The prechorus (1:47) chords are the same as the original, but they are similar to "Snowblind," so it fits in with Tony's style. Ronnie's vocal melodies are different than Carl's in the verses, but they are the same for the prechorus and chorus sections. The lyrics are similar, with some minor differences. Like the GBB version, Sabbath goes into a half-time feel for the middle part (3:55). However, GBB used the chords from the prechorus here, but in the Sabbath version there are two new riffs in two different keys. From 4:59 to 5:01, listen for "Vinny's fast twenty-four triplet lick" on the snare and toms, a similar fill heard at 3:19–3:22 in "Country Girl" and at 5:01–5:03 and 6:27–6:29 in "The Sign of the Southern Cross."

"Time Machine" is another fast one (163 bpm) with a driving riff on a crunchy palm-muted guitar. For that, it may remind the listener of songs such as "Neon Knights" or "Turn Up the Night." Additionally, Ronnie's entrance on "oh" (0:23) is not unlike his "oh no" entrance in "Neon Knights." The chorus (1:32) uses a pop-like chord progression, but any poppiness is negated with Geezer and Tony's chromatic riff (1:43) to close it. Comparing it to the *Wayne's World* version, not much was changed for *Dehumanizer*. The guitar solo is similar, as are many of the drum fills (e.g., 2:36, 2:55, and 3:55), showing that much of what they play is worked out and not improvised.

Although most of "Sins of the Father" is dark and heavy, the beginning has a Beatles-esque pop-like quality to it, especially the vocal melody on "fall" (0:26) and the vocal harmony on "crawl" (0:40). It certainly does not sound from the sixties, especially with Geezer's low notes on the five-string and Vinny's gated drums. This material never returns, and the song takes on a dark tone at 1:15 after Ronnie sings the song's title. Some of the lead guitar work in this song is unlike most of Tony's output; instead of melodies and licks, he approaches it like a soundscape of sound effects (1:53–2:10) or with key-less/atonal lines (2:31–2:38). The second "solo" is more Iommi-like, but he does bring back the atonal lick (3:32–3:34). At 2:24, it goes into a double-time feel for the third part of the song, never returning to the slower tempo. Ronnie brings back the verse from 1:29 at 3:49, but because it's in a new tempo over a new riff, it's reimagined in a different musical context. It's like when he brings back the "fool, fool" motif in "Heaven and Hell" but this time with an entire verse.

At nearly seven minutes, "Too Late" is the longest track on the album. It begins with atmospheric synth sounds from Geoff on what sounds like a Korg M1, a popular keyboard at the time. Tony sets up the verse chord progression on acoustic guitar at 0:28 for what the band called "some nice light and shade" for the album.[13] The chords take an eerie turn at 0:58 when Ronnie sings "night." Here, the "promises made in the night" are a deal with the devil, which the song's protagonist wishes to back out of, but "it's too late" for that. Geezer plays some nice lines in the song, such as the melodic approach in the second verse (1:39) and the fill along with Vinny at 6:07. It gets heavy for the second chorus (2:14), and the riff is even darker (especially 2:28 and 2:44). The next part of the song (2:58) starts in a new key, giving it a different flavor. The riff backing the guitar solo (3:49) is based on the verse riff but placed in a third key (compare 4:11–4:15 to 0:58–1:03, for example). Perhaps the most defining feature of this solo is the guitar scream (3:50 and 3:54). At 4:40, it returns to the original key, briefly recalling the atmospheric synth, and adds a clean guitar lick and vocal "ooh." The final verse is extended at 5:13 for "let me go" over a beautifully dissonant chord, a jazz chord, really. Geoff's keyboard sounds here give the overall sound an interesting timbre. In contrast, it makes the final chorus (5:18) sound especially heavy. Vinny plays the "fast twenty-four triplet lick" at 5:33, which he hinted at earlier (4:38). The song closes with light cymbal work, a couple of guitar "cries," and the atmospheric synth sounds.

"I" begins with a reverse piano like the beginning of Yes's "Roundabout" but with a digital piano instead of an acoustic one. At 0:20, Ronnie sings "ooh" with the guitar, treating his voice like an instrument. He reaches his lowest note on the album at 0:31 to close the intro. Ronnie's anaphoric lyrics repeat the word "I" on several lines, providing a different type of rhyme. With the exception of its appearance at the end of the guitar solo (3:02–3:12), notice the chorus increases in length each time: 1:05–1:15, 1:36–1:56, and 3:33–4:13. Although most of the song is pretty straightforward, the bridge (1:56) is very chromatic and in an unusual meter of "seven." Compare this to the "Computer God" intro riff, also in "seven."

The main riff for "Buried Alive" is Sabbath's most chromatic and arguably their most sinister sounding. It is also really heavy. The intro sounds almost atonal, but the key becomes clearer once Ronnie enters, even though his melody is also quite chromatic. Vinny plays wonderfully simple here, leaving plenty of space for Geezer and Tony. At 2:37, 4:01, and 4:26–4:32, he does something clever with his simple beat, shifting it over to the offbeats as does Led Zeppelin's John Bonham in "Black Dog," making it not so simple. The chorus is simple, but Geezer plays quite busily in parts (1:31–1:39 and 3:31–3:37). He is also busy in Tony's second solo, but that is to be expected from him. Ronnie's vocals on the verses appear to be run through an octave pedal, providing a second evil-sounding vocal far below. His departing scream "I'm buried alive" at 4:21 is incredibly dramatic, a fine way to end the album.

DEHUMANIZER TOUR AND THE DIO YEARS

The set list for the *Dehumanizer* tour included Ozzy-era songs, early eighties songs, and new material. There are many bootlegs from this tour, so it is possible to hear and see this material performed live. Sabbath was scheduled to be the opening act for Ozzy on the last two nights of the tour. Ronnie, refusing to open for Ozzy, quit the band and was replaced by Rob Halford (Judas Priest) for these concerts (November 14 and 15, 1992). It is worth checking out the bootlegs of these concerts to see and hear this rare version of Sabbath.

Over a decade had passed, and in 2005 when Sabbath was touring with Ozzy, Geezer and Tony had agreed that "it would be nice to do some other shows" as they have been "doing the same show for [several] years."[14] Later that year the record company approached Tony about putting together a compilation of Ronnie-era songs, and they asked if Sabbath had any unreleased tracks. In one interview Tony says that they hadn't any, but in another interview he says they do have some unreleased recordings but "it'd be better to write some new stuff."[15] In 1992, Tony said they "ended up not using a lot of really great material"[16] for *Mob Rules*, so perhaps there are demos or completed tracks from those sessions. Tony approached Ronnie with the idea of writing two new songs for the compilation. In October 2005, Ronnie announced publically that they would proceed with creating new material. Geezer was brought on board, as was Bill for a time, but Geoff was not. Any songwriting contributions Geezer may have made were not credited on the album or with the American Society of Composers, Authors and Publishers (ASCAP), as only Ronnie and Tony were given credit. To help prepare the tracks, Tony hired Mike Exeter, an engineer-producer he used for his albums *DEP Sessions* (2004) and *Fused* (2005). To the delight of the fans, Sabbath ended up writing three songs instead of two.

In November 2006 after working on material with the band, Bill quit, citing musical differences. Specifically, he said it was requested of him to "play a straight beat through" on a song that he described as "pretty fast" (likely "Ear in the Wall").[17] Bill said Tony was "pushing his guitar," which I suspect refers to the anticipated offbeat hits in that song. "If he's punching, I punch with him," he said. "I never go through him like he [doesn't] exist."[18] In other words, he did not want to play a simple rock beat, effectively ignoring the musical gesture and the person playing it for the sake of keeping time. "What was being asked of me was disrespectful to Tony as a player," he said.[19] As discussed in the first five chapters, Bill "plays to the riff" and rarely plays a straight beat, especially when there are offbeat hits in the guitar part. However, as noted in chapter 5, he does play that way on parts of *Heaven and Hell*, so one might think it would be a reasonable request for a reunion of the lineup from that album. At any rate, Bill called it an "intolerable request" and quit the project. Soon thereafter Vinny was brought in, essentially reuniting the *Mob Rules* and *Dehumanizer* lineup, albeit without Geoff. With Ronnie and Tony producing and Mike engineering, Sabbath recorded the three songs at Tony's home recording studio, thirty miles southeast of Birmingham.

The Dio Years (2007) compilation consists of five songs from *Heaven and Hell*, four from *Mob Rules*, three from *Dehumanizer*, one from *Live Evil*, and the three new songs. The new tracks are loud throughout, which is due to modern production techniques and how the songs are constructed. The one exception is a softer middle section of "Shadow of the Wind," which, at only thirty-six seconds long, is less than 4 percent of the total time of the three songs. The variance of soft and loud that Tony describes as "light and shade" is largely absent from these songs, but some older songs from the compilation provide that contrast. Another element different about the new songs is that they lack the expressive elasticity of tempo heard on earlier albums. Whereas the band would stretch out a phrase, have small variances in tempos for verse and chorus riffs, or drop into a slightly less than half-time feel, these tracks were done to a click track with no variance programmed in. In other words, each song remains at exactly the same tempo throughout, which is very much unlike how they play. For as solid as Vinny is with his tempos, there has always been room for expressive playing when the music calls for it, especially when following Geezer and Tony.

"The Devil Cried," as Ronnie described it, has the "unusual premise" that "if you can make the Devil cry, he'll send you back to heaven."[20] At 0:48, his first vocal line sets the scene: "one fine day in hell." Underneath the heavy, sustained power chord riffs in the intro, notice a guitar melody played four times (0:16–0:46). When Tony palm-mutes for the verse riff, it sounds heavier yet leaves room for Ronnie. The single-line riff that opens the middle section is classic Sabbath (2:44).

Geezer plays simpler than he normally does, but you can hear Geezer-isms such as bending of the string (e.g., 0:54).

"Shadow of the Wind" is another slow song (53 bpm), even slower than "The Devil Cried" (61 bpm). The first five seconds of the intro riff is almost the same as "Electric Funeral" (about 61 bpm). One of the key differences to note is that Tony's riffs are quite long in comparison to his seventies ones. Notice that it seems as if the riff is nine seconds long, but it changes at 0:12. Thus, the riff lasts eighteen seconds, eleven times as long as the main riff in "Johnny Blade," for comparison. The vocal melody is very similar to Dio's "Rainbow in the Dark" (1983) but in a lower key. Compare, for instance the notes and rhythm of the two songs' refrains: "and the shadow of the wind" (1:22) to "like a rainbow in the dark." The title "Shadow of the Wind" seems to recall the line "shadows of the night" from the same Dio song. The middle section (3:45–4:21) offers a break from the loudness of the rest of the song, opening up space for Geezer to play melodically. There are some nice synth sounds in here as well. According to a source close to the band, Geezer said Mike, the engineer, played the keyboards. This section gives a nice contrast to the other songs as well. It also makes the return of the main riff especially doomy (4:53).

The album closes with "Ear in the Wall," a fast song at 164 bpm, comparable in speed to "Time Machine." For a brief time, only four-teen seconds, they drop into a half-time feel at 2:03 (82 bpm). Knowing their style, this is a moment that I suspect would have been played differently if a click track had not been used. I also wonder if the held chord at 2:14 would have been stretched out a bit before Vinny's fill at 2:15. This riff is very syncopated, with most of it played on the offbeats. Perhaps this is the "pushing" that Bill described when he said he didn't want to play a "straight beat through."[21] Vinny does a fine job of incor-porating the offbeats into a "straight beat": notice how he is very simple at first with the bass–snare alternating (2:03–2:06). He progressively gets more complex, adding different rhythms and faster hi-hat work, and then by 2:12, he plays all the syncopated parts in the bass drum without disrupting the backbeat of the snare drum.

2007 TOUR AND *THE DEVIL YOU KNOW*

In October 2007, during the tour to promote *The Dio Years*, the band decided to make another album. They started writing material in 2008 before their brief "Metal Masters" tour that August. Geezer, Ronnie, and Tony individually put their ideas on CD and then shared their work with one another. Tony said that although Vinny "didn't write as such," he was "very much involved."[22] Although the genesis of those ideas came separately, Geezer said they wrote the music "as a band."[23] Tony said that "most of the songs were group efforts."[24] Ronnie estimated the total time of the writing process at fifteen to sixteen weeks. Geezer said, "When we're writing the stuff, we make sure the album isn't just one track sixty minutes long. If we write a fast one then we think the next one's got to be medium or slow, and that's the way we approach things."[25] After writing and rehearsing the songs in LA, the band returned to Rockfield Studios, where they had made *Dehumanizer*, to record that autumn.

The *Devil You Know* was released not as "Black Sabbath" but as "Heaven & Hell." Geezer said they changed the band name to "let people know we were only doing songs off the Dio albums."[26] Ronnie said they "wanted to eliminate any confusion about it" but conceded that "people are going to call us Black Sabbath at the end of the day anyway."[27]

Geoff did not return to record. They used Dio keyboardist Scott Warren for the tours but not for the album; Mike again covered those duties. Geezer said, "*Heaven and Hell*, *Mob Rules* and *Dehumanizer* had a lot of keyboards on there. This time we sort of stripped keyboards down. We only used them for intros and to pad out solo backing bits so it sounds a lot more raw than the old stuff."[28]

In respect to songwriting, production, and performance, *The Devil You Know* (*TDYK*) sounds like a logical continuation of the three new songs for *The Dio Years*. Overall, *TDYK* is mostly loud, but it has more variety in range of volume than the new songs on *The Dio Years*. A click track was used for this album as well. With the exception of the first part of "Bible Black," the click track does not accommodate for the natural fluctuation of tempo from section to section. Thus, like the new songs on *The Dio Years*, it lacks the elasticity of tempo and feel heard on this lineup's 1981 and 1992 albums. However, there are moments where you hear Tony pull ahead of the beat, especially in the postverse, chorus, and bridge sections where the energy tends to ramp up a bit. In these instances, Vinny will either follow Tony and compensate later or he will hold back and stay with the click. In that sense, there is a sense of elasticity, but it always goes back to the unwavering click.

Like *Mob Rules* and *Dehumanizer*, Vinny is the first to be heard on *TDYK*. His opening fill for "Atom to Evil," using rhythms different than what he uses for most of the song, almost teases the ear by nearly implying a different tempo for the unsuspecting listener. He brings back those rhythms with Geezer in the verse at 1:30 and similar fills at 3:19 and 3:57. The feel is solidified at 0:04 when he starts the drumbeat. It is slow (60 bpm, one beat per second), similar in speed to "Letters from Earth" and "The Devil Cried."

Ronnie wrote the music and lyrics for this song; notice how the vocal line in the verse follows the riff (0:37–0:43). He harmonizes himself on the second phrase (0:45–0:51). The riff changes for the third and sixth vocal phrases (0:52 and 1:16), but the fourth and fifth phrases (1:00 and 1:08) are like the first two. The verse ends with a brief extension for the refrain ("atom and evil") lasting only two beats (two seconds), followed by a simple synth melody and drum fill.

The second verse (1:30) has a new vocal melody and guitar part. The bass part is also different, incorporating rhythms derived from the opening drum fill but much more choppy. Vinny lines up some of those in his drum parts at 1:37 and 1:44. Instead of repeating earlier material for a second verse, the song is continually developing, showing maturity in Ronnie's songwriting and the band's arranging. At 2:02 and 2:28, for the second part of the verse, they bring back the original verse riffs. When Ronnie sings the refrain (2:26), his melody ascends and the band plays for three beats: one more than before but still one less than expected because the solo starts at 2:29.

The key changes for the solo, but the last phrase, which is extended by four beats, connects it to another verse so smoothly that the key change largely goes unnoticed (3:05). This verse is shortened to avoid bringing back the first two verse riffs. The refrain (3:37) is performed as the first time, only two beats long. This time, the synth melody is heard more clearly because there is no drum fill.

When Geezer plays the bass fill at 3:42, it sounds as if it will head into the second verse riff, but the bass oddly stops at 3:43. Instead, they bring back the intro riff (0:04–0:35), which hadn't been used in over three minutes. At 3:59, Ronnie sings new vocal melodies over this riff. At 4:15 he repeats the refrain over the riff, making it like a chorus. He harmonizes with himself on the fourth "atom and evil," and Vinny fills across the drum set to close this section. You can hear the space of his kit with the high tom in the left channel and the floor tom in the right (4:29–4:30). The intro/outro riff repeats as the song fades.

The single-line main riff of "Fear" sounds like something Geezer would have written, especially the ornamentation. The chorus melody and vocals harmony also sound as if they could be his contributions to the songwriting, reminiscent of songs such as "Sceance Fiction" from his solo album *Plastic Planet* (1994). Vinny's drumming for the intro sounds a lot like Bill's in that the snare and bass drums are placed on offbeats to match the riff, and also for the two tom hits as part of the drum part (0:21 and 0:23). His drumming over the same riff is much simpler in the verse. The end of the main riff is interesting because it has an extra beat in order to fit all four chord hits (0:27). It's performed that way at 1:42 and 4:42, but at 4:30 it's only lengthened by one-fourth of a beat; notice that they only play three of the four chord hits this time, making Ronnie's "fear" enter early—the effect is jarring and awesome. As the song stays with the click track at 78 bpm, these slight elongations provide a nice variety. The reverse reverb when Ronnie sings "fear" make it especially dramatic.

The soft beginning to "Bible Black" offers a nice "light and shade," as Tony might describe it, in the way the beginnings of "Children of the Sea" and "Southern Cross" offer contrast on *Heaven and Hell* and *Mob Rules*. At 1:05, listen for Geezer's melodic bass lines (the tone sounds like a fretless) and for Tony's background long-tone melodies that are similar to his e-bow-sounding work in "Die Young" and "Heaven and Hell." Also here, the key changes and tempo jumps up from 74 to 78 bpm. All of these elements increase the song's energy. When the drums enter suddenly at 1:31, it jumps further to 82 bpm. This is very much in the Sabbath style, so having the click track accommodate their jumps in tempo was an appropriate decision. Tony and Vinny have a brief musical conversation at the end of the song. Notice in the second guitar solo when Tony leaves space for Vinny's drum fill (5:57–5:59). Tony then incorporates those rhythms into his next phrase (6:00 and 6:02–6:04).

"Double the Pain" is a straightforward rock song alternating between a slow rock feel (62.5 bpm) and double the feel (125 bpm). It opens with Geezer through an effect plus other sounds. A second bass track is added at 0:08 with an even grittier tone. His solo part returns at 3:29, but this time Vinny enters on his "fast twenty-four triplet lick": six on the snare and the rest on the toms. In the middle of the song, the band does a variation of the intro riff, first in the slower feel (2:57) and then in the double-time feel (3:04). The song ends abruptly on the last note of this altered riff.

After the previous four songs starting in the same key, "Rock and Roll Angel" provides contrast by being even lower. Tony's guitar is down three half steps as in songs such as "Children of the Grave" and "Sabbath, Bloody Sabbath." Instead of tuning down, Geezer uses a five-string, providing a fat tone in some parts and a cutting tone in others. In the first part of the guitar solo (3:03–3:51) and in the acoustic outro solo (5:07–end), Vinny plays more like a percussionist than a drummer in that he avoids playing a drumbeat and instead uses the drums and cymbals only occasionally. Tony's outro solo is not in his jazz-like style as in "Planet Caravan"; he uses a slightly darker scale as at the end of "Heaven and Hell," which also uses acoustic guitar, for a classical guitar sound.

"The Turn of the Screw" is similar in structure to "Double the Pain," and both songs alternate between half-time and double-time feel (this one a bit slower at 59 and 118 bpm). It was written as a band in LA— "together on the spot,"[29] Tony described—instead of coming from ideas put down on the individual CDs. He said that "Eating the Cannibals" and "Neverwhere" were written this way as well. Listen for the way the band members interact with one another in these three songs, knowing they were created this way. For instance, notice how the break in Tony's verse riff (0:23, 0:30, 0:39, etc.) allows space for Ronnie's vocal lines. Also, listen how Vinny sets up Tony's dissonant chord with two fast bass drum hits (1:45). The way they hold out a chord at 4:49 and play a four-note tag at 4:52 to end the song gives it a "band" feel.

At 185 bpm, "Eating the Cannibals" is the album's fastest song, comparable in speed to "Turn Up the Night" and "Neon Knights." At only three and a half minutes, it's quite short, comparable in duration to those songs as well. Perhaps from creating the song as a band, there are some moments of interaction, such as the Geezer/Vinny fill at 2:43,

Tony's mini-solos between Ronnie's vocal lines in the third verse (2:48, 2:53, etc.), and the "Lady Evil"–like band ending (3:28). The riffs and vocals follow each other at the ends of verses and the bridge (0:40, 1:14, 1:45, and 3:03), and perhaps that's because the song was created as a band. At these four moments in the song, the phrases extend beyond the usual symmetrical grouping of bars (e.g., four, eight, sixteen, etc.), contrasting many Ozzy-era songs. In the seventies, Sabbath wrote the riffs before the lyrics, and the phrase lengths were more often symmetrical (e.g., a riff played eight times). In this song, phrases are also extended when Ronnie is not singing (0:21, 1:56, 2:29, 2:43, and 3:29), so clearly the band thought beyond regular phrase lengths for vocal and instrumental sections.

"Follow the Tears" is tuned down as in "Rock and Roll Angel." The other eight songs on the album begin in the same key, so it gives the ear a break from having too much of the same. The opening riff in the guitar is especially heavy and is backed by a dissonant rock organ part. Additional synthesizers are added at 0:15: synth pads and then what sounds like a modern Mellotron choir emulator. There is electronic percussion in this intro as well: MIDI timpani (0:13, 0:27, 0:41, and 0:49), samples of snare drum rolls (0:35, 0:38, 0:42, 0:45, and 0:49), and bass drum. The marching snare drum sounds like electronic samples as well, as neither it nor the bass drum match the sound of Vinny's kit. Also, the snare drum roll samples don't connect to the marching snare part. Although the intro may be only Mike and Tony, the whole band kicks in at 0:57. The verse riff is very heavy as well, thanks in part to the lower tuning and palm-muting. The song doesn't drudge along for its entirety; for instance, Geezer and Ronnie are especially melodic in the bridge (3:32–4:00). Mike said that the programmed drums in the demo had a double-time feel, but Vinny was told not to copy the drum machine.

"Neverwhere" is the album's other fast song (166 bpm), comparable in speed to "Time Machine" but not as fast as "Cannibals." The bridge (2:22) provides a break from the intensity with held-out chords and a half-time feel (83 bpm). The tricky transition into the bridge (2:17) also sets up a key change, allowing greater contrast for the bridge. Parts of the backing riff for Tony's solo (2:45) are like the "Sweet Leaf" and "Symptom of the Universe" solos, and his blues-inflected solo lines recall classic Sabbath.

"Breaking into Heaven" is the album's longest and slowest (57 bpm). Vinny makes the song seem even slower by barely playing between each beat or chord. It is so slow that the chorus doesn't appear until 3:49 in the song, long after most pop songs have ended. The old pop-song adage "don't bore us, get to the chorus" certainly doesn't apply here as Sabbath's music requires patience and long-range listening. The music takes a sudden turn at 4:22 when the tempo doubles and they change the key for the guitar solo. They return to the slower tempo after the solo, but the transition to the original key is cleverly subtle. The first part of the verse melody is very similar to "Computer God" (compare "someone said there's a lost horizon" at 0:39 to "waiting for the revolution"), but obviously slower.

RONNIE'S FINAL LIVE PERFORMANCES

Unlike the 1980s and 1992 tours, the tours for *The Dio Years* and *The Devil You Know* included no Ozzy-era songs. Before *TDYK*, Heaven & Hell released a live album and DVD from their March 30, 2007, performance in New York titled *Live from Radio City Music Hall*. Their June 16, 2009, performance was broadcast on German TV (Rockpalast) and is available. Recorded on July 30, 2009, they released *Neon Nights: 30 Years of Heaven & Hell* on CD and DVD after Ronnie's death in 2010. His final performance was in Atlantic City, New Jersey, on August 29, 2009, and only some footage from this concert exists. An interview with him after that concert revealed that they had plans to do another album and another tour.

9

TONY MARTIN RETURNS

In 1991, when Black Sabbath was working up material for *Dehumanizer*, Tony Iommi asked Tony Martin to rejoin the band, as things weren't working out with Ronnie James Dio. Martin was busy working on his solo album, *Back Where I Belong*, so he declined. This solo album includes a version of "Jerusalem" and guest appearances from Geoff Nicholls, Laurence Cottle, and Neil Murray. Iommi phoned Martin again months later, and this time he agreed. They rewrote lyrics and vocal melodies, and Martin recorded vocals on a few songs. These recordings have yet to surface, and it would be fascinating to hear *Dehumanizer* songs with different vocal parts. Martin said the band had completed the rhythm tracks, meaning it must have been some time in the final six weeks of the recording sessions at Rockfield. However, his timeline regarding Iommi's invitations implies that these recordings occurred in July, so unless these were demo recordings from the pre-production phase in Henley-in-Arden, it seems Ronnie had rejoined earlier than he knew.

Martin also said that they were putting together songs for a new album before Ronnie had rejoined for the 1992 *Dehumanizer* tour, material that would end up on their 1994 album *Cross Purposes*. The bridge riff in "Psychophobia" (1:32 and 2:08), for instance, dates back to 1991. It had been the verse riff for a song labeled "The Next Time" on *Dehumanizer Rehearsals*, a bootleg from when Cozy Powell was still in the band. The main riff for "The Next Time" is very similar to Led Zeppelin's "Dancin' Days," and riffs in the remainder of the song (such as the two-chord chorus) aren't very striking, so it's not surprising that they extracted the verse riff for use in a new song.

With Ronnie and Vinny Appice gone after the *Dehumanizer* tour, Sabbath invited Martin to resume work on the new material. They auditioned drummers and eventually hired Bobby Rondinelli in 1993. Bobby had worked with Ray Gillen in the mideighties and recorded an album with him in the early nineties but most notably—and almost ironically—replaced Cozy in Rainbow in 1981. He is the sixth Rainbow alum to work in Sabbath (the others are Bob Daisley, Cozy, Craig Gruber, Don Airey, and Ronnie). Iommi says Bobby is "a similar drummer to Vinny, very precise."[1] I agree with this assessment, especially in reference to his execution of fills and drumbeats. However, as much as he may play a straightforward rock beat along the lines of Cozy, Eric Singer, and Vinny, Bobby incorporated more syncopation and groove-oriented feel into his playing, which, in a way, evokes Bill Ward. When asked about the unusual meter in "Immaculate Deception," Bobby said they would "not bother" counting the meter and instead "just play," keeping it "very earthy" and "not mathematical." To come up with a drum part in that unusual meter, Bobby said he would "play to the riff."[2] Therein lies the important connection to Bill's approach: "playing to the riff," just as Bill has described it.

Sabbath returned to Henley-in-Arden to rehearse and work up the new material. Some of the songs were written by the time Bobby got involved, but others only had riffs, and the band was still coming up with material. He said he could contribute ideas as well. Bobby said Iommi was open to different ways the drum parts would go, describing him as "very easy going."[3] Bobby would try two different approaches to a drum part and present both. Unlike *Tyr* where the songs were credited to the entire band, the songs on *Cross Purposes* were credited to Geezer Butler and the two Tonys, excluding Bobby and Geoff. Perhaps Geoff was less involved in the songwriting process this time, but it could have to do with the change in management since then or contractual agreements. There are moments on the album with prominent keyboard parts, so the omission is curious, but not shocking, because Geoff did not receive songwriting credits for the first five Sabbath albums on which he played.

Bobby said he had spent about six weeks rehearsing with them. Eddie Van Halen came to rehearsal on April 26, his day off between

Van Halen's Birmingham and Sheffield concerts. They jammed on what became "Evil Eye," for which Geoff and Martin said Eddie cowrote, albeit uncredited. Bobby recalls rehearsing for another week, taking a week break, and then spending about a month recording the album, with the possibility of rehearsing some more just before recording sessions began. This dates the rehearsal/songwriting sessions with Bobby from late March to early May, and the recording sessions from about mid-May to mid-June. Iommi recalls finishing writing the songs in the summer, which makes sense considering they were likely still crafting and honing aspects of the songs in the studio. Also, they probably recorded vocals and guitar solos after Bobby had left, so recording could have continued well into the summer. Sabbath recorded the album at Monnow Valley Studios, where they had recorded some demos for *Dehumanizer*.

CROSS PURPOSES

The album opener, "I Witness," opens with guitar, bass, and drums providing an up-tempo (about 180 beats per minute [bpm]) groove underneath an ascending line in the keyboards and lead guitar. The vocal melody starts in Tony Martin's lower register, but he works his way higher by the end of the verse. Showing off his vocal range, Tony sings higher for what is labeled in the lyric sheet as the chorus (e.g., 1:21). Geezer plays some amazing, busy bass lines behind the verse vocals (e.g., 0:22–0:27). The riff played in the verse between vocal phrases is Sabbath's shortest ever, at only 1.3 seconds in duration. For that, it is like the "Johnny Blade" riff, which is only longer because of the slower tempo. A contrasting half-time feel emphasizes the sections starting at 2:46 and at 3:55. Bobby plays some nice fills in these parts, for example, the fast double-bass drum fill (4:09) and a more rhythmically complex one at 4:19 with accents in unusual places. Bobby also hits accents with Geezer and Tony in unexpected places (e.g., 1:07 and 2:45). Both Tonys hit a "dark" note (cf. "When Death Calls" and "The Sabbath Stones"), giving the half-time sections an interesting flavor (2:55, 4:04, and 4:25). Iommi introduces an even darker riff at 4:41, and then the song closes with the main riff played three times as a tag.

Geoff's synth choir and Tony's acoustic guitar open "Cross of Thorns," and Martin starts in his low register, the three keeping the volume low. Geezer and Bobby join in for the second verse (1:22), and notice how well locked in they are with each other here. The rhythm is simple, and Geezer only plays two different notes, but any more than that would have gotten in the way of the vocals. The chorus (0:42 and 2:04) is much louder and heavier, and Bobby, Geezer, and Tony play a funky groove during the first and third phrases (e.g., 0:42–0:48 and 0:54–1:00); pay special attention to the bass drum here. The riff for the second half of the bridge (2:46) is very similar to the half-time riff in "I Witness," which remarkably also occurs at 2:46 in that song. Listen for the similarity in rhythm and contour. The song begins to fade at 4:10 when they mix elements from the intro and chorus. The final "cross of thorns" vocal part is nearly inaudible as the fade completes, an unusual musical or production choice.

The opening riff of "Psychophobia" is the unusual (for rock) meter of three. Most rock songs in three are either felt in a slower one (e.g., "Lucy in the Sky with Diamonds") or have a backbeat (e.g., "War Pigs"), making it not *really* in three. Rarely do rock songs in "three" have three evenly stressed beats as in "Psychophobia." The main/verse riff was written before Bobby had arrived, as he said that the band told him some of the auditioning drummers tried playing it in "four," effectively costing them the job before the audition had finished. The vocal phrases are temporally close to one another, and with Bobby's snare hit on "two," it gives a tense, anxious feeling as if there's a missing beat. The song relaxes each time the chorus starts (0:28, 1:13, 1:59, and 2:36) because it's in a comfortable "four" feel and the guitars and drums are lighter. The lyric "it's time to kiss the rainbow goodbye" is presumably a snarky comment directed at Ronnie but is also awkward because Bobby was a former member of Rainbow. As mentioned before, the bridge riff (1:32 and 2:08) had an earlier life as the verse riff in a pre-*Dehumanizer* song.

"Virtual Death" begins with Geezer alone, his bass with a rich, menacing tone. Iommi called writing the music for this song a "joint effort" between him and Geezer.[4] The evil-sounding bridge (2:36–3:33) sounds as if it could have been on Geezer's solo album *Plastic Planet* (also released in 1994; cf. "Sceance Fiction"). Geezer penned the lyrics, unlike most of the *Cross Purposes* lyrics, which were written by Martin.

At only about 50 bpm, the song is almost uncomfortably slow. The lead and background vocals in the verses may remind the listener of Alice in Chains due to the register in which Tony sings, the scale used in the vocal parts, and the way the lead vocal relates to the background vocal part. The listener might notice the unusual phrasing in the riff and vocal phrases of the chorus (1:17 and 2:16). The reason is the highly unusual meter of "seventeen" (at about 100 bpm); with seventeen being a prime number, the division is unequal (eight plus nine and then nine plus eight). For the use of unusual meters and rhythms, Bobby thinks of *Cross Purposes* as being Sabbath's "most progressive album." He considers the seventies Sabbath to be more "jazzy" than progressive rock (prog).[5]

"Immaculate Deception" is another song with unusual phrasing and meter. It begins in a slow (about 60.5 bpm) "five" feel, but it can be felt as a faster (about 121 bpm) groove in "ten," divided four plus three plus three. Rather than starting the vocal part at the beginning of the riff (0:20), Tony enters at the end (0:23), cleverly navigating the unusual groove. He reaches the apex of his vocal melody with the song's title, triggering a double-time (or quadruple-time) feel at 0:57, where Bobby batters the double-bass drums. The song really opens up at 2:31 when they drop from 242 bpm to 60.5 bpm. Geezer takes this opportunity to play some nice bass fills around the vocal melody (2:36 and 2:52). At 2:58, Bobby plays a huge drum fill to take it back to 242 bpm for the guitar solo. To end the song, they recall the main riff (the one in "five" or "ten").

"Dying for Love" is a sophisticated track, but listeners wanting heavy metal throughout every song on an album might easily write it off and miss out on some fine musical moments. It starts with a minute-long guitar solo over a simple accompaniment from Bobby, Geezer, and Geoff. It may remind listeners of "Feels Good to Me" or "No Stranger to Love," as these songs also begin with a guitar solo over synth pads. With the addition of bass and drums, there are more things happening musically and interactively. For instance, on the surface it sounds as if Bobby is merely playing a simple bass–snare–bass–snare pattern, as some drummers might do. But notice how he incorporates the rhythm of Tony's melody and plays a little tom hit at 0:17 and an "extra" bass drum hit at 0:18 right along with him. Then at 0:27, he and Geezer hit a syncopated note together. It's these little things that take what could be a very boring texture and make it something aurally interesting.

Tony's guitar solo is phrased very patiently (e.g., the note at 0:10 lasts until 0:14, and then there's a two-second pause); the artfully executed bends are an important aspect thereof. The first note of the solo is bent up, and at 0:05–0:06, he releases the bend downward. These sigh-like bend releases (another one at 0:21) give a nice, smooth shape to the contour by keeping it from being too angular. I especially like how he hits a note at 0:26, bends it up and back down at 0:27, and then sustains the note into the chord at 0:28 to create a lush harmony. He also colors his solo by altering timbre, like the partial harmonics at 0:42 and 0:54. Repetition is used sparsely but effectively (e.g., the lick at 0:49 immediately repeated at 0:50). The solo mixes long, slow tones (e.g., 0:10) with faster licks (e.g., 0:45). His rhythms are more free than rigid, letting Bobby's consistent hi-hat be the anchor of time.

The combination of the synth pads and the guitar solo give it a Journey-like texture, but there are other elements at play that seem to echo Neal Schon and Jonathan Cain. The chord progression is like "Who's Crying Now," only slightly changed and reordered. There are some melodic moments that evoke "Send Her My Love" (0:34–0:39). The way Tony bends and sustains the note, and the way it relates to the supporting chord, is something Neal does (as do countless other players, of course)—for example, the ends of the first two phrases of the "Who's Crying Now" solo. These observations may be more abstract than literal, but it's important to acknowledge Iommi and the others as multifaceted musicians.

The transition from the intro to the verse section is cleverly smooth thanks to Geezer. The repeated chord pattern (0:01–0:10, 0:10–0:19, etc.) gives the expectation of going back to the first chord, and it could loop indefinitely. Thus, the ear expects the chord from 0:01 to return at 0:56, but all we get is a crash from Bobby. After a brief pause, Geezer gives us the note we expect to hear (1:00). However, Iommi plays a different chord, yet one that includes Geezer's note. The song has changed key almost imperceptibly thanks to Geezer. He plays a brief bass solo, gradually descending from that pivot note to a much lower note for the start of the verse.

Geezer's low note (0:11, 0:27, 0:29, and 0:38) means that he is probably playing a five-string as on "Computer God." The low and slow dramatic slide at 3:29 almost confirms that. His tone is different, and perhaps it's a chorus to give it the smooth sound of a fretless. At 1:33, he plays a short lick in the upper register of the bass, and with that tone, it is reminiscent of Bob in "The Shining." Geezer utilizes the full range of his instrument—low to high—but never abuses the outer extremities.

At 1:53, the key change is much less subtle than at 1:00. This abrupt-but-not-too-distant change helps to propel the energy into the chorus, but it is still "light." The addition of drums here also helps build the energy. When the music changes key for the second verse, it is less abrupt and acts to relax the music slightly. As expected, it changes key for the second chorus, which of course is not as abrupt because it had already happened. It retains the same key for the heavy riff (3:23), making the change in heaviness and loudness, not the harmony, the focal point. At 3:41, the song changes key yet again, arriving at the fourth different key used in the song. This section is brief, only eighteen seconds long, and features a simple, direct guitar melody. The key change back to the verse is fairly abrupt, but Martin keeps Iommi's directness and energy (3:59). The final key change comes at 4:18 for the final chorus, and by now it sounds expected and natural. The reasons for these gradations of abruptness are beyond the scope of the book, but understanding where and why a band would change keys helps illuminate deeper musical meaning.

At 2:13, Tony sings an Alice in Chains–like vocal harmony part. It sounds similar to that band for the same reasons it did in "Virtual Death": register, scale used, and the way the background part relates/interacts to the lead part. The scale implied by Tony's vocal parts is the same one used by Iommi when evoking a jazz style (Dorian), but clearly this music sounds nothing like jazz. The background vocal part follows his lead part but is lower. Although this is a centuries-old technique (similar to *fauxbourdon*), we tend to relate this instead to Alice in Chains because *Cross Purposes* was released only two years after *Dirt* and the same year as *Jar of Flies*.

The whole song seems to lead to the final chorus (4:53–5:30). Instead of ending the song with a double chorus as do so many pop songs, they fuse the elements from the "heavy" section (3:23–3:40), the verse (1:17, 2:11, and 3:59), and the chorus (1:53, 2:47, and 4:17) to create a new, heavy version of the chorus. The listener expects the heavy section to return at 4:53 because it came in the last time they played the chorus.

The heavy riff does come in at 4:53, but they artfully incorporate the verse riff at 4:55 and the chorus riff at 4:57. This combinatorial section sounds like the goal of the song: its climactic point. Tony sings his highest note of the song at 5:23, giving additional emphasis to this section.

"Back to Eden" starts off with a classic Sabbath blues-inspired-style riff with elements of a funk-rock feel but not to the extent of, say, Red Hot Chili Peppers. The bluesy riff faintly sounds like the Band of Gypsys' "Who Knows" riff but played with straight rhythms and is less funky and more rock. On the topic of funkiness, listen for the abrupt syncopated tight breaks at 2:29 and 3:50; this is not something Sabbath does, so I wonder if this was Bobby's influence as the newest member. Likewise, check out his three syncopated hi-hat/bass drum accents at 3:27. Not all of the drumming is funk oriented on this track; his fill at 3:38 (six snare hits and then six bass drum hits) sounds like something Cozy would play (cf. 5:24 in "Headless Cross").

"The Hand That Rocks the Cradle" is about Beverly Allitt, a children's nurse at a hospital in England who, in May 1993, was convicted of murdering four of her patients and attempting to kill nine more. "The hand that rocks the cradle" that should "save, not steal, a life," as Martin's lyrics say, is Beverly, and the "young life" is of course the children. The music already has a very serious tone (e.g., the synth, guitar, and bass intro), but knowing the meaning behind the lyrics makes the song creepier. As in "Virtual Death," Iommi calls writing the music a "joint effort" with Geezer.[6] The main riff (0:54) is a single-line riff (i.e., not using chords), so considering his riffs such as "A National Acrobat," it makes sense that Geezer would have contributed to the writing.

"Cardinal Sin," or "Sin Cardinal Sin" as it was supposed to have been labeled on the album, is about Eamon Casey, an Irish Catholic bishop who, in 1992, was exposed for having a secret love affair in 1973 that produced a son. The woman said that exposing Bishop Casey was about his lack of financial support, his hypocrisy, how celibacy doesn't work, and showing "the human side of priests."[7] Tony's lyric "you're no better than the rest of the human race" addresses this hypocrisy. The intro is made dramatic with big, heavy chords in the guitar and synth choir, accented by drums and bass. The harmonies are also dramatic because of the way they relate to one another, like the chords in "The Battle of

Tyr," a piece that also has a symphonic-like texture. Keeping with the symphonic sound, the verse riff (0:26) is very similar to Led Zeppelin's "Kashmir." For the long tones at 1:08 and 1:32, the heavily processed guitar tone almost sounds like a synth (like the synth-y long tones in "Eternal Idol"). At 2:10, Bobby plays a big drum fill to bring in the faster tempo (182 bpm), which is about two and a half times as fast as the first part of the song. Thus, when they drop into half time at 2:23, it is still faster than the first part, effectively giving the song three distinct feels. Geezer plays especially well on this track, such as the five-second-long fill during Tony's guitar solo (3:37). Bobby and Geezer interact naturally, for instance, at 0:57 when they both suddenly go into a triplet rhythm after playing the first minute of the song with straight rhythms. The drum fill at 1:55 is a good example of Bobby accenting in unusual places, creating an interesting syncopated rhythm in the crash cymbals. With the use of pinch harmonics, palm-muted melodic lines, and other elements, the guitar solo (3:16) has echoes of Eddie Van Halen, and I wonder if this solo was recorded after having done "Evil Eye." Listen, for instance, for the bends, rhythm, and vibrato in the phrase at 3:27. Iommi's style had evolved over the previous fifteen years, and there are plenty of instances of pinch harmonics on *Dehumanizer*. The solo fades out at 3:42 as if he wanted to continue with another cycle through the riff.

The album ends with "Evil Eye," a song that Eddie Van Halen helped write on the day he came to rehearsal. Martin said Eddie cowrote it, and Geoff said that Eddie "put quite a bit of work into it" but that Iommi "reworked the track."[8] Songwriting credits went to Geezer and the two Tonys but not Eddie. He was thanked in the liner notes, however. After a classic Sabbath-sounding riff, a brief guitar solo is heard before the first verse begins. The lick at 0:15–0:17 sounds very Van Halen–like for its particular style of bends, vibrato, and treatment of the timbre (the partial feedback/harmonic squeals), but then not so much for the next ten seconds. A similar lick at 1:30–1:32 also is in the Van Halen style (e.g., 0:25 in "Eruption"). The opening lick of the second solo (1:24–1:30) is very Iommi-like, especially how the melodic line emerges out of the riff. The breakdown at 3:17 allows the listener to truly hear Geezer's tone and how much vibrato he uses when he plays (i.e., the bends and shakiness of the pitch, e.g., at 3:22). Out of the breakdown returns the main riff, but this time it is harmonized by an additional guitar as done in "A National Acrobat" and "Supernaut." In fact, the riff starts like the "A National Acrobat" riff but without the swung rhythms.

The Eddie Van Halen Mystery

Fans have speculated that Van Halen played the solos on the album, assuming he was uncredited for contractual reasons. Geoff said, "I don't think that first solo is Eddie because Tony redid that again and again so [he] probably just duplicated what Eddie had done before."[9] Iommi wouldn't have had Eddie's solo as a reference, because he said they did not record the rehearsal. Geoff said that Tony learned the parts that Eddie came up with so he could record them in the studio, so maybe Sabbath did record the rehearsal session that day and Tony had forgotten. By the time Sabbath entered Monnow Valley Studios to record the album, Eddie was probably back in LA resting and gearing up for the U.S. leg of Van Halen's tour. It is highly unlikely he would have flown to Wales to record a few brief solos, but it is possible that he recorded the solos in an LA studio and shipped the tapes overseas. Bobby said he was "under the impression" that Eddie played on the track, thinking that it was "probably done later." "Sure sounds like him," he continued.[10] Martin said Eddie played on it, but maybe he was "under the impression" as well. Bobby wasn't there when the guitar solos were recorded, but it seems that Geoff was present, based on his comments. Considering Geoff's explanation of Tony learning Eddie's parts and recording the opening solo in multiple takes, it seems it was indeed Tony playing on the track but that he used some of the aforementioned Van Halen–isms as a sort of "hat tip" to Eddie.

An additional song from these sessions, titled "What's the Use," appeared on the Japanese release of *Cross Purposes*. It starts off with a Cozy-like fill (cf. "Heaven in Black" and Rainbow's "Stargazer") and heads into up-tempo, heavy riffing. Oddly enough, Tony sings with some Ronnie-like inflections such as the vibrato and distinctive growl.

CROSS PURPOSES TOUR AND TYR REUNION

At the time Sabbath wrote and recorded *Cross Purposes*, negotiations for a reunion with Ozzy Osbourne were underway, until he backed out of the deal in August. The album was completed by summer, but it was not released until early the next year. Sabbath toured from February to June 1994 promoting *Cross Purposes*. The April 13 concert in London was recorded and released as a CD/VHS combo pack titled *Cross Purposes—Live* in 1995. The set list is a mix of Ozzy-, Ronnie-, and Martin-era songs, even including a performance of "The Wizard" with Martin playing the harmonica part. It's an opportunity to hear Bobby interpret drum parts originally played by Bill, Cozy, and Vinny and to hear Geezer approach songs originally played by Laurence and Neil ("Anno Mundi" on the VHS and "Headless Cross" on the CD and VHS). Contractual disagreements found Bobby off the dates in South America, so Bill came back to play the final four performances.

After the *Cross Purposes* tour, Geezer left, and the *Tyr* lineup reunited to make another album. Management suggested they enlist Ernie C (Body Count) to produce the next record, and Iommi said they were "talked into it."[11] Body Count is a Sabbath-influenced heavy metal band fronted by rapper Ice-T, yet his vocals were only quasi-rap with that group. Ernie said Iommi came to Sheffield to hear the band, and they talked about doing something together. This must have been Body Count's October 1, 1994, concert, only four weeks after Sabbath finished their brief South American tour.

Later that month, the band went to Bluestone Studios in Pembrokeshire County (West Wales) to work up material for the new album. Ernie came to some of the songwriting sessions to offer direction. Neil said Cozy wanted to "work the songs out" but that Ernie preferred what he called an "organic" approach.[12] Iommi said the songwriting was done mostly among Geoff, Martin, and himself, as Cozy and Neil weren't present all the time. Cozy was much more involved with *Headless Cross* and *Tyr*, having composed and produced with Iommi on those albums. Cozy explains, "I came in a bit late for this one so basically just went in and did my thing, kept my mouth shut."[13] The liner notes said "all songs by Black Sabbath," but the American Society of Composers, Authors and Publishers (ASCAP) credits various combinations of band members, which may offer some insight into the creation, so they are listed below. The liner notes say that lyrics were by Martin, with the exception of "The Illusion of Power," which was credited to Ice-T as well. Neil said, "Cozy wanted *Headless Cross* Part III but the record company were very resistant to that. Tony Iommi didn't want that either. He thought that style was all a bit old hat and eighties."[14] Iommi said they rehearsed for three weeks coming up with ideas. Then, Tony would sing over what they had written to come up with the vocal parts and lyrics. He tried a new process that involved no pen or paper, just coming up with lyrics and vocal melodies by singing. This sounds similar to how Ozzy came up with vocal ideas before Geezer would revise. Martin said that Paul Banfield, Sabbath's manager, suggested they include Ice-T as a guest vocalist. He appears on the opening track, "The Illusion of Power."

In early December, the band went to Parr Street Studios in Liverpool to record the album. Iommi said it was recorded in only eight days, explaining that they "wanted a live feel, to get back to setting up and just playing," rather than having the band record separately, overdubbing their parts.[15] Without the rest of the band, he went to LA to mix the album, but the studio was flooded so they mixed at Ridge Farm in England instead (where they began writing *Technical Ecstasy* and likely recorded the *Wayne's World* version of "Time Machine"). The liner notes state that additional recording was done at Devonshire Studios, the North Hollywood studio where Body Count mixed their 1994 album *Born Dead*. Rather than flying Ice-T to Liverpool, maybe they recorded Ice-T's vocal parts there. Iommi in another interview states the album was done in ten days, not eight, so perhaps the Devonshire sessions were some guitar overdubs done in a couple days before it flooded.

FORBIDDEN

The stately intro to "The Illusion of Power" features guitars with added light percussion, including a couple of tam-tam hits at 0:19 and 0:27. When it suddenly changes key for the verse riff (0:36), the guitar goes higher, but the bass goes lower—the space between the two instruments uncommon for Sabbath. Neil plays notes only available to a five-string or a detuned four-string bass, making it especially heavy and full.

Notice how Neil bends the string in a Geezer-like fashion, following Tony's string bends, an aspect integral to the riff. The verse begins at 0:52 with Tony using his speak-singing (*sprechstimme*) voice (cf. 2:16 in "Ancient Warrior"). Guest vocalist Ice-T performs a spoken-word part in the first half of the bridge section (2:24–2:38). It is not rap, as it lacks the rhythmical and rhyming aspects found in that vocal style. Ice-T's vocals are slowed down in places (e.g., the laughs at 3:56); compare Body Count's "Masters of Revenge" on *Born Dead* (1994), which also has slowed-down vocals and laughs. The contour, the bends, and the chromatic nature of the verse riff lend itself well for Tony's *sprechstimme* vocals and sounds like a riff Geezer would have come up with. Thus, I was not surprised to find out that he is credited as a cowriter in ASCAP with Ice-T and both Tonys. With Geezer's input, riffs from this song likely dated back to the *Cross Purposes* or *Dehumanizer* writing sessions.

The first half of the main riff to "Get a Grip" (0:00–0:01) is similar to the main "Zero the Hero" riff and is only slightly (about 8 percent) faster than the 1983 song. Cozy plays a double-bass-drum-driven fill at the end of the second bridge (2:58) to set up a double-time feel at 3:00, and they stay at the faster tempo for the remainder of the song. As in "Black Sabbath," "Heaven and Hell," and "The Sabbath Stones," they switch to fast tempo about three-fourths of the way through the song and stay there, giving it a climactic feeling to the final part. It is very heavy and intensified by the low note from Neil's five-string at 3:04 and 3:09. Like "I Won't Cry For You" and "Forbidden," this song is only credited to the Tonys on ASCAP.

Iommi's first note in "Can't Get Close Enough" is the lowest he ever played Sabbath, studio or live. His lowest string is three whole steps below standard tuning, twice as far as they had detuned in the seventies (e.g., "Sabbath, Bloody Sabbath")! It makes the intro sound especially rich. Martin's entrance (0:09) clarifies the harmonic ambiguity of the incomplete chords of Iommi's intro. The harmony takes a slight turn for the brief chorus (0:26–0:34), its first part not unlike the bridge in "Tomorrow's Dream." Tony's vocal melody elegantly navigates the new harmonies, ending on the note with which he started. Like "Lucy in the Sky with Diamonds," the music is in a fast "three" (168 bpm) but felt like a slow "one" (56 bpm). It changes to a moderate "four" feel (124 bpm) for Iommi's heavy riff, of which the first half (1:24–1:26) is like the heavy riff of the second part of "Megalomania." It sounds especially heavy because of his very low bottom string. The use of the seven-string guitar was becoming popular in heavy metal in the early nineties, so it's not surprising that such a low note would appear in a Sabbath riff in 1995. It drops into half time (62 bpm) for the chorus (2:11, 3:05, and 3:20). Notice how the harmony is basically the same, but Iommi plays heavy power chords instead. It's clever how they transformed the chorus into the new tempo and meter while keeping the same vocal melody and essentially the same harmony. When they abruptly return to the intro material at 3:27, it sounds surprisingly smooth and natural. Another thing to notice is Ernie C's production on the vocal effects, for example, the delay on "away," giving the sense that he fades away into the distance (0:35, 1:19, etc.). This track is credited to Cozy, Geoff, and both Tonys on ASCAP.

"Shaking Off the Chains" begins with an atonal riff from Iommi, soon joined by Neil in the bottom register of his bass. The vocals in a way harmonize the riff, but his line does not help clarify the uncertainty of key. Also unsettling is the unusual meter of "seven" (172–175 bpm). The meter "evens out" to a standard "four" rock feel (90 bpm) at 0:39 to give some stability, but the atonal quality remains throughout this highly dissonant section. The relative instability of the key and meter give the music tension, something they maintain until 1:29 when a new riff clearly establishes a key and when Cozy takes the band into a double-time feel (180 bpm). When the opening riff returns at 3:11, it doesn't sound as atonal because we hear it in context of the middle section. Iommi's solo explores this idea by sometimes suggesting a key and incorporating atonal ideas at other times (e.g., 3:52). Another thing to listen for is how Neil's active bass line complements Iommi's riff instead of merely doubling it (1:29–2:11). Curiously, neither this track, "Rusty Angels," nor "Sick and Tired" are registered with ASCAP.

Geoff starts "I Won't Cry for You" with what sounds like a Korg 01/W electric guitar sound, and his synth pad accentuates the descending three-note figure (0:01–0:03). Neil follows the synth pad part at 0:09, with the occasional ornament (0:15 and 0:32). The music builds gradually, Tony sings higher, and they reach a heavy chorus by 1:14. They bring the volume and energy back down—but add Cozy—for another verse and chorus, and build it up again. At 3:24 the music changes key for a brief guitar solo using the chord progression from the bridge and solo of "You Won't Change Me." They descend a tritone for a surprise chord at 3:51 to send it back to the original key, a transition that is aided by Tony's vocal line on "cry" (3:53). Cozy's bass drum–heavy fill at 3:50–3:54 adds an exclamation point to this middle section.

"Guilty as Hell" harkens back to Sabbath's eighties style with Neil's pulsating pedal bass part and Cozy's simple bass–snare–bass–snare drumbeat. Considering style, it's the "Headless Cross III" as Neil described, but on the production side of things, it lacks the eighties gated drum sound of Headless Cross, so it sounds more nineties. That intro bass part isn't entirely stationary; listen for when Neil and Tony play the four-note "Heaven and Hell" lick at the end of the riff (0:09). A highlight of the song happens at the start of the middle section when they base a new riff off of a little motif from the verse (e.g., 0:26–0:27). Neil and Tony transform it into a six-note motif (2:08–2:10) and shift it down twice (2:11–2:13 and 2:13–2:16) to create one long, chromatic riff (2:08–2:16). As with the "chromatic" riff in "All Moving Parts (Stand Still)," it uses ten different pitches, which, as mentioned in chapter 4, is far more than normal for Sabbath. This track is credited to Geoff and both Tonys on ASCAP.

Cozy's drum fill at the beginning of "Sick and Tired" may easily trick the ear in the same way his intro to "Heaven in Black" does. Notice how similar the second half of the fill (0:03–0:06) is to the opening fill of "Heaven in Black." Thus, it could be setting up a fast triplet-galloping rocker like "Heaven in Black" but faster (160 bpm) as in "In for the Kill." But his fast rhythms seem to imply he is setting up a fast rocker (240 bpm) such as "Turn to Stone," "Immaculate Deception," or "The Law Maker," or perhaps it suggests a medium rock song at half that speed (120 bpm) such as "Lady Evil." This fill is actually setting up none of these three likely possibilities but instead is setting up a moderately slow blues shuffle at 80 bpm, with its inner pulse at about 240. The riff comes in at a slightly slower pace (75 bpm) at 0:06. The lyrics, by Geoff and Martin, have a double meaning: romantic relationships and the music business. If a listener or performer is "sick and tired" of a typical blues chord progression, that isn't the case here because the main riff, verses, and solo are in different keys, giving the ear a bit of variety.

With the absence of drums, the opening riff and vocal phrase of "Rusty Angels" make it uncertain if the song will be slow (about 74 bpm) or fast (about 148 bpm), as it could go either way. If it were seventies-era Sabbath, Bill and Geezer would almost certainly choose the former and play at a "Sweet Leaf"–like pace. When Cozy and Neil enter, they choose the latter for a pace similar to "Hard Life to Love." One of the big differences with post-Ozzy Sabbath is the predilection for faster tempos. Adding emphasis for the chorus, they drop into half-time feel (1:19–1:45). Here, they use a variation of the "Gimme Some Lovin'" chord progression (Spencer Davis Group, 1966), a variation of the "House of the Rising Sun" chord progression. Notice the top two notes of Tony's guitar chords ringing out, one string at a time (e.g., at 1:24 just before the second "rusty angels"). For Iommi, long, sustained, arpeggiated chords usually imply a half-time feel (cf. the final few minutes of "Dirty Women"). The song sounds as if it could end at 2:50—and for many bands it would—but Sabbath continues with a bridge and solo before going into a final chorus and outro solo. Martin's idea for "rusty angels" came from seeing a picture of one of the so-called airplane boneyards, or aircraft graveyards.

Like "Guilty as Hell," the title track "Forbidden" has remnants of eighties Sabbath, but it has elements of an early nineties style as well. For example, the prominent use of the synth pads in the verse gives it an eighties sound. Neil's pulsating pedal bass in the verses and Cozy's drumming throughout most of the song is stylistically eighties. Conversely, the brief bits at 1:47–1:48 and 1:56–1:59 sound very current for its time (cf. Alice in Chains, Soundgarden, etc.). Tony's bottom string is tuned down two whole steps, which is lower than in the seventies, but not as low as "Can't Get Close Enough." The low note can be heard in the intro riff (0:01, 0:04, and 0:06) and on the first of every four beats in the main riff (0:10, 0:12, 0:15, etc.). Perhaps this was Ernie C's influence to help give it a more nineties sound, as seven-string and tuned-down guitars were more common at the time.

At over six minutes in duration, which isn't remarkably long for Sabbath, "Kiss of Death" is the longest track on *Forbidden*. Like some of their Ozzy-era songs, it is quite involved, having seven different riffs in five distinct sections. Once it goes to the bridge at 3:00, it doesn't return to the earlier material until 5:25, giving the feeling of having a middle part lasting nearly as long as the first part of the song. Although there are moments in the rest of the album that are more remarkable, this is *Forbidden*'s most ambitious track and, I think, the most structurally interesting. I find it very noteworthy that it is the only song on the album credited to all five members on ASCAP. Could this have been the only true, total collaborative effort on the album? Maybe that's why I find it to be the most intriguing.

There are several similarities to "The Sign of the Southern Cross," starting with the guitar intro. Although the chords are different, the key, timbre, tempo, and general mood are the same. Both songs feature an eight-second guitar phrase that is repeated for the intro and opening verse. In the first half of the verse (0:17–0:31), Tony sings in the same register as Ronnie. There are also similarities in the two songs' melodies. For instance, compare Tony's "just another life" (0:26–0:27) to Ronnie's "then how can I know what" and "somehow must reflect." Geoff plays some long synth string pads, and Neil plays melodically in the upper register of his bass.

The next section, a postverse riff, comes in loudly at 0:53. Not only does the sudden boost of volume heighten the song, but also its slightly (7.5 percent) faster tempo gives it an extra bit of energy. The riff begins with two exclamatory hits, the same rhythm as the hits in "War Pigs" or the middle section of "The Sign of the Southern Cross" (4:08). The riff is similar to the chorus of "I Won't Cry for You" in that it starts with held chords (0:53–0:54), then several fast hits in the second quarter of the riff (0:55–0:56), and then held chords in the latter half (0:57–1:00). In both riffs, the several hits occur immediately after beat "three." At 1:13 and 2:16, Tony hits a certain chord against Neil's sustaining note, which also happens in the middle part of "Southern Cross" (4:04).

The volume comes down, and the tempo drops to the original 59 bpm for a second verse. The melody and chords are different, so one could think of this as the first verse; and the opening, as an intro verse. Tony uses the electric guitar instead of acoustic and picks at half the rate as he did for the intro. The repeated guitar part is sixteen seconds long instead of eight, and the latter half (1:32–1:39) uses the "James Bond theme" chords (the distinctive moving notes at the top of his chord). The vocal melody is different, but it resembles the earlier verse and "Southern Cross." For instance, compare Tony's melody on "you tried to touch me" (1:24–1:26) to Ronnie's "isn't light where no one." This section is colored with Geoff's synth string pads and two little guitar bits, mostly in the right channel (1:37 and then lower at 1:47).

The postverse riff returns, so the music becomes louder and slightly (7 percent) faster. The volume and tempo drop for another verse at 2:27. The vocal melody here is essentially the same as the verse from 1:24. Tony uses almost exactly the same vocal phrasing for the last line (2:53–3:00) as it appeared before (1:49–1:56), as they share the same lyrics. At 2:34, the extra right-channel guitar continues its descent from 1:37 to 1:47, but it returns to the high register at 2:50. Geoff's synth is suddenly loud in the mix at 2:31 and again at 2:44, and Cozy adds some cymbal work at 2:43 and 2:51.

Instead of another postverse riff, they go to a bridge that is also loud and slightly (9 percent) faster. Iommi's first chord (3:00–3:01) might sound familiar, as he has used it in a similar way in several songs, but most prominently at the beginning of his solo intro to "Black Sabbath" in live performances (e.g., *Live Evil*). His third chord and the last melody note of Martin's "before" (3:05) imply that the music has changed key. The key change is so subtle that it takes seven seconds for the ear to realize it (3:00–3:07). Remarkably, the bridge for "Southern Cross" (3:48–3:56) does the same subtle change, and both songs transition back in the same way (compare 3:20–3:22 here to 3:53–3:56 in "Southern Cross"). A combination of key change, Martin's highest notes (3:01 and then even higher at 3:16), and the fastest tempo thus far, give this section a heightened feeling.

The next section (3:22–3:57) starts with the two ascending hits as in the postverse riff, but with the chords from "War Pigs" and "Southern Cross," and continues with three descending hits as in "Sweet Leaf" (3:25). The tempo has gradually crept up to 66 bpm by now, stimulating the music. Cozy's best drumming on the album can be heard in this section. He plays hits with Neil and Tony as most drummers would (e.g., 3:36), but instead of playing a standard rock beat in the remaining space, he plays some interesting fills (3:30–3:32, 3:38–3:40, and 3:46–3:47). As the last chord rings, Cozy's ride cymbal continues, and other layers of ride cymbals are superimposed.

Iommi introduces another riff at 3:28 in a much faster tempo: 136 bpm. His rhythms here are interesting as some divide each beat into threes (as in "Black Moon," "Devil and Daughter," "Children of the Grave," or the end of "Black Sabbath"), and some divide each beat into fours (as in the fast part of "Iron Man"). This is also how it's played in the demo for the album. When Cozy enters, he plays a rock beat that implies only the latter, so his rhythmical feel is incongruent with what the guitar is doing. It seems they never were in agreement about the groove because in the demo, it sounds as if Neil sometimes follows the "threes" of the guitar and other times follows Cozy's feel. Moreover, at 4:05, Cozy and Neil enter at 5 percent faster (143 bpm) than what the guitar was doing, so the feel is even more unsettling. I suspect the odd use of the layers of ride cymbals from 3:53 to 4:05 was to intentionally obscure the guitar riff so it didn't sound so out of place when Cozy and Neil enter. This fast section alternates between two riffs, and Tony sings over the other one, his verses split into two parts (4:19–4:26 and 4:32–4:39). The section from 3:32 comes back at 4:52 with the same vocal parts; it has a feeling of a chorus for its heightened quality and for the simple fact that it returns. Again, Cozy has some of his best work showcased in this section (5:00–5:01, 5:07–5:09, and 5:15–5:16).

At 5:25, it goes back to the very beginning, but slightly (7 percent) faster, retaining some of the energy of the middle part (3:00–5:24). Tony sings the same lyrics and vocal melody as before but only the first half. Thus, it ends on the lowest note of the song on the word "time." As a play on the lyric, the sound of a ticking clock is heard and fades away as the album comes to a close.

FORBIDDEN TOUR AND THE END OF AN ERA

Forbidden was released in June 1995. After a couple of festival perfor-mances in Europe, Sabbath left for the United States and Canada for a five-week summer tour. I remember seeing the *Forbidden* tour T-shirt for sale in my neighborhood rock T-shirt store. My hometown was listed on the back as one of the cities, and I was thoroughly disap-pointed they never came, as it would have been my first Sabbath con-cert. They ended that leg of the tour just prior to that never-to-be Las Vegas concert in LA, which was Cozy's last show. Bobby attended that concert and rejoined the band for the remainder of the tour. It wasn't a surprise to those in the band, as Bobby met with Iommi in Manhattan well in advance (either five weeks prior, just before the New Haven, Connecticut, concert, or three weeks prior on July 10 when they played Manhattan). Audio and video footage exist from the tour, including some with Cozy and some with Bobby. By the end of autumn, the tour ended, and this version of the band was no more.

There has yet to be a reunion of a Martin-led Sabbath, though various Sabbath alumni have worked together since 1995. For instance, Bobby, Neil, and Martin did an album together, Rondinelli's *Our Cross Our Sins* (2002), and Geoff has been involved in Martin's solo work, studio and live concerts. Cozy, Geoff, and Martin recorded the song "Raising Hell" for Martin's 2005 solo CD *Scream*. However, the drum tracks were recorded in 1992 when Martin and Cozy worked together in Hammer, so it's not as if this is a "reunion." The reason for the thirteen-year gap is that Cozy died in a car accident in 1998. Iommi said in March 2016 that he would like to record a couple of new songs with Martin for rereleases of *Headless Cross* and *Tyr*, but those plans have yet to materialize.

10

REUNIONS WITH OZZY AND THE END

The first reunion of the original lineup of Black Sabbath was the *Live Aid* concert on July 13, 1985. The set consisted of only three songs ("Children of the Grave," "Iron Man," and "Paranoid"), as there were numerous acts as part of the benefit festival. Plans to continue the reunion never came into fruition; Ozzy Osbourne and Geezer Butler returned to their solo careers, Tony Iommi made *Seventh Star*, and Bill Ward eventually made his solo album *Ward One: Along the Way* (1990).

Seven years later, Ozzy toured to promote his 1991 album *No More Tears* billed as his farewell tour, "No More Tours." With the expectation that Ozzy would retire, Bill, Geezer, and Tony joined him for a reunion for the final night of Ozzy's tour, November 15, 1992. This set was slightly longer at four songs: "Black Sabbath," "Fairies Wear Boots," "Iron Man," and "Paranoid." Their performance of "Black Sabbath" was released on Ozzy's *Live and Loud* album and VHS (later DVD).

Ozzy's retirement did not last long, and by 1997 he had reunited with Geezer and Tony for over twenty dates on the Ozzfest '97 tour. Geoff remained on keyboards and likely occasional backing vocals and rhythm guitars. On drums was Mike Bordin, who also played in Ozzy's solo band on the tour. Shannon Larkin (Ugly Kid Joe) filled in on drums for one date, as Mike was unavailable that evening. Shannon said the experience was "one of the best things that ever happened to me in my whole life."[1]

Later that year, Bill joined up with the band for a full reunion. They performed two nights in Birmingham, and the performance was recorded and released on *Reunion* in 1998. Geezer said, "I don't think I felt that much energy and felt so alive in years."[2] Their performance of "Iron Man" on this album was awarded a Grammy Award for Best Metal Performance. They recorded two studio tracks for *Reunion*, "Psycho Man" and "Selling My Soul," in April and May at A&M Studios in LA, produced by Bob Marlette. Unlike their seventies songs where songwriting credits went to the full band, these two songs were credited only to Ozzy and Tony, so Bill and Geezer's involvement in the writing process was likely minimal. Bob was also given writing credit with the American Society of Composers, Authors and Publishers (ASCAP) for "Psycho Man," the first studio track recorded by the original four members in two decades. "Selling My Soul" was the first Sabbath studio track to use a drum machine. Apparently, they were not pleased with Bill's recorded parts, so they programmed the drum parts instead.

With twenty years since *Never Say Die!*, "Psycho Man" was a highly anticipated studio track. They answer their decades-long silence with the classic Sabbath style. The song opens with the chorus riff, heavy as ever. This comes as no surprise, especially considering Geezer's heavier-than-Sabbath solo albums *Plastic Planet* and *Black Science* released in the years leading up to it. Bill is bashing away, accenting with crash cymbals and snare drum and giving an earthy pulse on the bass drum and toms. Just before the end of the riff (0:20), Bill hits a cowbell, and at 0:21, the chord is held out. After three cymbal hits, Bill and Ozzy lead into the first verse (0:25). The verse is very subdued, due in part to Ozzy singing in his low register. The first couple of lines are in the same register as the soft parts of "Hand of Doom." He goes even lower for "when he appears" (0:36) in the same baritone register as the end of "Never Say Die," but even lower for "when" and the first syllable of "appears." Ozzy jumps to his medium-high register for the chorus (0:59) when the band kicks in, just as in "Hand of Doom." The vocals are doubled in the lower register, as in "The Writ" and "Megalomania," but this is done naturally instead of tape-speed or electronic manipulation. Additional overdubbed vocals provide a second melody line ("psycho man"). For the second verse (1:18), there are two Ozzys: one low and the other in his medium register. When the chorus returns

(1:32), there are multiple Ozzys (low and medium-high registers) as it was done in the first chorus.

The tempo picks up slightly (less than 8 percent) for the postchorus riff (2:12), just enough to increase momentum into the guitar solo. Here, Bill plays the pulse on the bass drum, accents on snare drum and toms, and the occasional crash cymbal. He approaches the drum kit the same way as the intro but offers more interesting rhythms. The tempo is a hair faster in the solo, which continues over the postchorus riff (3:00).

The last note of the solo is held over into part two of the song (3:08). The guitar in the right channel plays a new riff at a new tempo over two and a half times as fast (158 from 60 beats per minute [bpm]). A second guitar enters in the left channel at 3:17, and Bill and Geezer enter at 3:22. At 3:23, Bill plays a half-time feel, so it becomes a medium-slow groove (79 bpm), still considerably faster than the first three minutes of the song (54 to 60 bpm). Here, Ozzy sings a third verse in his medium register, the same as "Children of the Grave," for example.

The postverse/refrain section that follows has two riffs over which Ozzy repeats the refrain "when he's killed again." The first (3:47–3:56) functions in a similar way to the chorus of part two of "Megalomania" (4:17, 5:29, 6:10, and 7:21) in that the chord leaps up and walks back down (their blues and rock 'n' roll roots are present but dressed in metal). The second (3:56–4:14) includes full-band hits that are repeated at the end as Ozzy holds out "again." Bill stops at 4:14, and Tony's chord sustains. At 4:19, Ozzy yells "watch out," and the main riff of part two starts up again. This is another similarity to "Megalomania," when Ozzy yelled "stick me" and the main riff of part two restarted (4:35). All that's missing from that section of the 1975 song is Bill's incessant cowbell, although we did hear it once in the intro.

The riff is only heard twice before Bill and Geezer come in (4:25), and instead of playing the half-time feel as at 3:23, Bill keeps the faster feel of Tony's riff. At 4:31, Sabbath does something they hadn't done before: they bring back the chorus from part one, yet they stay in the new tempo and use the new riff. In other words they use part two material to accompany vocal parts from part one. Ozzy sings the chorus melodies at about 50 percent faster to match the new tempo. By singing the melody at a considerably faster tempo over a different feel and riff, they reinterpret the chorus and give it a different character. This is not unlike when the guitar bends from the opening of "Iron Man" are reinterpreted in the fast part at the end, or when the verse in "Sins of the Father" comes back near the end. Also, the chorus has two components: the background "he's the angel of death" and the foreground "psycho man." This time, unlike before, the background part is heard first; then at 4:44 the "psycho man" part comes in on top of it. It is a very clever way of bringing back a chorus and making it sound fresh.

The other track on *Reunion*, "Selling My Soul," is musically less involved, perhaps due to limited input by Bill and Geezer. The main riff is used for the verse and guitar solo, and the chorus is in two parts. There are no postverse riffs, interludes, bridges, or other ancillary sections that Sabbath usually uses. The drum machine programming was quite good in that it sounds like what a drummer would play. Some of the parts are very much like Bill in style, and I wonder if it was programmed based on what he had recorded. What is very uncharacteristic of Sabbath and Bill, however, is that the song remains at the same tempo throughout, exactly 60 bpm the entire song. If they had dropped the tempo a bit for the first part of the chorus (the relaxed, lighter bit) and sped up during the guitar solo, it would have sounded more natural, more Sabbath-like and more Bill-like. The slight changes in tempo that Sabbath does from section to section give the music life. On my car is a bumper sticker that reads, "Drum Machines Have No Soul"; I suppose if a drum machine were used, a title "Selling My Soul" would be most appropriate.

Bill suffered a heart attack before the release of *Reunion*, so Vinny Appice was brought in for the summer 1998 European tour. In addition to his keyboard work, Geoff Nicholls can be heard on background vocals on bootlegs from this tour. Bill was back in the band by fall for a performance on the *Late Show with David Letterman*, and they toured throughout 1999 with some dates as headline act, and other dates as part of the Ozzfest '99 tour. Some of the dates from that tour were filmed and released on VHS and DVD as *The Last Supper*. It is an excellent document of how the original lineup sounded and looked at the end of the millennium. Vinny was present backstage on the tour in case Bill had health problems, but he never had to play.

In 2000, Tony released a solo album titled *Iommi*. It includes several well-known musicians such as Kenny Aronoff, Matt Cameron, Jimmy Copley, Dave Grohl, Billy Idol, Brian May, Peter Steele, and many more. Sabbath alum Laurence Cottle, the bassist on *Headless Cross*, appears on six of the ten tracks. Bob Marlette, who produced the two studio tracks on *Reunion*, engineered and produced this album and played bass on one track. The song "Who's Fooling Who" could be thought as a Sabbath lineup because Ozzy is on vocals, Bill is on drums, and Laurence is on bass. It was not intended to be a Sabbath song, but neither were the tracks that became *Seventh Star*, so it is worth inclusion here. The change of tempo and feel to a fast shuffle halfway through the song is classic Sabbath. The tolling bell at the beginning and at the end recalls the song "Black Sabbath." The opening lyric "is the end beginning?" looks ahead to the line "Is this the end of the beginning" from the song "End of the Beginning" from their 2013 album *13*. Who's fooling whom? Kidding aside, it is interesting to listen to the album in relation to Tony's work with Sabbath, especially with the guest appearances by Bill and Ozzy. As Tony has recycled riffs from earlier Sabbath rehearsal and writing sessions for use on later Sabbath albums and his 1996 solo album, it is possible that some of the material on *Iommi* was originally conceived for use in Sabbath.

The Bill/Geezer/Geoff/Ozzy/Tony lineup toured as part of Ozzfest 2001. It was to be the last tour with Geoff, as he died in 2017 from lung cancer. In rehearsals for the tour, they wrote new material with the intention of making a studio album. One of those songs, "Scary Dreams," made its way into the live set and it is available on bootlegs. If you recall from chapters 1 to 4, previewing one or more songs on a tour before an album is recorded or released was regular practice in the 1970s for Sabbath. Except in the Chicago show and perhaps in other performances as well, "Scary Dreams" begins with a slow jazz hi-hat pattern (as at the beginning of "Wicked World" but less than half the tempo). Tony enters softly on a single-line melody/riff using very little distortion. When Geezer comes in, Bill adds a backbeat on the snare drum implying a half-time feel (about 50 bpm). The interlude riff between the two choruses has a sinister sound, recalling the first three notes of "Electric Funeral" but in a lower key. Like the intro riff to "Cornucopia," it emphasizes two different tritones for an especially "scary" sound. Unlike 1970s-era Sabbath, Ozzy sings in a very low register for the verses. The guitars are detuned three semitones, as in songs such as "Children of the Grave" and "Snowblind," and Ozzy keeps mostly to his low register. Only on the third line of the verses does he reach the middle register; this part of the melody is like "Johnny Blade" (on the word "twisted" and other places) or like "free now" in "Sweet Leaf," but "Scary Dreams" is in a much lower key. Ozzy goes a bit higher for the chorus on the word "scary." The highest note comes in the prechorus, and it is hit and miss in the various bootlegs. Thus, what used to be his middle register became his high register twenty to thirty years later.

The original lineup of Sabbath was on the 2004 Ozzfest tour, but they employed Adam Wakeman (son of Rick) in place of Geoff. The presence of keyboards is occasional, but there are times you can hear the rhythm guitar parts behind Tony's solos. Rarely discussed by the band or fans, this practice dates back to the midseventies when Jezz Woodroffe would play Tony's riffs on keyboards. Adam was originally hired to play keyboards, but he eventually played rhythm guitar as well. The set was short (only nine or ten songs) and included only songs from the first four albums, aside excerpting the main riff of "Sabbath, Bloody Sabbath." Ozzy was sick for the August 26 concert, so Rob Halford (who stepped in twelve years prior) sang that night; the footage of this concert is worth checking out. The same Adam/Bill/Geezer/Ozzy/Tony lineup toured again in 2005, including Ozzfest dates.

After Ronnie had passed away, Tony and engineer-producer Mike Exeter showed the demos they had been working on to Ozzy. They went to LA and created more demo tracks using drummer Tommy Clufetos (who was working in Ozzy's band at the time) and Mike temporarily on bass. According to Mike, "Dear Father" was the first song that they had worked on, dating it to February 2011. Mike and Tony returned to England for more writing: Tony would write a riff and then Mike would program drums and add bass and keyboards. Mike elaborates: "I program parts sympathetic to the riffs coming out of Tony's guitars within my workstation. . . . The parts are NEVER intended to be the template for the drummer, just a means to keeping a vibe for Tony and myself to put guitars and bass, and sometimes keyboards" for demo purposes.[3]

Bill and Geezer got involved in the project, and a full reunion was on the horizon. They worked at Ozzy's home studio, and Mike and Tony returned to LA to work on more tracks with them. Although Ozzy told *Melody Maker* in 1975, "I can't be doing Black Sabbath when I'm 58,"[4] at age sixty-two, he is back working with them again. Sabbath announced the reunion on November 11, 2011, at 11:11 a.m. at a press conference at the famous Whisky a Go Go club in West Hollywood. Unfortunately, just before Christmas, Tony was diagnosed with cancer. In early January 2012, with the original four members working on the new material in Los Angeles, they made plans to move the writing sessions to Birmingham due to Tony's illness. By the end of the month, Geezer, Mike, Ozzy, and Tony head to England. Mike explains Bill's absence: "It was just writing sessions and Bill didn't need to come over to England for that. Ozzy and Geezer came over and they worked on the days which Tony felt good."[5] One week later, however, Bill posted on Facebook that he is removing himself from the project due to receiving an "unsignable contract." They continued to write in the UK without Bill until April, after which they played a few concerts with Tommy on drums.

Rick Rubin was brought in as producer with Mike still involved as engineer. Drummer Brad Wilk (Rage Against the Machine) was given the demos, and according to him, it was seven months from when he was invited to "jam" with the band to the time it actually happened. They auditioned several drummers, but when Rick heard Brad with the band, he said to Mike, "This is the best I ever heard them sound. This is incredible. This is what they need."[6] Rick said later, "All I want is for this to be the best Black Sabbath album ever."[7] Rick heard the demos and said "forget about [all] that," and then he played the band their first album and said "imagine you're going to follow that."[8] Ozzy said Rick "wanted a feel of the blues."[9] Although they had been working with a computer in the songwriting process, Rick requested they not work to a click track (metronome) and play in one room. This gave the music a more natural feel than on *The Dio Years* and *The Devil You Know* because the tempos could fluctuate and the musical phrases could breathe.

In mid-August, the band resumed writing and began the recording process (now with Brad on drums). Mike said, "We did all the initial songwriting using the computer, but the songs evolved into the recorded versions once the band played them."[10] After a short break, they resumed recording sessions in mid- to late October. As it was done in their early years (e.g., *Paranoid* and *Master of Reality*), the band recorded live with Ozzy providing a guide vocal that would later be replaced once lyrics were completed. By mid-December, the drums, bass, rhythm guitars, some guitar overdubs, and much of the vocals were complete. Then, Mike and Tony returned to England to work on additional parts. According to LA-based harmonica player Stanley Behrens, Ozzy's harmonica part on "Damaged Soul" was unusable, so a studio musician, possibly Lynwood Slim, was brought in. The producers were apparently still unsatisfied, so they brought in Stanley to record in early 2013.[11] Mixing was done from late January to mid-March 2013, the single "God Is Dead?" was released in April, and the album was released in June titled *13*. It was their first number one album in the UK since *Paranoid* and their first ever number one album in the United States. The album *13* was at number one in multiple countries, a testament of their staying power and importance to the history of heavy metal music. Ozzy called it "quite possibly the most important album of [his] career."[12]

According to Geezer, the title *13* comes from the record company pressuring them to write thirteen songs although they wished to stop at ten. The title was to "piss them off,"[13] he explained, but it was a moot point because they ended up recording sixteen, over ninety-seven minutes of music and enough music for two full albums. The album *13* contains only eight tracks, but some releases have additional songs such as "Methademic," "Naïveté in Black," "Pariah," and "Piece of Mind." The four other songs, "Cry All Night," "Isolated Man," "Season of the Dead," and "Take Me Home," became the first half of their next album, *The End* (2016), the second half of which consisted of live recordings from the 2013/2014 tour.

13

With fifteen years since the last studio track and thirty-five years since the last full studio album with Ozzy, the opening strains of *13* cathartically release years of anticipation. "End of the Beginning" is clearly reminiscent of the song "Black Sabbath" as if it were an artistic statement about returning to their roots as a band. The primary difference between the two songs is that, lyrically, "End of the Beginning" is about cloning and technology. The song is very slow (44 bpm) but not as slow as "Black Sabbath." The first third of the song is structured in the same way as "Black Sabbath" in that the main riff alternates between loud and soft. In both songs, the soft sections use single notes on the guitar, but "End of the Beginning" uses five different notes instead of only two. Both songs have tom-focused drum parts in the soft sections; Brad channels Bill's approach to drums here. Both songs go into a faster section in a shuffle feel, and both songs start the faster section at 124 bpm, remarkably. The primary difference is that the fast part of "End of the Beginning" is much more involved, with several sections, and even a tempo and key change. Near the end of the guitar solo, it changes key and goes into a half-time feel (still faster than the first part). With the guitar strings ringing out and the half-time feel, it has an expansive feel, "epic" if you will, along the lines of the ending of "Dirty Women."

Ozzy came up with the idea for using the line "God is dead" as a lyric in the song, and Geezer said to him, "You can't sing that!"[14] However, Geezer kept it and wrote the rest of the lyrics around it. The line "God is dead" quite famously comes from late nineteenth-century philosopher Friedrich Nietzsche, but as Geezer explained, the song is about a religious fanatic who has been told that God is dead and wants to prove that God is alive and well.

At nearly nine minutes in duration, "God Is Dead?" is one of Sabbath's longest songs. "The Writ" is also nearly nine minutes and "Megalomania" nearly ten, but those songs are structured as if they were two separate songs that were connected, as material from the first few minutes never returns. "God Is Dead?" on the other hand, brings back the chorus after the middle part. It's like "Snowblind" in that it has a middle section in a fast shuffle feel, and it returns to earlier material. It also stays in the same key, so it sounds like one song. From that perspective, "God Is Dead?" is Sabbath's longest and slowest-developing song. It is incredibly patient; by the time the first chorus finishes, it is two minutes and fifty seconds into the song. Compare that to "Paranoid," which lasts two minutes and fifty seconds in its entirety. The appearances of choruses are three minutes apart: 2:16, 5:15, and 8:10. In other words, one could listen to an entire pop song in that space of time! The middle part and tempo change does not come until 6:19, a point at which most Sabbath songs would have finished. The maturity of their songwriting is demonstrated here in their ability to be expansive yet keep the music continually developing and interesting.

The band enters lightly and calmly in a slow tempo. Tony plays a simple pattern on guitar with the strings ringing out and without heavy distortion. Geezer's tone is fat and fills up the sound even though he plays long tones. His bass line is inventive because he plays different notes from Tony's pattern and sometimes a note different than Tony creating dissonance. His bass line contains two tritones, as in "Cornucopia" and "Scary Dreams," all of which have that sinister sound. Brad uses the unassuming cross-stick rimshot, as Bill used on "Hand of Doom" but without the funky rhythms, and places each with the changing note in Tony's pattern, adding emphasis to it. From 0:07 to 0:17 and 0:24 to 0:33, you will hear some "howling" from a software emulator of a Minimoog. Mike created the sounds and added many effects so it sounds, as he described it, like an "eerie effect without being obvious [keyboards]."[15] The "howling" synth returns at 1:54 for a few seconds, its appearances occasional and tasteful.

The band comes in very loudly at 0:33 in a "War Pigs"–like declaration but slower and with the chords held out. Here, Geezer's tone becomes bright in order to cut through the texture, his low notes growling like a beast. His slide at 0:55 is especially menacing. Brad crashes the hits with Geezer and Tony, but while the chord rings out, he focuses on a tribal-like tom pattern, not unlike the middle, slow section of "Children of the Grave." Near the end of the riff (1:02), the evil-sounding "flat 5" that was part of the opening guitar part (0:04, 0:07, etc.) returns in a heavy state and signals Brad to stop the groove and bring it back down in volume.

The verse guitar pattern uses only the first two chords from the intro part, and they alternate. Geezer goes back to playing long tones but with extra activity. Brad plays some nice "ghost" notes on the snare drum, that is, the soft snare drum hits between the hi-hat pulse. Ozzy begins in his middle register ("lost in the darkness") but goes into his low register for the second half of the phrase ("I fade from the light"). The word "light" is even lower than his lowest notes in "Warning" and "Hand of Doom" from the first two albums. There is a delay on the words "night" and "shrine" at 1:37 and 2:09, respectively. The delay is set at one second, so it repeats every beat in this slow, about 60 bpm, tempo. Ozzy used the slow delay effect on select words previously in his solo career.

At 2:16, the band comes in heavy again without any warning or setup, the surprise factor for the chorus effective. Geezer plays a moving line in his classic, personal style under Tony's held-out chords. Brad's work is tom driven with several crashes. Ozzy goes up to his middle register in order to project above the loud guitars and drums. The second half of the chorus riff is a single-line melody played by Geezer and Tony. It uses the same notes as the postverse riff of "Into the Void," albeit in a different key and rhythm. The two-part riff is repeated under Ozzy's line "the voices echo in my head 'Is God alive, or is God dead?'"

Notice at 3:08 that Tony changes the guitar pattern during the second verse by incorporating an element from the intro (0:13–0:14) but approaching it differently. Geezer also makes the adjustment to his bass line to match Tony's variation. They do the same variation at 3:25, 3:41, and 3:57–3:58. Instead of simply repeating material verbatim, they develop it ever so slightly.

When the listener expects the chorus at 4:03, Tony alters his chord from the chorus slightly and uses it to start the bridge. Ozzy reaches the vocal climax of this section on the line "Is God really dead?" (4:26) and goes even higher when he repeats it (4:33). The first vocal climax sets up a new guitar riff (4:27). Brad and Tony come down in volume at 4:43 to make room for Ozzy as he returns to his lower register for the second part of the bridge, labeled as "M8 / BRIDGE B" in the lyric sheet in the CD and LP releases. "M8" is short for "middle eight," a term used in the UK in the same way that "bridge" is used in the United States.

As patient songwriters, the chorus returns at 5:15, three minutes after its first appearance, but the second verse and bridge do not seem long. The lyrics are changed, and Ozzy sings, "I don't believe that God is dead." However, by repeating only the end of the phrase, "God is dead," it seems to contradict "I don't believe that God is dead" and follow Nietzsche instead.

To close this part of the song, they recall the heavy material from the intro (0:33) at 5:48. This leads into the double-time shuffle part, starting at 6:35. It is similar to "Hole in the Sky" in feel, tempo, and rhythm. Even the first few notes (the opening gesture) are the same but in a different key. The riff changes at 6:35, but it has a similar feel. It's a rock shuffle along the lines of "Fairies Wear Boots" but without the jazz-like hits. The lyric sheet labels it "swing riff," referencing the swing rhythms that give it a shuffle feel. At 7:05, Ozzy repeats the "God is dead" line in his medium-high register, which for Ozzy in 2012, is near the top of his range. He goes even higher at 7:14, the highest of the song.

They introduce a new riff at 7:22, which is quite late in the song, even for Sabbath. However, it is based on the heavy intro riff from 0:33 but with much variation. Brad leaves plenty of space for Geezer to shine here. The guitar solo at 7:38 is very melodic, and quite brief, especially considering the long duration of the song.

They close this part of the song by recalling the riff from 6:35. Via an abrupt tempo change, they play the chorus for a third time at 8:10. As before, it had been about three minutes before the chorus's previous appearance, so its return sounds fresh and logical. Ozzy recalls his vocal climax from 7:14 at 8:41, but it's over a different feel. The song ends abruptly on the final chord of the riff.

"Loner" is a midtempo rocker beginning with a classic power-chord riff from Tony. Ozzy's verse melody has a nice shape to it. He descends into his lower register at the end of the second and fourth lines (0:32 and 0:51) but goes into his higher register for the third line (0:37). A syncopated postverse riff is heard only once in the song (0:55), as after the second and third verses, they instead head into the bridge. The first part of the bridge (1:51 and 3:42) features some nice lines from Geezer and tasteful hi-hat and tom work from Brad. Ozzy colors the end of his second phrase with a little "vocal fry" at the end of the word "advocate" (2:09). The second part of the bridge (2:12) has Brad "riding" on the toms, more vocals from Ozzy, and Tony playing a classic rock–style riff. Here, Tony plays "inverted" power chords with the open fifth string, as in "Cat Scratch Fever," giving it that sound. The third part of the bridge (2:39) has Brad bringing his experience with Rage Against the Machine to the fore. Drenched with flanger effect, Tony plays a brief solo over the bridge part two riff before heading to the third verse. After an extended part one of the bridge, Tony plays a second solo over the verse riff to end the song.

The connections between "Zeitgeist" and "Planet Caravan" are quite apparent, with elements found in both songs such as space-themed lyrics, a mellow vibe, acoustic guitars and bongos, piano introduced late in the song (3:29), and a guitar solo to end. Ozzy's voice isn't as treated as on "Planet Caravan," but effects such as reverse reverb are used. The biggest difference is that "Zeitgeist" has multiple sections (verse, chorus, and bridge) and "Planet Caravan" simply alternates between two chords for a couple of verses and a solo. The bridge, starting at 2:56, takes the music in a different direction. The goal of the song is at 3:17

when Ozzy sings "goodnight." The way Tony's chords and Ozzy's melody navigate toward 3:17 is beautiful, especially when Ozzy dips down lower for the word "kiss." There are other nice touches, such as Mike's synthesizer (3:38, 3:55, etc.), Brad's shaker and tambourine, Geezer's bass fills, and Tony's guitar overdubs (1:43, 2:13, 2:47, etc.). Tony used a Gibson ES-175 and slightly thicker strings to achieve more of a jazz tone for the end solo.

"Age of Reason" has the essence of progressive (prog) metal with tempo changes, eight different sections/riffs, and Mellotron-like sounds. Brad starts the song off with a tom-based pattern that plays nicely off the intro riff that is added at 0:08. Ozzy enters aggressively for a verse in his medium-high register. The postverse section (1:06–1:20) is like the postverse section in "Into the Void" in that it alternates a new postriff (1:06) with the verse riff (1:10). The postverse riff actually starts like the "Into the Void" postverse riff and the transitional riff in "Electric Funeral" (1:56). After a second verse and postverse, they recall the intro riff with an added SampleTron choir from Mike, re-creating the sounds of a 1970s-era Mellotron. The SampleTron returns at 5:50 during the guitar solo. The elaborate middle part has several sections. First, there's a new riff (2:44) and a verse over it (3:00). Then, a transitional riff (3:27) based on the postverse brings it to a faster riff based on a tritone (3:34). At 3:59, they introduce yet another riff with a very "N.I.B."–like "oh yeah" from Ozzy at 4:04. After a verse over this new riff, they recall the tritone riff (4:35) to close the middle part. After a return to the intro riff and original tempo, Tony plays a guitar solo instead of a verse. They close the song with the riff that accompanied the guitar solo.

"Live Forever" begins with a strange riff, fairly ambiguous about its key, but it soon settles into a "Hole in the Sky"–like groove. The feel, tempo, and key change for the chorus (1:20). In the middle of the guitar solo, the key goes up to add excitement and momentum, not unlike for the guitar solos in "After Forever" and "Under the Sun/Every Day Comes and Goes." Instead of returning to the original key, they remain higher to make Ozzy's vocal parts in the chorus (3:49) more intense. The verse riff returns for the outro, but by remaining in the higher key, the intensity is retained. Tony plays some simple, tasteful guitar parts (bends, pick slide, etc.) around Ozzy's vocal parts here. Although the feel, tempo, and key are different here than in the chorus, Ozzy superimposes lines from the chorus onto the verse riff for the outro. It is a clever reimagining of earlier material for an effective close to the song.

"Damaged Soul," with its working title "Satanic Blues," is essentially a hard-rock version of the blues, taking them back to the early days of the band. In fact, before *13* came out, Ozzy described the style of the album as "Satanic blues."[16] The groove is like a slow blues but with a hard-rock edge. The main riff has a Zappa-like sound to it in the way it's played, the rhythms, the shape, and so forth. The verse riff is simpler, but Brad fills it in with some nice "ghost" note work on the snare. The postverse riff (1:28), a variation of the main riff, brings the volume back up. Stanley's harmonica enters for the second postverse (2:42, 2:52, and 3:03); his tone and bends are certainly in the blues style, magnifying the band's blues roots. Matching the band's intensity, the harmonica is played aggressively to "throw it your face," as he described it.[17] After a bridge section with some nice vocal harmonies, the harmonica is featured (3:26–3:48) just before Tony's first guitar solo. After a third verse and a second solo from Tony, they transform the main riff by setting it to a faster blues shuffle feel (6:08). The harmonica returns (6:22), Tony takes a third solo (6:37), and the song closes with the main riff. Regarding the first twelve seconds of the track, it sounds like a recording played in reverse of Tony strumming chords from the chorus of "Zeitgeist" and Ozzy and at least one other person talking.

Ozzy and Tony blend rather nicely in the verses of "Dear Father." Unlike "Iron Man" or "Electric Funeral" where Ozzy followed the existing guitar riff for his vocal melody, this guitar part for "Dear Father" was written later, so Tony followed the first half of each vocal phrase for the first half of his riff (0:23–0:26, etc.). Ozzy's melody is very similar to the verse melody of "Lord of This World" in terms of tempo, rhythm, and phrasing; one could interchange them, and they would fit well. The guitars and drums of these two songs, however, are quite different in feel. For a few reasons, the chorus echoes the chorus and middle section of "No More Tears" from Ozzy's 1991 solo album. One of the interesting aspects to *13* is the confluence of elements from the various members' musical experiences between 1979 and 2012. The middle part of the song (2:42–4:49) has riffs reminiscent of early Sabbath. The first two-thirds of the first transitional riff are like a faster and slower "Black Sabbath" (2:42–2:47 and 2:49–2:54). The riff starting at 3:03 is like a riff from "War Pigs" for its similar rhythm and leap to a high note.

At 3:52, after Ozzy sings "die," the band hits two chords that may remind the listener of the two hits in the "Children of the Grave" riff. Interestingly, the band immediately goes into a double-time swing feel with a riff that is nearly identical to "Children of the Grave" but without the two hits. I mention these similarities not as a criticism of being derivative but only to make connections across songs and decades. The most obvious homage to their early days is when *13* closes as *Black Sabbath* began. Aside for the extra thunderclap at 6:40, the sound effects from the beginning of "Black Sabbath" (0:03–0:37) are used for the end of "Dear Father" (6:39–7:13).

Some releases of *13* contain additional songs, so they are mentioned here briefly. "Methademic," as in "Hand of Doom," paints drug use in a very ugly light. The main riff wouldn't feel out of place on a Geezer solo album for its aggressive nature. Tony's subtle guitar part in the verses creates an eerie atmosphere for the song's serious tone. "Piece of Mind" could be heard as either a two-part song or an unfinished one. After a transitional section (which has some of Brad's best drumming at 1:55–1:58), the song changes tempo and key (2:15), so it sounds like a middle part. But around 3:26, the listener expects it to go back to the original tempo and key of the first part, or perhaps to continue developing the second part. Instead, the song ends at 3:35 leaving the listener wanting more. "Pariah" makes nice use of a volume change (3:23–3:59) during the bridge, a much-needed aspect because nearly all of *13* is very loud, unlike their seventies albums that have wide dynamic ranges. "Naïveté in Black" is an up-tempo rocker whose riffs sound as if they were written for a Ronnie James Dio–era album; compare, for instance, a part of the riff at 1:38 with the intro riff to "Time Machine." The title references that so many people thought "N.I.B." was an abbreviation for "nativity in black." With the three other additional tracks being in the same key, "Naïveté in Black" being a bit higher gives it a nice contrast. Thirteen of the sixteen songs for the album are in the same key, which may cause "key fatigue" when listening to all of them in a row, as the ear may wish for more contrast.

GATHERED AT THEIR MASSES

The CD, DVD, and Blu-Ray release *Gathered at Their Masses* comes from their performances in Melbourne, Australia, in Spring 2013, several weeks before the album's release. It is an excellent document of how the band sounded and looked fourteen to fifteen years after *Reunion* and *The Last Supper*, although it was likely doctored a bit in the studio, as Ozzy sings more in tune here than in other performances from this time as heard on audience recordings. It is an opportunity to hear and see tracks from *13* such as "End of the Beginning," "God Is Dead?" "Loner," and "Methademic." These concerts were the first to include "Loner" and "Methademic," May 1 and April 29, respectively, so what appears on the DVD is actually the world premiere of these songs. The rarely heard "Under the Sun/Every Day Comes and Goes" was also performed, but it only appears on the deluxe version of the release. It also includes an instrumental performance of the first part of "Symptom of the Universe" that leads into a drum solo from Tommy. Although Brad played on *13*, Tommy did the tour. Tommy adheres to some of Bill's and Brad's drum parts, but there are some differences. Stylistically, Tommy is a very different drummer than Bill; whereas Bill is more reactionary to Geezer and Tony and plays more improvisationally, Tommy is more pattern based in approach and is a more straightforward rock drummer like Vinny Appice, Bobby Rondinelli, and Eric Singer.

With the exception of "Children of the Grave" and the new material, every song was played in a lower key than the studio recording for this tour. By detuning the guitars, it made it easier for Ozzy to hit some of the higher notes and made the guitars even heavier. Whereas Tony and Geezer already tuned down three semitones for some songs in the seventies, "Into the Void" and "Snowblind" were detuned an additional half step for this tour. "Into the Void" is particularly heavy as Geezer stays in the low register instead of going into Tony's range as he did on the album. "Symptom of the Universe" and "Sabbath, Bloody Sabbath" were actually played higher than the original, but these were done without vocals. With "Children of the Grave" in its original key, Ozzy changes the melody in certain places in order to avoid the high notes.

THE END

Lyrically, "Season of the Dead" is *The End*'s answer to "War Pigs" and "Children of the Grave." Musically, it's closer to "After All (The Dead)," as both have brutally slow tempos at the beginning of the song. Although Tony's riff could be heard in a moderately slow tempo (67 bpm), Brad's snare drum implies a half-time feel so it's felt at a mere 33.5 bpm. It is so slow that the riff is only played twice over the course of twenty-nine seconds. The riff is vaguely similar to the intro to "Under the Sun" for a variety of reasons, if not only for the very slow tempo.

When the tempo picks up at 0:30, it seems fast because of how slow the intro is, but it's actually fairly slow at 75 bpm. At 0:46, Brad plays a marching rhythm on the snare and bass drums, connecting his part thematically to the war-themed lyrics such as "marching off to war." Geezer comes in at 0:42, and there is a sound effect with the crash cymbal at 0:43. It is pitch-less, but it sounds as if it falls. When it is heard again at 0:49, the effect rises. Ozzy's verse begins at 0:56, and he sings in his middle-low register, akin to the verses to "War Pigs." The second part of the verse keeps the same riff but has a different vocal melody. Ozzy uses a similar exotic scale as in "Am I Going Insane (Radio)," which is the same register. Ozzy harmonizes with himself on select lyrics at 1:27–1:33 and 1:40–1:47, giving additional color to his vocal work. The band continues with a postverse riff, hits a dark chord at 1:52, and holds out the next chord at 1:54.

Brad leads the band back into the verse riff with a drum fill. The sound effect on the crash cymbals can be heard again at 2:05 and 2:49, nice production work that gives the cymbals another color. In the second part of the second verse, Brad continues his drum fill longer than most drummers would. Notice how the fill at 2:48 goes all the way past the start of the riff into the second syllable of "season"—a nice touch to extend the usual length of a drum fill. He does an extended drum fill again in the third verse during the words "it's like treason" (5:27–5:29).

After another postverse section, Brad leads the band into the bridge with a drum fill. The bridge riff has an unusual feel for Sabbath. The meter is in "six," and no other Sabbath riff approaches the groove in this way. Within this riff Geezer plays soloistically in some parts and foundationally in others: notice how each time he plays a soloistic fill at the end of the first half of the riff (3:18), but at the end of the second half (3:20), he hits the three big chords with Tony. After the riff is played four times, they enter the second part of the bridge for Ozzy's vocal parts (3:35). The groove here is different, although it is still in "six." Although Bill didn't play a groove like this, Brad captures Bill's approach to drumming by playing to the riff instead of a straightforward beat.

After returning to the first part of the bridge (4:12), they play a brief transition (4:30–4:40) back to the verse riff. Brad recalls the marching drum parts at 4:46, and verse 3 begins at 4:53. In the second part of the verse, Ozzy harmonizes all of the vocal parts instead of waiting six seconds for the second half of the phrase. The new harmony part gives extra interest to the third verse.

The postverse section is altered to include new, transitional material (5:50), taking it back to the original tempo to use the intro material as an outro. The band ramps up the energy here but keeps it very slow. For instance, listen for Geezer's fill at 6:23, and then Brad plays a fast fill from 6:24 to 6:26. This fill is similar to the twenty-four-note fill Vinny plays on "The Sign of the Southern Cross," "Master of Insanity," and "Double the Pain" as mentioned in earlier chapters. Brad extends that fast fill to four seconds (6:50–6:54) to end it. To add another layer and to help build the song to the end, an additional guitar enters at 6:26 and plays the riff as a single-line melody in a higher register, just as did the third guitar on "Sweet Leaf." The final chord hits at 6:54, and by 7:03, the guitar beautifully begins to feedback. Amidst the sustaining chord is Brad's marching snare and bass drums fading out.

After the slow intro to "Cry All Night," a new riff at a little more than twice as fast takes over. It is drenched with wah-wah effect, as in "Electric Funeral." The volume starts to come down at 2:46, and Ozzy adds a nice "vocal fry" to color his voice as he fades out. Tony controls the feedback artistically and shapes his guitar with some volume swells; the lower volume and intensity allows him to build his solo over time. Brad has some nice hi-hat work in this section as well. A bell as in "Black Sabbath" sounds when Ozzy comes back in (3:40) and again at 3:57. When the bell returns at 6:30, the sound effects from the beginning of "Black Sabbath" fade in, but with the pitch raised in order to match the key of the song. It's as if this song was an alternate choice as the final track of 13.

Brad really channels Bill in "Take Me Home" when he uses the drumbeat from the verses of "Wheels of Confusion" (0:16 and 0:29, respectively). Notice the "double" snare drum hit and the delayed snare hit that Bill and Brad play. The song is heavy throughout, never letting up, and Ozzy remains at the top of his new vocal range. What is most striking is Tony's nylon-string guitar solo juxtaposed against the heavily distorted guitars. The guitar lines and chords evoke a Spanish style, as in "Am I Going Insane (Radio)," but more overtly. Geezer has some nice moments as well, such as the bass fills at 1:57, 4:18, and 4:35.

Lyrically, "Isolated Man" is like "Loner" but set in first person instead of second. Ozzy's double-tracked vocals are like in "Psycho Man" where one is his low register and the other at the top of his modern range. At 2:34, there is a moment of silence before the band comes back in big. Many modern producers would edit out the amp and fret noise, but it's left in so you really get a sense of it being live. The noise is different in each channel, so there are two guitars in the mix. From 3:30 to 4:02, the Brad/Geezer/Tony trio really gets to shine; there aren't any background guitars so everything is quite clear. This is one of Sabbath's finest stripped-down instrumental performances on record.

The remaining four tracks on *The End* are live performances of songs from previous albums, which is beyond the focus of this book. It is worth checking out, as it includes the rarely heard "Under the Sun/Every Day Comes and Goes" and three songs from *13*. Tommy is on drums, and Adam is credited for keyboards and guitar.

THE END TOUR AND CLOSING THOUGHTS

Using the same lineup as with the *13* tour, Sabbath embarked on what they've announced as their final tour, finishing in their hometown of Birmingham in February 2017. This tour focused on the early seventies material, replacing the new material with "After Forever" and "Hand of Doom." With "Rat Salad" replacing "Symptom of the Universe" as the drum feature, "Dirty Women" became the only song from their 1973–1978 albums. Three songs in a row in the set were exceptionally low (at two whole steps down than standard tuning): "After Forever," "Into the Void," and "Snowblind." Even with the additional detuning, in the concert I attended (September 4, 2016, in Chicago), Ozzy still struggled with the high notes and sang all of "Into the Void" roughly a whole step below the rest of the band for the entire song (i.e., he sang in the wrong key the entire song). Audience recordings of other concerts reveal Ozzy struggling to sing in tune, but for the most part, he was okay. With "Children of the Grave" already tuned down three semitones, instead of tuning down even further, Ozzy changed parts of the melody in order to avoid the higher notes, a solution that seems to work better for him.

They titled the tour "The End" and sold *The End* album exclusively at their shows (i.e., not in stores or online). The individual members will likely continue recording and performing, but they announced that they will no longer tour as Black Sabbath. It was announced in August 2016 that Tony's cancer went into remission, so perhaps he will begin another solo project. In January 2017 he released a composition for choir, pipe organ, cello, synthesizers, and guitar titled "How Good It Is." Ozzy expressed interest in doing another solo album once *The End* tour is complete. Geezer says he would like to do another solo album, as he has "hundreds of half-written ideas taking up space on [his] computer." [18]

If *The End* really is the end for Sabbath, the world will still have the studio albums, live albums, and audience recordings that document their contributions to music for us to enjoy and continue to get to know better. There have been Black Sabbath tribute albums with contributions from various bands and solo artists. Countless Black Sabbath tribute bands around the world continue to play the music live. For instance, "Black Sabbitch" is an all-female Sabbath tribute band out of LA. Mac Sabbath, also from LA, is a must-see McDonald's-themed Sabbath tribute band with fast-food-themed versions of Sabbath songs such as "Lord of the Swirl," "Cherries Are Fruits," and "Sweet Beef." Not all of the bands performing Sabbath's music are metal. For instance, the jazz group The Bad Plus recorded "Iron Man" for their 2004 album *Give* and have included it in their live performances. Rondellus, an early music ensemble from Estonia, released *Sabbatum* in 2003, an album of twelve Sabbath songs performed in a medieval style. Having two generations of fans is an accomplishment, but not too many bands can claim three generations of fans as Sabbath can. With the Sabbath catalog still available, and with tribute and cover bands keeping their music alive in a live format, there will be a fourth generation of fans by the 2020s and 2030s.

NOTES

INTRODUCTION

1. Sharpe-Young 2006, 172
2. *Classic Albums: Paranoid*
3. Sharpe-Young 2006, 172–73
4. Cleveland 2010, 137
5. Bronson 1972, 10
6. Wictor 1999, 20
7. Wright 2013
8. Welch 1982, 50
9. Ibid., 17
10. Plummer 1971, 25
11. Sprague 2006
12. Osbourne/Ayres 2011, 166
13. Iommi/Lammers 2011, 161
14. Gabriel 1996, 33
15. Bronson 1972
16. Marshall, n.d.
17. Iommi/Lammers 2011, 53
18. Welch 1982, 72
19. Iommi/Lammers 2011, 62
20. *Inside Black Sabbath* (not to be confused with *Inside Black Sabbath 1970/1992: An Independent Critical Review*, also from 2002)
21. *The Last Supper*
22. *Classic Albums: Paranoid*
23. Ibid.

24. Ibid.
25. Ibid.
26. Rosen 1996, 39
27. *The Last Supper*
28. *Classic Albums: Paranoid*

1. THE BIRTH OF METAL

1. Nalbandian/Mille 2002
2. Iommi, unidentified video interview
3. McIver 2016, 20
4. The term "key" ought to be defined here, as it used throughout this book to describe the music. It is closely related to the concept of the scale, a collection of notes. One of the notes from the scale is treated as the primary one, and the ear tends to focus on it, as does the band when they play. In many of Sabbath's songs, the key will change, effectively changing the primary note and the collection of notes that are used. For example, notice in "Wasp/Behind the Wall of Sleep" that the primary note of the first part (0:00) is higher than the primary note of the next part (0:37). At this point in the music, the key has changed.
5. Osbourne/Ayres 2011, 83
6. Turner 2004 (1970), 28
7. *Classic Albums: Paranoid*
8. Ibid.
9. Ibid.
10. Ibid.
11. Iommi, Tony. 2011. Interview by Dave Lawrence, November 3, WNYC 93.9 FM (New York). Available as a YouTube video: "Black Sabbath Tony Iommi 2011 Interview Part 2." https://www.youtube.com/watch?v=BUPnrPXrvYI
12. *Classic Albums: Paranoid*
13. Wall 2015, 70
14. *Classic Albums: Paranoid*
15. Ibid.
16. Green 1970, 13
17. *Classic Albums: Paranoid*
18. Ibid.
19. Ibid.
20. Ibid.
21. Ibid.

22. Ibid.
23. Simpson 2016
24. *Classic Albums: Paranoid*
25. Ibid.
26. Ibid.
27. Ibid.
28. Ibid.
29. Ibid.
30. Ibid.
31. Ibid.
32. Angle 2015, 52
33. Green/Carr 1970, 14

2. SWEET LEAF AND SNOWBLIND

1. Anon. 1972, 65
2. Iommi/Lammers 2011, 95
3. Popoff 2006, 96
4. Iommi/Lammers 2011, 94
5. Osbourne/Ayres 2011, 124
6. Popoff 2006, 62
7. Wilkinson 2007, 113
8. Iommi/Lammers 2011, 94
9. Rosen 1996, 83
10. Popoff 2006, 114
11. Iommi/Lammers 2011, 109
12. Anon. 1972, 65
13. Meadows 1972
14. Holman 1972, 10
15. Plummer 1972, 11
16. Popoff 2006, 70
17. Green 1971, 6
18. Plummer 1972, 10
19. Tangye/Wright 2005, 73
20. Ibid., 63
21. *Inside Black Sabbath*
22. Ferrante 2004, 50
23. Tangye/Wright 2005, 78
24. Osbourne/Ayres 2011, 132
25. Popoff 2006, 96

26. Ibid., 71
27. Tangye/Wright 2005, 71
28. Meadows 1972
29. Kelleher 1971, 64
30. *The Last Supper*
31. Tangye/Wright 2005, 77
32. Iommi/Lammers 2011, 110
33. Ibid., 110
34. Bangs 1972, 48
35. Stark 2002, 21
36. Popoff 2006, 79

3. PROG SABBATH

1. Iommi/Lammers 2011, 111
2. Ibid., 136
3. Popoff 2006, 114
4. Rosen 1996, 83
5. Altham 1973, 6 (based on the audio in Iommi/Altham 1973, this seems to be a paraphrase, not a direct quote as implied in Altham 1973)
6. Popoff 2006, 96
7. Black Sabbath. 1974. Unidentified interviewer, November 12, Radio 3XY 1420 AM (Melbourne, Australia).
8. Osbourne/Ayres 2011, 169
9. Iommi/Lammers 2011, 130
10. Ward 1973, 24
11. Popoff 2006, 97–98
12. Iommi/Altham 1973
13. Popoff 2006, 98
14. Iommi/Altham 1973
15. Harrigan 1975, 8
16. Houghton 1975, 24 (reprinted in Hoskyns 2004, 49)
17. Doherty 1975, 30
18. Robinson 1975, 3
19. Popoff 2006, 112
20. Ibid., 111
21. Iommi/Lammers 2011, 146
22. Popoff 2006, 112
23. Robinson 1975, 3
24. Ibid., 114

25. Robinson 1975, 3
26. Elliott 2012
27. Osbourne/Ayres 2011, 170
28. Houghton 1975, 24 (reprinted in Hoskyns 2004, 49)
29. Popoff 2006, 122

4. JAZZ SABBATH AND OZZY'S DEPARTURE

1. Osbourne/Ayres 2011, 186
2. Popoff 2006, 150–1
3. Osbourne/Ayers 2011, 172 and Simmons 1979, 11-D
4. Simmons 1979, 11-D
5. Popoff 2006, 132
6. Ferrante 2004, 53
7. Blasko 2013, 34
8. Popoff 2006, 149
9. Thomas 2013, 18
10. Iommi/Lammers 2011, 171

5. ENTER RONNIE JAMES DIO

1. *The Black Sabbath Story Vol. 2*
2. Popoff 2006, 164
3. Simmons 1979, 11-D
4. *Inside Black Sabbath*
5. *Neon Knights: 30 Years of Heaven & Hell*
6. Tepedelen 2008, 65 (page 6 in Tepedelen/Mudrian 2009)
7. Ibid., 66 (page 8 in Tepedelen/Mudrian 2009)
8. Sharpe-Young 2006, 26
9. Ibid., 26
10. Ibid., 26
11. *Neon Knights: 30 Years of Heaven & Hell*
12. Sharpe-Young 2006, 31
13. Popoff 2006, 170
14. Wall 2015, 176
15. Iommi/Lammers 2011, 192
16. Popoff 2006, 274
17. Sharpe-Young 2006, 30

18. Ibid., 30
19. *Inside Black Sabbath*
20. Popoff 2006, 167
21. Ibid., 169
22. Iommi, Tony. 2016. Interview by Chris Jericho. *Talk Is Jericho*, Episode 300 (November 16), podcast.
23. Cramer 2012
24. Drummer Connection 2013
25. *Neon Knights: 30 Years of Heaven & Hell*
26. Popoff 2006, 183
27. Ibid., 185
28. Anon. 1994. Unpublished interview. "Ronnie James Dio Brutally Honest Tour Bus Interview 1994 Part 3 of 4." Uploaded February 4, 2010. https://www.youtube.com/watch?v=GGqz9CYXalQ

6. STONEHENGE AND THE REVOLVING DOOR OF MUSICIANS

1. Kitts 1992, 77 and *The Black Sabbath Story Vol. 2*
2. Cope, Malcolm. 2016. Personal interview (phone), May 30.
3. Ibid.
4. Popoff 2006, 203 and 207–8
5. Sharpe-Young 2006, 141
6. Ibid., 143
7. Gillan, Ian. n.d. (2005 or earlier). "Wordography: 50 Disturbing the Priest." *Caramba!* http://www.gillan.com/wordography-50.html
8. Popoff 2006, 210
9. Sharpe-Young 2006, 143
10. Ibid., 210–11
11. Sharpe-Young 2006, 143
12. Gillan, Ian. n.d. (2003 or earlier). "Wordography: 34 Digital Bitch." *Caramba!* http://www.gillan.com/wordography-34.html
13. Popoff 2006, 212
14. Sharpe-Young 2006, 189
15. Ibid., 225
16. Ibid., 258
17. The Associated Press, March 27, 1986: "Group Protests Good Friday Concert by Black Sabbath," http://www.apnewsarchive.com/1986/Group-Protests-Good-Friday-Concert-by-Black-Sabbath/id-673af9ccc88386e8b595323c569ba94c

18. Hochanadel, Mike. 1986. "Electric Music." *Schenectady Gazette*, March 28, TV Plus—Supplement: 27

19. Sharpe-Young 2006, 257

7. A TONY MARTIN TRIPTYCH

1. In chapters 7 and 9, I will refer to Tony Iommi as "Iommi" and Tony Martin as "Martin" except when it is clear that the discussion is about the guitar or vocals, in which case only the first name will be used.

2. Popoff 2006, 235

3. Sharpe-Young 2006, 279

4. Iommi/Lammers 2011, 260

5. Sharpe-Young 2006, 253

6. Daisley 2013, 217

7. Ibid., 217

8. Sharpe-Young 2006, 304–5

9. Iommi, Tony, and Cozy Powell. 1989. Interview by Mick Bailey and Dez Bailey, April, MTV, *Metal Hammer*

10. Ibid.

11. Sharpe-Young 2006, 375

12. Cottle, Laurence. 2016. Personal communication, June 2 (in-person) and June 29 (e-mail)

13. Popoff 2006, 251

14. Yurchak, Alexi. 2006. *Everything Was Forever, Until It Was No More: The Last Soviet Generation*. Princeton University Press, pg. 215.

15. Sharpe-Young 2006, 320

16. Ibid., 320

17. Ibid., 320

18. Popoff 2006, 263

8. RONNIE RETURNS

1. Sharpe-Young 2006, 329 and 332

2. Popoff 2006, 269

3. Alternate version of *The Black Sabbath Story, Vol. 2*

4. Ibid.

5. Butler, Geezer, and Tony Iommi. 1992. Interview, June 21(?), MTV, *Headbangers Ball*

6. Ibid.
7. Ibid.
8. Black Sabbath. 1992. Interview by Riki Rachtman, August 6(?), MTV, *Headbangers Ball*
9. Sharpe-Young 2006, 327
10. Flans 2007, 150
11. Ibid., 150
12. *The Black Sabbath Story, Vol. 2*
13. Popoff 2006, 279
14. *Live from Radio City Music Hall*
15. Ibid.
16. Kitts 1992, 77
17. Anon. 2009. "Bill Ward Says 'Musical Difference' Was The Main Reason He Dropped Out of Heaven & Hell." Posted August 11. http://www.blabbermouth.net/news/bill-ward-says-musical-difference-was-the-main-reason-he-dropped-out-of-heaven-hell/ Quotes come from Ward, Bill. 2009. Interview by Eddie Trunk, August 7, Q104.3 FM (New York), *Friday Night Rocks*
18. Ibid.
19. Ibid.
20. *Live from Radio City Music Hall*
21. Anon. 2009 (Ward/Trunk)
22. Iommi/Lammers 2011, 352
23. *Bonus Best Buy Exclusive DVD: Making of The Devil You Know*
24. Iommi/Lammers 2011, 353
25. *Bonus Best Buy Exclusive DVD: Making of The Devil You Know*
26. Smith 2009, 31
27. Crawford 2009, 77
28. Smith 2009, 31
29. Iommi/Lammers 2011, 353

9. TONY MARTIN RETURNS

1. Iommi/Lammers 2011, 291
2. Rondinelli, Bobby. 2016. Personal interview (phone), August 10
3. Ibid.
4. Iommi/Lammers 2011, 291–2
5. Rondinelli/Stolz 2016
6. Iommi/Lammers 2011, 291–2

7. Hays, Constance L. 1992. "Mother of Bishop's Son Tells of Irish Love Affair." *The New York Times*, May 9, Late Edition, Section 1: 2

8. Sharpe-Young 2006, 359

9. Ibid., 359

10. Rondinelli/Stolz 2016

11. Popoff 2006, 302

12. Sharpe-Young 2006, 376

13. Ibid., 375

14. Ibid., 372

15. Popoff 2006, 304

10. REUNIONS WITH OZZY AND THE END

1. Ouellette 2012

2. *The Last Supper*, Interview with Henry Rollins (DVD only: "Reunion EPK")

3. Exeter, Mike. ("mike.x") 2012. "'Substitute Drummer engaged' Tony, Ozzy and Geezer Respond." *Black Sabbath Online Forums*. September 7, 2:42 pm. http://www.black-sabbath.com/vb/showthread.php?37142-Substitute-Drummer-engaged-Tony-Ozzy-and-Geezer-Respond/

4. Doherty 1975, 30

5. Mike Banks. 2014. "Producer/Engineer Mike Exeter Talks About Recording Black Sabbath." Interview with George Shilling. Uploaded January 11. https://www.youtube.com/watch?v=Mfb40y6Tr2o

6. Ibid.

7. Ibid.

8. Ibid.

9. Gundersen 2013, 2D

10. Exeter, Mike. ("mike.x") 2012. "Questions for Mike Exeter." *Black Sabbath Online Forums*. December 19, 4:36 am. http://www.black-sabbath.com/vb/showthread.php?37506-Questions-for-Mike-Exeter

11. Behrens, Stanley. 2016. Personal interview (phone), September 10, and follow-up electronic communication on January 5, 2017.

12. Black Sabbath. 2013. "An Inside Look at Black Sabbath in the Studio." Uploaded February 13. https://www.youtube.com/watch?v=3GLqS7yjyMw

13. Levine 2013

14. NME. 2013. "Black Sabbath: 'We Said To Ozzy 'You Can't Sing 'God Is Dead!.'" Uploaded June 14. https://www.youtube.com/watch?v=r3NO3V8R_ak

15. Exeter, Mike. ("mike.x") 2013. "Geezer and the Mellotron." *Black Sabbath Online Forums*. May 17, 2:05 pm. http://www.black-sabbath.com/vb/showthread.php?39907-Geezer-and-the-Mellotron

16. Brown 2013

17. Behrens/Stolz 2016

18. Carson, Nathan. 2016. "Five Things Geezer Butler Wants to Do After Retiring from Black Sabbath." *Willamette Week*, September 6. http://www.wweek.com/music/2016/09/06/five-things-geezer-butler-wants-to-do-after-retiring-from-black-sabbath/

SELECTED READINGS

Cope, Andrew L. 2010. *Black Sabbath and the Rise of Heavy Metal Music*. Burlington, VT: Ashgate.

Daisley, Bob. 2013. *For Facts Sake*. Moonee Ponds, VIC, Australia: Thompson Music.

Hoskyns, Barney, ed. 2004. *Into the Void: Ozzy Osbourne and Black Sabbath; A Rock's Backpages Reader*. New York: Omnibus Press.

Iommi, Tony, and T. J. Lammers. 2011. *Iron Man: My Journey through Heaven and Hell with Black Sabbath*. Cambridge, MA: Da Capo Press.

Osbourne, Ozzy, and Chris Ayres. 2011. *I Am Ozzy*. New York: Grand Central Publishing.

Popoff, Martin. 2006. *Doom Let Loose*. Toronto: ECW Press.

———. 2011. *Black Sabbath FAQ*. Milwaukee, WI: Backbeat.

Sharpe-Young, Garry. 2006. *Sabbath Bloody Sabbath: The Battle for Black Sabbath*. New Plymouth, New Zealand: Zonda.

Stolz, Nolan. 2015. "Black Sabbath." In *The 100 Greatest Bands of All Time: A Guide to the Legends Who Rocked the World*, edited by David V. Moskowitz, 76–82. Santa Barbara, CA: Greenwood.

———. 2016. "Progressive Rock Elements in Black Sabbath's Music from 1972 to 1980." In *Prog Rock in Europe: Overview of a Persistent Musical Style*, edited by Philippe Gonin, Chris Atton, Sarah Hill, Allan F. Moore, and Justin Williams, 143–50. Dijon, France: Editions Universitaires de Dijon.

Tangye, David, and Graham Wright. 2005. *How Black Was Our Sabbath: An Unauthorized View from the Crew*. London: Pan.

Welch, Chris. 1982. *Black Sabbath*. New York: Proteus.

ADDITIONAL SOURCES

Altham, Keith. 1973. "Sabbath Days of Rest." *New Musical Express*, September 1: 6.

Angle, Brad. 2015. "Iron Men: Tony Iommi & Geezer Butler Recall the Rise and Fall of the First—and Greatest—Incarnation of Heavy Metal's Originators." *Guitar World* 37/3 (March): 44-50, 52, 54, 55, 158, 160.

Anon. 1972. "Black Sabbath Undergoes an Image Change and It Works Magic." *Billboard*, July 22: 65.

Bangs, Lester. 1972. "Bring Your Mother to the Gas Chamber Part Two: Black Sabbath and the Straight Dope on Blood-Lust Orgies." *Creem*, July: 47–49, 78–80.

Blasko, Rob. 2013. "The Wizard Returns: Geezer Butler and Black Sabbath Reconvene to Conjure the Magic Once More." *Bass Player* 24/7 (July): 28–30, 32, 34–36, 38, 40, 42.

Bronson, Harold. 1972. "The Wit & Wisdom of Ozzy Osborne or For the Best Coke Call Black Sabbath." *UCLA Summer Bruin*, June 30: 10.

Brown, David. 2013. "Black Sabbath's Dark, Twisted Resurrection." *Rolling Stone*, February 10. http://www.rollingstone.com/music/news/black-sabbaths-dark-twisted-resurrection-20130210

Cleveland, Barry. 2010. "Something Wicked This Way Comes: Traversing Heaven & Hell with Tony Iommi." *Guitar Player* 44/1 (January): 58–62, 64, 66, 68, 70, 72, 74, 137.

Cramer, Jeff. 2012. "A Very Candid Conversation with Vinny Appice," *Stone Cold Crazy*, July 3, http://jeffcramer.blogspot.com/2012/07/very-candid-conversation-with-vinny.html

Crawford, Jeff. 2009. "Dark Musical Patterns for Dio." *Southern-Times Messenger*, June 24, Features: 77.

Doherty, Harry. 1975. "Paranoid." *Melody Maker*, October 11: 30.

Drummer Connection. 2013. "Vinny Appice - Black Sabbath, Heaven & Hell, Dio, Axis, John Lennon - Drummer Connection Interview." Interview by Eric Rosebrock. Uploaded June 1. https://www.youtube.com/watch?v=FwQUc5PAygo

Elliott, Paul. 2012. "Black Sabbath: Mirror, Mirror on the Wall." Posted May 23. http://teamrock.com/feature/2012-05-23/black-sabbath-mirror-mirror-on-the-wall

Ferrante, John. 2004. "Sabbath Bloody Sabbath: Geezer Butler Riffs on Black Sabbath." *Bass Player* 15/7 (July): 46–48, 50–53.

Flans, Robyn. 2007. "Vinny Appice: Back in Heaven." *Modern Drummer* 31/9 (September): 146–148, 150, 152, 154–156.

Gabriel, Paul. 1996. "Sabbath, Bloody Sabbath: The Enduring Riff Rock of Black Sabbath." *DISCoveries*, June: 32–40.

Green, Richard. 1970. "Black Sabbath Win Struggle Against Black Magic Tag." *New Musical Express*, September 26: 13.

———. 1971. "Following Recent Sensational London Concert Black Sabbath Admit: U.S. Tour Got Us Together—We're Into Some Nice Things Now." *New Musical Express*. May 8: 6.

Green, Richard, and Roy Carr. 1970. "Plumpton Succeeds with Good Music." *New Musical Express*, August 15: 14-15.

Gundersen, Edna. 2013. "Black Sabbath: Dark Past, Colorful Reunion, Hazy Future: New Album '13' Puts Them Back on the Metal Map." *USA Today*. June 11, Life: 2D.

Harrigan, Brian. 1975. "Sabbotage." *Melody Maker*, June 21: 8.

Holman, Pamela. 1972. "Pamela Holman Talks to Ossie Osbourne." *New Musical Express*, January 22: 10.

Houghton, Mick. 1975. "Sabbath's Sabotage: Rock Magicians On Tour–End Sabbatical with Devilish LP." *Circus Raves*, October: 20–24. Reprinted in Hoskyns 2004 as "Sabbath's Sabotage: An Interview with Tony Iommi," 45–51.

Iommi, Tony. 1973. Interview by Keith Altham, August 2. Audio available at: https://www.rocksbackpages.com/Library/Article/black-sabbaths-tony-iommi-1973

Kelleher, Ed. 1971. "Black Sabbath Don't Scare Nobody." *Creem*, December: 34–37, 64.

Kitts, Jeff. 1992. "Master of Reality: Evil Guitar Genius Tony Iommi, the Heart and Soul of Black Sabbath, Recalls the Best and the Worst of the Heaviest Band South of Heaven." *Guitar World* 23/8 (August): 76–77.

Levine, Nick. 2013. "Black Sabbath: 'We Named New Album '13' to Piss Off Record Company'." *New Musical Express*, June 10. http://www.nme.com/news/music/black-sabbath-60-1251275

Marshall, Brandon. n.d. "Never Say Die: An Interview With Bill Ward." http://www.sonicexcess.com/BILL_WARD_BLACK_SABBATH_interview.html

McIver, Joel. 2016. *The Complete History of Black Sabbath: What Evil Lurks*. New York: Race Point Publishing.

Meadows, Dick. 1972. "Black Sabbath: Sabbath Ready to Rejoin the Rock Machine." *Sounds*, January 22.

Nalbandian, Bob, and Mark Mille. 2002. "Bill Ward Interview." http://www.hardradio.com/shockwaves/ward9.php3

Ouellette, Mary. 2012. "Godsmack's Shannon Larkin on Drumming for Black Sabbath: One of the Best Things That Ever Happened to Me." Posted August 5. http://loudwire.com/godsmacks-shannon-larkin-on-drumming-for-black-sabbath-one-of-the-best-things-that-ever-happened-to-me/

Plummer, Mark. 1971. "Remember the Sabbath Day." *Melody Maker*, September 11: 24–25.

———. 1972. "Honour the Sabbath." *Melody Maker*, October 14: 10–11.

Robinson, Joe. 1975. "Sabotage: Black Sabbath Go Mental." *Circular* 7/23 (July 7): 2–4.

Rosen, Steven. 1996. *Wheels of Confusion: The Story of Black Sabbath*. Chessington, Surrey, UK: Castle Communications.

Simmons, Sylvie. 1979. "After 10 Years, Black Sabbath Dissolves." *Evening Independent*, November 10: 11-D.

Simpson, Dave. 2016. "Tony Iommi: 'We Used to Get Witches at Black Sabbath Shows'." *The Guardian*, June 2. https://www.theguardian.com/music/2016/jun/02/tony-iommi-black-sabbath-final-tour

Smith, Mark. 2009. "In One of Just a Handful of Australian Interviews, Founding Black Sabbath Bassist Terence 'Geezer' Butler Talks to Mark Smith about His New Band." *Whittlesea Leader*, April 29, News: 31.

Sprague, David. 2006. "Black Sabbath: Ozzy Osbourne Recalls His Band's Heavy, Scary Journey." http://www.rollingstone.com/music/news/rock-and-roll-hall-of-fame-2006-black-sabbath-20060306

Stark, Mike. 2002. *Black Sabbath: An Oral History*. Edited by Dave Marsh. New York: HarperEntertainment.

Tepedelen, Adem. 2008. "Holy Hell: The Making of Black Sabbath's *Heaven and Hell*." *Decibel* 47 (September): 62–68. Reprinted in *Precious Metal*, edited by Albert Mudrian, 1–14. Cambridge, MA: Da Capo Press, 2009.

Thomas, Skylar. 2013. "Don Airey, Master of Heavy Metal Keyboards." *Keyboard* 37/11 (November): 18. Extended interview available at: http://www.keyboardmag.com/artists/1236/don-airey-master-of-heavy-metal-keyboards/29437

Turner, Steve. 2004 (1970). "Black Sabbath (1970)." In *Into the Void: Ozzy Osbourne and Black Sabbath: A Rock's Backpages Reader*, edited by Barney Hoskyns, 27–29. New York: Omnibus Press.

Wall, Mick. 2015. *Symptom of the Universe*. New York: St. Martin's Press.

Ward, Jeff. 1973. "Caught in the Act: Bloody Sabbath." *Melody Maker*, December 22: 24.

Wictor, Thomas. 1999. "Bass Notes: Black Sabbath: Geezer Butler." *Bass Player* 10/3 (March): 20, 22.

Wilkinson, Paul. 2007. *Rat Salad: Black Sabbath, The Classic Years, 1969–1975*. New York: Thomas Dunne Books/St. Martin's Press.

Wright, Jeb. 2013. "Producer Tom Allom: From Sabbath to Priest." http://www.classicrockrevisited.com/show_interview.php?id=978

SELECTED LISTENING AND VIEWING

STUDIO ALBUMS

Black Sabbath, 1970
Paranoid, 1970/1971
Master of Reality, 1971
Black Sabbath Vol. 4, 1972
Sabbath, Bloody Sabbath, 1973/1974
Sabotage, 1975
Technical Ecstasy, 1976
Never Say Die!, 1978
Heaven and Hell, 1980
Mob Rules, 1981
Born Again, 1983
Seventh Star, 1986
The Eternal Idol, 1987
The Eternal Idol: Deluxe Expanded Edition (disc 2 recorded with
    Ray Gillen on vocals), 2010
Headless Cross, 1989
Tyr, 1990
Dehumanizer, 1992
Cross Purposes, 1994
Forbidden, 1995
The Devil You Know (as Heaven & Hell), 2009
13, 2013

LIVE ALBUMS (AUDIO ONLY) AND COLLECTIONS WITH NEW SONGS

Past Lives (recorded in 1970, 1973, and 1975), 2002/2010/2016

Heaven and Hell: Deluxe Expanded Edition (disc 2 recorded in 1980), 2010

Live at Hammersmith Odeon (recorded in 1981/1982), 2007

Live Evil (recorded in 1982), 1982/1983

Seventh Star: Deluxe Expanded Edition (disc 2 recorded in 1986 with Ray Gillen on vocals), 2010

Reunion (recorded live in 1997 with two new studio tracks), 1998

The Dio Years (collection with three new studio tracks), 2007

The End (recorded live in 2013 and 2014 with four new studio tracks from the *13* sessions), 2016

CONCERT VIDEOS AND DOCUMENTARIES

Never Say Die (recorded in 1978), 2003

The Black Sabbath Story Vol. 1 and *Vol. 2* (1992), 2002

Cross Purposes—Live (recorded in 1994; VHS/CD combo pack), 1995

"Sabbath Bloody Sabbath," episode 2 of *Rock Family Trees* series 2, 1998

The Last Supper, 1999

Inside Black Sabbath, 2002 (directed by Graham Holloway)

Live from Radio City Music Hall (as Heaven & Hell; also available on CD), 2007

Bonus Best Buy Exclusive DVD: Making of The Devil You Know, 2009

Neon Knights: 30 Years of Heaven & Hell (as Heaven & Hell; recorded in 2009; also available on CD), 2010

Classic Albums: Paranoid, 2010

Live . . . Gathered in Their Masses (also available on CD), 2013

INDEX

ABOUT THE AUTHOR

Nolan Stolz is a composer, scholar, and drummer with a background in classical, jazz, and rock. Stolz grew up in Las Vegas, where he worked for several years as a freelance jazz drummer. He has been a Black Sabbath fan since 1994, when he first heard Bill Ward's heavy-hitting, jazz-infused drumming on "Rat Salad."

Specializing in music written since 1966, Stolz has published articles and essays and has presented at numerous conferences on a variety of musical topics. He presented on Black Sabbath at the 2016 College Music Society National Conference (Santa Fe, New Mexico) and at the First International Conference on Progressive Rock (Dijon, France). His essay "Progressive Rock Elements in Black Sabbath's Music from 1972 to 1980" appears in the book *Prog Rock in Europe: Overview of a Persistent Musical Style*. His essays on Black Sabbath, Genesis, Rush, and Frank Zappa and the Mothers of Invention appear in *The 100 Greatest Bands of All Time: A Guide to the Legends Who Rocked the World*.

As a drummer, Stolz has performed with a variety of bands ranging in style from the avant-garde electroacoustic Southern California ensemble Caravan to the Tokyo-based J-Pop band Swinging Popsicle. He plays on several rock and jazz albums including Art Rock Circus's *Tell a Vision* and *Variations on a Dream*; Coalition's *Point of View*; Halloween Town's *Zafra Ct.* (with members of the Killers and Louis XIV); Johnny Pate's *80th Birthday Celebration* (with Monty Alexander, Kenny Burrell, Ron Carter, James Moody, Phil Woods, etc.); a solo album *Nolan Stolz Rock Orchestra*; and many albums as a session musician.

   Stolz's compositions are rooted in the contemporary classical tradition yet clearly influenced by his performance background in jazz fusion
and progressive rock. His works may be heard on releases from a variety
of labels, some of which include *Catharsis II* (for piano quartet), Con-
certo for Electric Guitar and Symphonic Band, *Lincoln Highway Suite*
(for orchestra or symphonic band), *Lullaby for Sam* (for guitar), and
Princess Ka'iulani (for flute).

   Dr. Stolz holds degrees in music composition and jazz studies from
The Hartt School, University of Oregon, and University of Nevada, Las
Vegas. Stolz is currently assistant professor and coordinator of music at
University of South Carolina Upstate, where he teaches composition,
theory, popular music studies, and drum set. Previously, he taught at
the University of Nevada, Las Vegas, Southeast Missouri State Univer-
sity, the University of South Dakota, and at two community colleges in
Connecticut.

CPSIA information can be obtained
at www.ICGtesting.com
Printed in the USA
BVOW08*2128271017
498665BV00001B/1/P